THE ROSARY IN A YEAR
PRAYER GUIDE

with FR. MARK-MARY AMES, CFR

ASCENSION
West Chester, Pennsylvania

Litany of Loreto © 2024 *Amministrazione del Patrimonio della Santa Sede Apostolica* and *Dicastero per la Comunicazione, Libreria Editrice Vaticana, Città del Vaticano.* All rights reserved.

© 2024 Ascension Publishing Group, LLC. All rights reserved.

With the exception of short excerpts used in articles and critical reviews, no part of this work may be reproduced, transmitted, or stored in any form whatsoever, printed or electronic, without the prior written permission of the publisher.

Excerpts from the English translation of the *Catechism of the Catholic Church* for use in the United States of America © 1994 United States Catholic Conference, Inc.–Libreria Editrice Vaticana. Used with permission. English translation of the *Catechism of the Catholic Church: Modifications from the Editio Typica* © 1997 United States Conference of Catholic Bishops–Libreria Editrice Vaticana.

Scripture quotations are from the Revised Standard Version of the Bible–Second Catholic Edition (Ignatius Edition) copyright © 2006 National Council of the Churches of Christ in the United States of America. Used by permission. All rights reserved.

Excerpt(s) from LIFE OF CHRIST by Fulton J. Sheen, Ph.D., D.D., copyright © 1958 by Fulton J. Sheen. Used by permission of Doubleday, an imprint of the Knopf Doubleday Publishing Group, a division of Penguin Random House LLC. All rights reserved.

Ascension
PO Box 1990
West Chester, PA 19380
1-800-376-0520
ascensionpress.com

Cover and interior design: Ashley Dias

Printed in USA

25 26 27 28 29 8 7 6 5 4

ISBN 978-1-935940-59-3 (trade book)
ISBN 978-1-935940-60-9 (e-book)

TABLE *of* CONTENTS

How to Use This Book 1
Introduction *by Fr. Mark-Mary Ames* 4
A Roadmap for This Journey 9
   The Rosary in a Year Prayer Plan 11
The Basic Prayers of the Rosary 35
The Mysteries of the Rosary 36

PHASE 1: FORMING THE RELATIONSHIP 41
Introduction 42
Litanies 43
Days 1–7 51

PHASE 2: BIBLICAL ROOTS OF THE ROSARY 55
Introduction 56
The Biblical Foundation of the Prayers of the Rosary 57
The Biblical Foundation of the Mysteries of the Rosary 67
Days 8–68 81

PHASE 3: MEDITATING ON THE MYSTERIES 95
Introduction 96
Days 69–188 99

PHASE 4: FINDING FOCUS 293
Introduction 294
Days 189–208 296

PHASE 5: BUILDING UP THE DECADES 307
Introduction 308
Days 209–335 310

PHASE 6: PRAYING TOGETHER 359
Introduction 360
When to Pray Each Set of Mysteries 361
Days 336–365 362

How to Pray the Rosary 366
Prayers of the Rosary 367
Conclusion 369
Sources 370
Illustration Information and Credits 380

HOW TO USE THIS BOOK

This *Rosary in a Year Prayer Guide* contains everything you need to have the fullest experience with Ascension's *Rosary in a Year (with Fr. Mark-Mary Ames)* podcast (*RIY* for short). In the pages of this book you will find the proprietary **Rosary in a Year prayer plan**, **prayer assignments for each day**, all the **Scripture passages and reflections** read in the podcast, and every piece of **sacred art** prayed with throughout the podcast.

If you have journeyed through the Bible with us by listening to the chart-topping podcast *The Bible in a Year (with Fr. Mike Schmitz)*™ featuring Jeff Cavins, you will love discovering the connections between the Rosary and the Bible! Though many Catholics are unaware of it, this Marian prayer is steeped in Scripture. Throughout the course of this year, you will encounter its biblical roots.

Similarly, if you encountered the *Catechism* with us by listening to *The Catechism in a Year*™ *(with Fr. Mike Schmitz)* podcast, you know the importance of meditative prayer and contemplating the life of Christ.

Whether or not you have listened to these podcasts and are familiar with Scripture or the *Catechism*, in this *Rosary in a Year* podcast, you will find a new (or should we say centuries old!) way of meditating on significant moments in the lives of our Lord Jesus Christ and his mother. As the *Catechism* states, "Prayer is the encounter of God's thirst with ours" (CCC 2560). In the coming year, you will experience 365 days dedicated to growing in prayer with the Lord.

This book is meant to guide you through *The Rosary in a Year* podcast to help you achieve meaningful goals in your prayer life that can lead you closer to Christ through his Mother in the Rosary.

What you will find in this book:
- An introduction from Fr. Mark-Mary Ames to help you get started.
- A roadmap for this journey, including the *RIY* prayer plan, to show where you are headed.

- Introductions to the six phases of *The Rosary in a Year* podcast. Here, you will learn about each phase, its goals, what you will discover and accomplish, tips to get the most out of that phase, and any relevant assignments for that phase (prayer, meditation, or reading).
- Charts outlining the biblical roots of the prayers of the Rosary, line by line, to help you see their spiritual depths.
- The Scripture passages associated with each mystery of the Rosary to help you learn about the mysteries and pray with them.
- Two reflections from the saints on each mystery of the Rosary, as read verbatim in the podcast, to help you enter more deeply into the mysteries.
- Three sacred art images for each mystery of the Rosary, as mentioned and prayed with in the podcast, to help you visualize the mysteries with reflection questions to guide you in prayer.
- The daily prayer commitments associated with all 365 days of the podcast to guide you in a "slow build" toward a fruitful daily habit of praying the Rosary.
- The full text of the prayers of the Rosary.

How to get the most out of this book:

Keep this *Prayer Guide* handy as you listen to *The Rosary in a Year* podcast each day. Refer to the introduction to each phase to help guide you along your journey, and turn to each day's entry to be reminded of the day's prayer. When the podcast presents Scripture, reflections, or sacred art, you can read along or view the art in the pages of this book.

Each phase of the podcast is color-coded in this guide, from light blue to deep blue, to help you see your progress as you grow deeper in your prayer. Additionally, the four sets of Rosary mysteries are color-coded to make the day's prayers easier to follow.

Each of the six phases of *The Rosary in a Year* podcast, from "Forming the Relationship" to "Praying Together," are represented by deepening shades of blue. This color is traditionally associated with the Blessed Mother, and the colors represent how your love for and understanding of the rosary will grow and deepen along this journey.

Additionally, each of the four sets of Rosary mysteries from joyful to glorious is represented by a color that symbolizes a key aspect of those mysteries. The joyful mysteries are represented by rose, which is a liturgical color for rejoicing. Priests wear rose-colored vestments on Gaudete Sunday in Advent and Laetare Sunday in Lent. The luminous mysteries are represented by green, to symbolize Christ's earthly ministry. The sorrowful mysteries are represented by purple, which is a traditional penitential color that priests wear during Advent and Lent. The glorious mysteries are represented by gold, which symbolizes the glory and royalty of the Resurrection and Christ's Kingdom.

As you press play each day, we hope this book serves you in your journey to praying the Rosary like never before.

JOYFUL MYSTERIES:
Rose, representing rejoicing

LUMINOUS MYSTERIES:
Green, representing Christ's earthly ministry

SORROWFUL MYSTERIES:
Purple, representing repentance

GLORIOUS MYSTERIES:
Gold, representing glory

INTRODUCTION

One of the greatest gifts that Jesus has given us is the gift he gave in the final moments of his life: the gift of Mary, his mother, to be our mother as well. How the world and the Church—that is, each of us—could use a mother in a particular way in these days. She is a mother who comforts us, who encourages us, who speaks words of peace and hope, but also a mother who is strong, who fights for us, who reminds us of truth, and who helps us to grow in maturity. Now, as much as ever, we need Mary and her motherhood in our lives.

I really believe one of the most concrete ways we can experience the motherhood of Mary in our daily lives is through a holy and prayerful recitation of the Rosary. I love to think of the Rosary as going back to Nazareth, sitting with Mary, and with loving attention listening to her recount the truths and the mysteries of the life of Christ. We get to ponder the deep love, the deep affection that Mary has for her son. She points us back to Jesus. She unpacks the mysteries. She reminds us to stand firm in difficulties. To pray the Rosary is to allow Mary to mother us, and it is to make ourselves the recipients of these truths that she has pondered in her heart.

The Springtime of the Rosary

It is great news that there is a growing popularity, what Pope Benedict XVI referred to as the springtime of the Rosary, and I deeply believe that this is a work of grace. This is the work of the Holy Spirit, because in the most holy Rosary, and in an increased devotion to it, is going to be found the particular remedy and medicine for our times.

First and foremost, **the Rosary puts Jesus back in the center of our lives**. The Rosary brings us to ponder each day, again, the foundational truths of our faith, the foundational events in the life of Jesus. This is especially important in these modern times, where we receive so much information and so much news. There is such a temptation and tendency toward distraction and dissipation day in and day out. The world is communicating to us false promises, lies about our identity and our dignity, and lies about the goodness of God. It attacks our hope and the nature of God.

Through praying the most holy Rosary, we not only block those lies out, but we receive again and remain focused on the truth of the goodness of God, the power of God, the humility of God, and the surety of our hope.

The Rosary has often been called a weapon. One way it is a weapon is the way it takes down the dissipation and the distraction that bombard us each day.

Secondly, there is a component of the rosary that is medicinal—not just spiritually, but also humanly speaking. Certainly pondering the lives of Christ and his mother reminds us of the truth and helps us to transform our minds so that we can be conformed to Christ. But also, in the midst of this very busy world, there is an attack on our ability to contemplate, to be still, to focus, to receive, and to drink deeply of the truth, including to drink deeply of the truth of the life and love of God. It's just hard to focus. It's hard to pay attention. It's hard to be still. For this reason, the Rosary, with its prolonged meditation and recitation, can feel sort of like physical therapy. It can be hard to do it, but in the difficulty is the renewal and the healing.

It renews our ability to focus, our ability to be still. It helps to form, to strengthen, to purify our imagination. I really believe that the Rosary can help heal our humanity, which is so often wounded as we grow up in modernity. **The Rosary helps us be still in order to drink deeply of the truth of the life and love of God.** Devotion to the Rosary is growing, and God is continuing to bring us to the Rosary in these days and to bring Christ back into the center of our lives.

So, yes, there's this invitation again and again: "Let's pray the Rosary." But my personal experience, and maybe your experience as well, is that sometimes praying the Rosary can be difficult.

Whether getting started or persevering in it or doing it in a way that feels prayerful, praying the Rosary can actually be quite difficult. It can feel like I'm trying to do a lot of things all at once. Sometimes I feel as if praying the rosary is like running a 5K while writing a short story while saying a specific number of Hail Marys over and over again. Oftentimes this can make praying the Rosary an experience that is not super prayerful. This, at least, was a bit of my own experience with the Rosary as a young man.

As I had my deeper conversion to Christ, I knew I wanted to pray the Rosary and do it every day, and I felt like I should. I needed to pray the Rosary every day. But often I didn't really know how to do it. I didn't have the "muscle" formed. I didn't have an inner "library" or "archive" of knowledge or insight about the mysteries of Christ to bring to the Rosary and to bring to my meditation and contemplation. So, I battled and I white-knuckled it through the Rosary, but I don't know that it was particularly prayerful.

Pope Benedict XVI said that praying the Rosary can be so deeply fruitful as long as it is not done in a way that is just purely routine or "mechanical and superficial." Often, because we can be so focused on getting to the end when we are praying the Rosary, we don't necessarily pray it well. I think we need to know that saying Hail Marys isn't always synonymous with praying the Rosary. The invitation and the grace are not in just *saying* the Rosary, but in *praying* the Rosary. In other words, we receive grace in the real encounter with God that it facilitates.

How Will This Work?

For this reason, the approach we're taking is somewhat novel. We're going to start quite slow. We're going to start at the fundamentals and slowly build from there. The fundamentals include a meditation upon the principal prayers of the Rosary, the Our Father and the Hail Mary. This is a reminder of what we are called to contemplate as we pray the Rosary.

One of the components of *The Rosary in a Year* that I'm most excited about is a very intentional **building up an inner "library" or "archive"**

of sources of meditation that we can pull from as we are praying the Rosary. We are going to build up this archive through a prolonged meditation upon the scriptural passages where we encounter the mysteries of the Rosary. We're also going to pull from a variety of meditations and insights from the saints. Also, we're going to go through a guided meditation upon a number of holy images depicting these mysteries. The idea is that we will enter deeply into these mysteries.

As we have real prayerful encounters with the Gospels, as we receive and drink of the insights of the saints, as we visualize and ponder the beauty of the artwork, then it will be much more natural for our minds and hearts to contemplate the mysteries. We will be moved with greater ease to meditate on these mysteries as we are invited to do in the Rosary.

There are a couple of different ways you can go about this, depending on where you are. For example, I refer to praying the rosary as running a 5K. Maybe you're already a regular runner—that is, you are already praying the rosary, and you feel like it's a regular part of your life. Maybe you're praying more than one Rosary a day, and it's already very, very fruitful. If that's you, you have my full encouragement to continue to pray the Rosary as you're doing, but perhaps to incorporate *The Rosary in a Year* meditations to help deepen and strengthen and bring newness to your already beautiful routine of praying the Rosary.

For those who are just starting with the Rosary, just feeling invited to it, who don't have much practice with it or catechesis about it—or for those of you who, like me for a number of years, tried it but have found it quite difficult—perhaps you can start at the very beginning. I invite you to pull back from some of your practices where you may have picked up some bad habits with your approach to the Rosary, where it has become too routine or mechanical or shallow. **Take a step back to begin again, and do a slow build.**

The goal of the Rosary is not simply for you to be saying 50 Hail Marys a day as soon as possible. The hope is that you are able to fall in love with the Rosary because you experience in it the motherhood of Mary and you experience in it a deeper encounter in entering into relationship with Jesus. The slow build is just simply taking into account our humanity and how we grow. When we fall in love with anything, we naturally and joyfully make space for it in our day-to-day lives. That is my hope for you as you journey through *The Rosary in a Year*: for you to fall in love with the Rosary and slowly, day by day, incorporate it as a regular part of your spiritual life and your prayer for the rest of your life.

My brothers and sisters, I believe *The Rosary in a Year* is a personal invitation from Mary to me, to be renewed. I've been a religious for nearly 15 years, I've been praying the Rosary for nearly 20 years, and I even have Mary in my name. But this is an invitation to begin again. No matter where you are on your journey with the Rosary, there is room for renewal and increased love for Christ and his Mother.

My friends, I thank you for joining us. I thank you for praying with me through this year. I deeply believe and am deeply confident that for you and for me, it will be a deeper encounter with Mary as our mother and with Christ as our beloved Savior and the source of our peace and our hope.

Fr. Mark-Mary Ames, CFR

A ROADMAP FOR THIS JOURNEY

The Rosary in a Year podcast will guide listeners through six phases, doing a "slow build" to form a lasting habit of prayer and gain the tools to enter more deeply into fruitful meditation on the lives of Jesus and Mary through the Rosary. We will be equipped to pray the Rosary with fervor, putting Christ first in our lives as we still ourselves to drink deeply of the truth of God's life and love.

Goals for Each Phase

FORMING THE RELATIONSHIP: Phase 1 (Days 1–7)

In this phase, we will deepen our relationships with Jesus and Mary, the foundation of praying the Rosary and praying well.
We will pray 1 Our Father, 3 Hail Marys, and 1 Glory Be each day.

BIBLICAL ROOTS OF THE ROSARY: Phase 2 (Days 8–68)

In this phase we will learn about the biblical roots
of the prayers and the mysteries of the Rosary.
We will continue to pray 1 Our Father, 3 Hail Marys,
and 1 Glory Be each day.

MEDITATING ON THE MYSTERIES: Phase 3 (Days 69–188)

In this phase we will build up an inner "library" or "archive" of information, images, and insights as we meditate on the mysteries of the Rosary with the aid of Scripture, the saints, and sacred art.
We will pray 1 decade of the Rosary (1 Our Father,
10 Hail Marys, and 1 Glory Be) each day.

FINDING FOCUS: Phase 4 (Days 189–208)

In this phase, we will draw on our newly formed inner "library" or "archive" each day to independently meditate on a mystery for 10 minutes. Then, we will pray 1 decade of the Rosary each day.

BUILDING UP THE DECADES: Phase 5 (209–335)

In this phase, we will continue drawing on our inner "library" or "archive" each day to meditate while praying the prayers of the Rosary. We will build up the number of decades prayed each day, from 2 decades up to 5 decades each day.

PRAYING TOGETHER: Phase 6 (Days 336–365)

In this final phase, we will pray a daily Rosary, meditating on the mysteries of the day, using the prayer "muscles" we have built during this year.

And beyond…

After the podcast ends, we will be equipped with tools and skills to *pray,* not just *say,* the Rosary devoutly each day as we seek to grow closer to Christ through his Mother.

THE ROSARY IN A YEAR PRAYER PLAN

Day	Phase	Focus	Prayer	Mystery(s)
1	Phase 1: Forming the Relationship	Practicing the Presence of Jesus and Mary	1 Our Father 3 Hail Marys 1 Glory Be	None
2				
3				
4				
5				
6				
7				
8	Phase 2: Biblical Roots of the Rosary The Biblical Foundation of the Prayers of the Rosary	Hail Mary	1 Our Father 3 Hail Marys 1 Glory Be	None
9				
10				
11		Our Father		
12				
13				
14				
15				
16		Glory Be		
17		Sign of the Cross		
18				
19		Hail Holy Queen		
20				
21				
22		Fatima Prayer		
23		Apostles' Creed		
24				
25				
26				
27				
28				

29		Luke 1:26–38		The Annunciation
30		Luke 1:39–56		The Visitation
31		Luke 2:1–20		The Nativity
32		Luke 2:22–39		The Presentation of Jesus in the Temple
33		Luke 2:41–52		The Finding of Jesus in the Temple
34		Matthew: 3:13–17		The Baptism of Jesus
35		John 2:1–12		The Wedding at Cana
36		Mark 1:14–15		The Proclamation of the Kingdom and the Call to Conversion
37	Phase 2: Biblical Roots of the Rosary	Matthew 17:1–13		The Transfiguration
38		Luke 22:14–23	1 Our Father 3 Hail Marys 1 Glory Be	The Institution of the Eucharist
39	The Biblical Foundation of the Mysteries of the Rosary	Matthew 26:36–46		The Agony in the Garden
40		Matthew 27:26		The Scourging at the Pillar
41		Matthew 27:27–31		The Crowning with Thorns
42		Matthew 27:32		The Carrying of the Cross
43		Luke 23:33–46		The Crucifixion
44		Matthew 28:1–10		The Resurrection
45		Luke 24:50–53		The Ascension
46		Acts 2:1–13		The Descent of the Holy Spirit on Pentecost
47		Luke 1:46–56		The Assumption of Mary
48		Revelation 12:1–5		The Coronation of Mary as Queen of Heaven and Earth
49		Luke 1:26–38		The Annunciation
50		Luke 1:39–56		The Visitation
51		Luke 2:1–20		The Nativity
52		Luke 2:22–39		The Presentation of Jesus in the Temple

53		Luke 2:41–52		The Finding of Jesus in the Temple
54		Matthew 3:13–17		The Baptism of Jesus
55		John 2:1–12		The Wedding at Cana
56		Mark 1:14–15		The Proclamation of the Kingdom and the Call to Conversion
57	**Phase 2: Biblical Roots of the Rosary**	Matthew 17:1–13		The Transfiguration
58		Luke 22:14–23	1 Our Father 3 Hail Marys 1 Glory Be	The Institution of the Eucharist
59	**The Biblical Foundation of the Mysteries of the Rosary**	Matthew 26:36–46		The Agony in the Garden
60		Matthew 27:26		The Scourging at the Pillar
61		Matthew 27:27–31		The Crowning with Thorns
62		Matthew 27:32		The Carrying of the Cross
63		Luke 23:33–46		The Crucifixion
64		Matthew 28:1–10		The Resurrection
65		Luke 24:50–53		The Ascension
66		Acts 2:1–13		The Descent of the Holy Spirit on Pentecost
67		Luke 1:46–56		The Assumption of Mary
68		Revelation 12:1–5		The Coronation of Mary as Queen of Heaven and Earth
69	**Phase 3: Meditating on the Mysteries**	Luke 1:26–38	1 Decade of the Rosary (1 Our Father 10 Hail Marys 1 Glory Be)	The Annunciation
70		Luke 1:39–56		The Visitation
71		Luke 2:1–20		The Nativity
72	**Scripture (*Lectio Divina*)**	Luke 2:22–39		The Presentation of Jesus in the Temple
73		Luke 2:41–52		The Finding of Jesus in the Temple
74		Matthew 3:13–17		The Baptism of Jesus
75		John 2:1–12		The Wedding at Cana

76		Mark 1:14–15	1 Decade of the Rosary (1 Our Father 10 Hail Marys 1 Glory Be)	The Proclamation of the Kingdom and the Call to Conversion
77		Matthew 17:1–13		The Transfiguration
78		Luke 22:14–23		The Institution of the Eucharist
79	Phase 3: Meditating on the Mysteries Scripture (*Lectio Divina*)	Matthew 26:36–46		The Agony in the Garden
80		Matthew 27:26		The Scourging at the Pillar
81		Matthew 27:27–31		The Crowning with Thorns
82		Matthew 27:32		The Carrying of the Cross
83		Luke 23:33–46		The Crucifixion
84		Matthew 28:1–10		The Resurrection
85		Luke 24:50–53		The Ascension
86		Acts 2:1–13		The Descent of the Holy Spirit on Pentecost
87		Luke 1:46–56		The Assumption of Mary
88		Revelation 12:1–5		The Coronation of Mary as Queen of Heaven and Earth
89	Phase 3: Meditating on the Mysteries Reflections from the Saints and Others	St. Bernard of Clairvaux, *Four Homilies in Praise of the Virgin Mother* 4.8–9	1 Decade of the Rosary (1 Our Father 10 Hail Marys 1 Glory Be)	The Annunciation
90		St. Alphonsus Liguori, "On the Visitation of the Blessed Virgin," in *The Way of Salvation*		The Visitation
91		St. Leo the Great, *Sermon 21 (On the Feast of the Nativity, I)*		The Nativity
92		St. Cyril of Alexandria, *Homily 4*, in *Commentary on the Gospel of Saint Luke*		The Presentation of Jesus in the Temple
93		St. Augustine, *Sermons on Selected Lessons of the New Testament: Sermon 1*		The Finding of Jesus in the Temple
94		St. Ambrose, *On the Mysteries* 5.26–27		The Baptism of Jesus

95		St. Alphonsus Liguori, *The Glories of Mary* 6.1		The Wedding at Cana
96		St. Augustine, *On the Sermon on the Mount* 1.1.2		The Proclamation of the Kingdom and the Call to Conversion
97		St. Anastasius of Sinai, *Homily on the Transfiguration*		The Transfiguration
98		St. Catherine of Siena, *Dialogue*		The Institution of the Eucharist
99		St. Alphonsus Liguori, "Reflections and Affections on the Passion of Jesus Christ," in *The Passion and the Death of Jesus Christ* 6.1		The Agony in the Garden
100		St. Bridget, *Revelations* 16		The Scourging at the Pillar
101	Phase 3: Meditating on the Mysteries	St. Thomas Aquinas, *Commentary on the Gospel of Matthew* 2350	1 Decade of the Rosary (1 Our Father 10 Hail Marys 1 Glory Be)	The Crowning with Thorns
102	Reflections from the Saints and Others	St. Josemaria Escriva, "Second Station: Jesus Takes Up His Cross," in *The Way of the Cross*		The Carrying of the Cross
103		St. Alphonsus Liguori, "On the Fifth Dolour," in *The Glories of Mary*		The Crucifixion
104		St. John Chrysostom (attr.), Easter homily		The Resurrection
105		St. Thomas Aquinas, *Summa Theologiae* III.57.1		The Ascension
106		St. Ambrose, *On the Holy Spirit* 14.168–170		The Descent of the Holy Spirit on Pentecost
107		Ven. Fulton J. Sheen, *Meditations on the Fifteen Mysteries of the Rosary*		The Assumption of Mary
108		St. John Damascene, *Sermon 1: On the Assumption*		The Coronation of Mary as Queen of Heaven and Earth
109		St. Gregory Thaumaturgus, *On the Annunciation to the Holy Virgin Mary*		The Annunciation

110	Phase 3: Meditating on the Mysteries Reflections from the Saints and Others	St. Ambrose, *Commentary on the Gospel of St. Luke* 2.19–20, 22–23, 26	1 Decade of the Rosary (1 Our Father 10 Hail Marys 1 Glory Be)	The Visitation
111		St. Bernard, *On the Miraculous Nature of the Nativity*		The Nativity
112		St. Alphonsus Liguori, *The Glories of Mary* 2.6		The Presentation of Jesus in the Temple
113		St. Cyril of Alexandria, *Homily 5*, in *Commentary on the Gospel of Saint Luke*		The Finding of Jesus in the Temple
114		St. Gregory of Nazianzus, *Oration 39*		The Baptism of Jesus
115		John Henry Newman, "Sermon III," in *Sermons Bearing on Subjects of the Day*		The Wedding at Cana
116		St. John Eudes, *The Life and the Kingdom of Jesus* 6.4		The Proclamation of the Kingdom and the Call to Conversion
117		St. Augustine, *Sermons on Selected Lessons of the New Testament: Sermon 28*		The Transfiguration
118		St. Cyril of Jerusalem, *Catechetical Lecture 22 (On the Mysteries. IV.): On the Body and Blood of Christ*		The Institution of the Eucharist
119		St. Hilary of Poitiers, *The Trinity* 10.42		The Agony in the Garden
120		St. Faustina, *Diary* 445		The Scourging at the Pillar
121		Ven. Fulton J. Sheen, *Life of Christ*, chapter 47		The Crowning with Thorns
122		St. Thomas Aquinas, *Commentary on the Gospel of John* 2412–2414		The Carrying of the Cross
123		St. Bridget, *Revelations* 16		The Crucifixion
124		St. Augustine, *Sermon 8: In octava Paschatis ad infantes*		The Resurrection

A Roadmap for This Journey 17

125	**Phase 3: Meditating on the Mysteries** **Reflections from the Saints and Others**	St. Augustine, *Sermons on Selected Lessons of the New Testament: Sermon 41*		The Ascension
126		St. Alphonsus Liguori, "Novena of the Holy Ghost," in *The Way of Salvation*		The Descent of the Holy Spirit on Pentecost
127		St. Bernard of Clairvaux, *On the Solemnity of the Assumption of the Blessed Virgin Mary: Sermon One*		The Assumption of Mary
128		St. John Henry Newman, "Mary Is the *'Regina Angelorum,'* the Queen of Angels," in *Meditations and Devotions of the Late Cardinal Newman*	1 Decade of the Rosary (1 Our Father 10 Hail Marys 1 Glory Be)	The Coronation of Mary as Queen of Heaven and Earth
129		*The Annunciation*, Fra Angelico		The Annunciation
130		*The Visitation*, Rembrandt		The Visitation
131		Nativity painting in presbytery of Salesianerkirche, Vienna*		The Nativity
132	**Phase 3: Meditating on the Mysteries** **Sacred Art ("Visio Divina")**	Fresco of the Presentation in the Temple, Giulio Campi, in Chiesa di Santa Rita, Cremona, Italy*		The Presentation of Jesus in the Temple
133		Mosaic of Jesus Lost and Found in the Temple, in Rosary Basilica, Lourdes*		The Finding of Jesus in the Temple
134		Baptism of Christ scene in San Benedetto, Padua*		The Baptism of Jesus
135		*Wedding at Cana*, Carl Bloch		The Wedding at Cana
136		*Healing of the Lepers at Capernaum*, James Tissot		The Proclamation of the Kingdom and the Call to Conversion
137		Transfiguration stained glass window in Votiv Kirche, Vienna*		The Transfiguration

| 138 | Phase 3: Meditating on the Mysteries

Sacred Art ("Visio Divina") | *The Last Supper*, Giacomo Raffaelli* (based on Leonardo da Vinci) | 1 Decade of the Rosary

(1 Our Father 10 Hail Marys 1 Glory Be) | The Institution of the Eucharist |
|---|---|---|---|---|
| 139 | | Painting of Jesus in Gethsemane, Vicente Macip, in cathedral in Valencia, Spain* | | The Agony in the Garden |
| 140 | | Fresco of flagellation in Santa Prassede, Rome* | | The Scourging at the Pillar |
| 141 | | *Christ Crowned with Thorns*, Titian | | The Crowning with Thorns |
| 142 | | *The Procession to Calvary*, Pieter Bruegel | | The Carrying of the Cross |
| 143 | | Fresco of Crucifixion, Pietro Gagliardi, in San Girolamo dei Croati, Rome* | | The Crucifixion |
| 144 | | *The Resurrection of Christ*, Annibale Carracci | | The Resurrection |
| 145 | | Ascension mosaic on St. Mark's Basilica, Venice | | The Ascension |
| 146 | | *Pentecost*, Jean Restout | | The Descent of the Holy Spirit on Pentecost |
| 147 | | Assumption scene in Santa Maria dell'Orto, Rome* | | The Assumption of Mary |
| 148 | | *The Coronation of the Virgin*, Diego Velázquez | | The Coronation of Mary as Queen of Heaven and Earth |
| 149 | | *The Annunciation*, Henry Ossawa Tanner | | The Annunciation |
| 150 | | Visitation painting, Federico Maldarelli, in Chiesa dei Santi Severino e Sossio, Naples, Italy* | | The Visitation |
| 151 | | *Adoration of the Shepherds*, Gerard van Honthorst | | The Nativity |
| 152 | | Presentation painting in Kostel Svatého Havla, Prague, Czech Republic* | | The Presentation of Jesus in the Temple |

A Roadmap for This Journey   19

153		Scene of Jesus teaching in the Temple in St. Nicholas Church, Brussels*		The Finding of Jesus in the Temple
154		*The Baptism of Christ*, Andrea del Verrocchio and Leonardo da Vinci		The Baptism of Jesus
155		*The Wedding at Cana*, Gérard David		The Wedding at Cana
156		*The Adulterous Woman*, Lorenzo Lotto		The Proclamation of the Kingdom and the Call to Conversion
157		*The Transfiguration*, Raphael		The Transfiguration
158		*The Last Supper*, Juan de Juanes		The Institution of the Eucharist
159	Phase 3: Meditating on the Mysteries	Jesus in Gethsemane painting by Alessandro Maganza, in cathedral in Vicenza, Italy*	1 Decade of the Rosary	The Agony in the Garden
160	Sacred Art ("Visio Divina")	*The Flagellation of Christ*, Caravaggio	(1 Our Father 10 Hail Marys 1 Glory Be)	The Scourging at the Pillar
161		*Ecce Homo*, Caravaggio		The Crowning with Thorns
162		*Christ Carrying the Cross*, Orazio Gentileschi		The Carrying of the Cross
163		*What Our Lord Saw from the Cross*, James Tissot		The Crucifixion
164		*The Incredulity of St. Thomas*, Caravaggio		The Resurrection
165		Ascension painting, Bernardino Gandino, in Chiesa di Santa Maria del Carmine, Brescia, Italy		The Ascension
166		*Pentecost*, Titian		The Descent of the Holy Spirit on Pentecost
167		Assumption fresco, Cesare Mariani, in Chiesa di Santa Lucia del Gonfalone*		The Assumption of Mary
168		Glory of Mary scene in parish church of Santa Maria Assunta, Santa Maria Maggiore, Italy*		The Coronation of Mary as Queen of Heaven and Earth

169	Phase 3: Meditating on the Mysteries Sacred Art ("Visio Divina")	*The Annunciation*, Jan van Eyck	1 Decade of the Rosary (1 Our Father 10 Hail Marys 1 Glory Be)	The Annunciation
170		Mosaic of the Visitation on the Church of the Visitation, Ein Karem, Israel		The Visitation
171		*Nativity with St. Francis and St. Lawrence*, Caravaggio		The Nativity
172		*Simeon's Song of Praise*, Arent de Gelder		The Presentation of Jesus in the Temple
173		*The Finding of the Saviour in the Temple*, William Holman Hunt		The Finding of Jesus in the Temple
174		*The Appearance of Christ Before the People*, Alexander Ivanov		The Baptism of Jesus
175		*The Wedding at Cana*, Paolo Veronese		The Wedding at Cana
176		*Christ in the Storm on the Sea of Galilee*, Rembrandt		The Proclamation of the Kingdom and the Call to Conversion
177		*The Savior's Transfiguration*, Theophanes the Greek (attr.)		The Transfiguration
178		*Christ and the Disciples Before the Last Supper*, Henry Ossawa Tanner		The Institution of the Eucharist
179		*The Arrest of Christ (Kiss of Judas)*, Giotto		The Agony in the Garden
180		*The Flagellation of Our Lord Jesus Christ*, William-Adolphe Bouguereau		The Scourging at the Pillar
181		*The Crowning with Thorns*, Anthony van Dyck		The Crowning with Thorns
182		*Christ Falls on the Way to Calvary*, Raphael		The Carrying of the Cross
183		*The Descent from the Cross*, Peter Paul Rubens (1617)		The Crucifixion

A Roadmap for This Journey   21

184	Phase 3: Meditating on the Mysteries through Sacred Art ("Visio Divina")	*The Holy Women at Christ's Tomb*, Annibale Carracci	1 Decade of the Rosary (1 Our Father 10 Hail Marys 1 Glory Be)	The Resurrection
185		*Appearance on the Mountain in Galilee*, Duccio		The Ascension
186		*Pentecost*, Simone Peterzano (attr.), in Basilica of Santa Eufemia, Milan, Italy*		The Descent of the Holy Spirit on Pentecost
187		Assumption stained glass window in Burgos Cathedral*		The Assumption of Mary
188		Mary, Help of Christians fresco, Giuseppe Rollini, in Basilica Maria Ausiliatrice, Turin, Italy*		The Coronation of Mary as Queen of Heaven and Earth
189	Phase 4: Finding Focus	Now that you have practiced many ways of meditating on the mysteries of the Rosary, it's time to enter into prayer on your own. Remember that you can choose to focus on any of the following: Persons (Days 1–7) Prayers (Days 8–28) Mysteries (Days 69–188)	1 Decade	The Annunciation
190				The Visitation
191				The Nativity
192				The Presentation of Jesus in the Temple
193				The Finding of Jesus in the Temple
194				The Baptism of Jesus
195				The Wedding at Cana
196				The Proclamation of the Kingdom and the Call to Conversion
197				The Transfiguration
198				The Institution of the Eucharist
199				The Agony in the Garden
200				The Scourging at the Pillar
201				The Crowning with Thorns
202				The Carrying of the Cross

Day	Phase	Instructions	Count	Mystery
203	Phase 4: Finding Focus	Now that you have practiced many ways of meditating on the mysteries of the Rosary, it's time to enter into prayer on your own. Remember that you can choose to focus on any of the following: Persons (Days 1–7) Prayers (Days 8–28) Mysteries (Days 69–188)	1 Decade	The Crucifixion
204				The Resurrection
205				The Ascension
206				The Descent of the Holy Spirit on Pentecost
207				The Assumption of Mary
208				The Coronation of Mary as Queen of Heaven and Earth
209	Phase 5: Building Up the Decades		2 Decades	• The Annunciation • The Visitation
210				• The Nativity • The Presentation of Jesus in the Temple
211				• The Finding of Jesus in the Temple • The Baptism of Jesus
212				• The Wedding at Cana • The Proclamation of the Kingdom and the Call to Conversion
213				• The Transfiguration • The Institution of the Eucharist
214				• The Agony in the Garden • The Scourging at the Pillar
215				• The Crowning with Thorns • The Carrying of the Cross
216				• The Crucifixion • The Resurrection
217				• The Ascension • The Descent of the Holy Spirit on Pentecost
218				• The Assumption of Mary • The Coronation of Mary as Queen of Heaven and Earth
219				• The Annunciation • The Visitation
220				• The Nativity • The Presentation of Jesus in the Temple
221				• The Finding of Jesus in the Temple • The Baptism of Jesus
222				• The Wedding at Cana • The Proclamation of the Kingdom and the Call to Conversion
223				• The Transfiguration • The Institution of the Eucharist

224			• The Agony in the Garden • The Scourging at the Pillar
225			• The Crowning with Thorns • The Carrying of the Cross
226			• The Crucifixion • The Resurrection
227			• The Ascension • The Descent of the Holy Spirit on Pentecost
228			• The Assumption of Mary • The Coronation of Mary as Queen of Heaven and Earth
229			• The Annunciation • The Visitation
230			• The Nativity • The Presentation of Jesus in the Temple
231			• The Finding of Jesus in the Temple • The Baptism of Jesus
232			• The Wedding at Cana • The Proclamation of the Kingdom and the Call to Conversion
233	Phase 5: Building Up the Decades	2 Decades	• The Transfiguration • The Institution of the Eucharist
234			• The Agony in the Garden • The Scourging at the Pillar
235			• The Crowning with Thorns • The Carrying of the Cross
236			• The Crucifixion • The Resurrection
237			• The Ascension • The Descent of the Holy Spirit on Pentecost
238			• The Assumption of Mary • The Coronation of Mary as Queen of Heaven and Earth
239			• The Annunciation • The Visitation
240			• The Nativity • The Presentation of Jesus in the Temple
241			• The Finding of Jesus in the Temple • The Baptism of Jesus
242			• The Wedding at Cana • The Proclamation of the Kingdom and the Call to Conversion
243			• The Transfiguration • The Institution of the Eucharist
244		3 Decades	• The Agony in the Garden • The Scourging at the Pillar • The Crowning with Thorns

245			• The Carrying of the Cross • The Crucifixion • The Resurrection
246			• The Ascension • The Descent of the Holy Spirit on Pentecost • The Assumption of Mary
247			• The Coronation of Mary as Queen of Heaven and Earth • The Annunciation • The Visitation
248			• The Nativity • The Presentation of Jesus in the Temple • The Finding of Jesus in the Temple
249			• The Baptism of Jesus • The Wedding at Cana • The Proclamation of the Kingdom and the Call to Conversion
250			• The Transfiguration • The Institution of the Eucharist • The Agony in the Garden
251			• The Scourging at the Pillar • The Crowning with Thorns • The Carrying of the Cross
252	Phase 5: Building Up the Decades	3 Decades	• The Crucifixion • The Resurrection • The Ascension
253			• The Descent of the Holy Spirit on Pentecost • The Assumption of Mary • The Coronation of Mary as Queen of Heaven and Earth
254			• The Annunciation • The Visitation • The Nativity
255			• The Presentation of Jesus in the Temple • The Finding of Jesus in the Temple • The Baptism of Jesus
256			• The Wedding at Cana • The Proclamation of the Kingdom and the Call to Conversion • The Transfiguration
257			• The Institution of the Eucharist • The Agony in the Garden • The Scourging at the Pillar
258			• The Crowning with Thorns • The Carrying of the Cross • The Crucifixion
259			• The Resurrection • The Ascension • The Descent of the Holy Spirit on Pentecost
260			• The Assumption of Mary • The Coronation of Mary as Queen of Heaven and Earth • The Annunciation

A Roadmap for This Journey

261			• The Visitation • The Nativity • The Presentation of Jesus in the Temple
262			• The Finding of Jesus in the Temple • The Baptism of Jesus • The Wedding at Cana
263			• The Proclamation of the Kingdom and the Call to Conversion • The Transfiguration • The Institution of the Eucharist
264			• The Agony in the Garden • The Scourging at the Pillar • The Crowning with Thorns
265			• The Carrying of the Cross • The Crucifixion • The Resurrection
266			• The Ascension • The Descent of the Holy Spirit on Pentecost • The Assumption of Mary
267			• The Coronation of Mary as Queen of Heaven and Earth • The Annunciation • The Visitation
268	Phase 5: Building Up the Decades	3 Decades	• The Nativity • The Presentation of Jesus in the Temple • The Finding of Jesus in the Temple
269			• The Baptism of Jesus • The Wedding at Cana • The Proclamation of the Kingdom and the Call to Conversion
270			• The Transfiguration • The Institution of the Eucharist • The Agony in the Garden
271			• The Scourging at the Pillar • The Crowning with Thorns • The Carrying of the Cross
272			• The Crucifixion • The Resurrection • The Ascension
273			• The Descent of the Holy Spirit on Pentecost • The Assumption of Mary • The Coronation of Mary as Queen of Heaven and Earth
274		4 Decades	• The Annunciation • The Visitation • The Nativity • The Presentation of Jesus in the Temple
275			• The Finding of Jesus in the Temple • The Baptism of Jesus • The Wedding at Cana • The Proclamation of the Kingdom and the Call to Conversion

276			• The Transfiguration • The Institution of the Eucharist • The Agony in the Garden • The Scourging at the Pillar
277			• The Crowning with Thorns • The Carrying of the Cross • The Crucifixion • The Resurrection
278			• The Ascension • The Descent of the Holy Spirit on Pentecost • The Assumption of Mary • The Coronation of Mary as Queen of Heaven and Earth
279			• The Annunciation • The Visitation • The Nativity • The Presentation of Jesus in the Temple
280			• The Finding of Jesus in the Temple • The Baptism of Jesus • The Wedding at Cana • The Proclamation of the Kingdom and the Call to Conversion
281	Phase 5: Building Up the Decades	4 Decades	• The Transfiguration • The Institution of the Eucharist • The Agony in the Garden • The Scourging at the Pillar
282			• The Crowning with Thorns • The Carrying of the Cross • The Crucifixion • The Resurrection
283			• The Ascension • The Descent of the Holy Spirit on Pentecost • The Assumption of Mary • The Coronation of Mary as Queen of Heaven and Earth
284			• The Annunciation • The Visitation • The Nativity • The Presentation of Jesus in the Temple
285			• The Finding of Jesus in the Temple • The Baptism of Jesus • The Wedding at Cana • The Proclamation of the Kingdom and the Call to Conversion
286			• The Transfiguration • The Institution of the Eucharist • The Agony in the Garden • The Scourging at the Pillar
287			• The Crowning with Thorns • The Carrying of the Cross • The Crucifixion • The Resurrection
288			• The Ascension • The Descent of the Holy Spirit on Pentecost • The Assumption of Mary • The Coronation of Mary as Queen of Heaven and Earth

A Roadmap for This Journey 27

289			• The Annunciation • The Visitation • The Nativity • The Presentation of Jesus in the Temple
290			• The Finding of Jesus in the Temple • The Baptism of Jesus • The Wedding at Cana • The Proclamation of the Kingdom and the Call to Conversion
291			• The Transfiguration • The Institution of the Eucharist • The Agony in the Garden • The Scourging at the Pillar
292			• The Crowning with Thorns • The Carrying of the Cross • The Crucifixion • The Resurrection
293			• The Ascension • The Descent of the Holy Spirit on Pentecost • The Assumption of Mary • The Coronation of Mary as Queen of Heaven and Earth
294	Phase 5: Building Up the Decades	4 Decades	• The Annunciation • The Visitation • The Nativity • The Presentation of Jesus in the Temple
295			• The Finding of Jesus in the Temple • The Baptism of Jesus • The Wedding at Cana • The Proclamation of the Kingdom and the Call to Conversion
296			• The Transfiguration • The Institution of the Eucharist • The Agony in the Garden • The Scourging at the Pillar
297			• The Crowning with Thorns • The Carrying of the Cross • The Crucifixion • The Resurrection
298			• The Ascension • The Descent of the Holy Spirit on Pentecost • The Assumption of Mary • The Coronation of Mary as Queen of Heaven and Earth
299			• The Annunciation • The Visitation • The Nativity • The Presentation of Jesus in the Temple
300			• The Finding of Jesus in the Temple • The Baptism of Jesus • The Wedding at Cana • The Proclamation of the Kingdom and the Call to Conversion
301			• The Transfiguration • The Institution of the Eucharist • The Agony in the Garden • The Scourging at the Pillar

302	Phase 5: Building Up the Decades	4 Decades	• The Crowning with Thorns • The Carrying of the Cross • The Crucifixion • The Resurrection
303			• The Ascension • The Descent of the Holy Spirit on Pentecost • The Assumption of Mary • The Coronation of Mary as Queen of Heaven and Earth
304		5 Decades	• The Annunciation • The Visitation • The Nativity • The Presentation of Jesus in the Temple • The Finding of Jesus in the Temple
305			• The Baptism of Jesus • The Wedding at Cana • The Proclamation of the Kingdom and the Call to Conversion • The Transfiguration • The Institution of the Eucharist
306			• The Agony in the Garden • The Scourging at the Pillar • The Crowning with Thorns • The Carrying of the Cross • The Crucifixion
307			• The Resurrection • The Ascension • The Descent of the Holy Spirit on Pentecost • The Assumption of Mary • The Coronation of Mary as Queen of Heaven and Earth
308			• The Annunciation • The Visitation • The Nativity • The Presentation of Jesus in the Temple • The Finding of Jesus in the Temple
309			• The Baptism of Jesus • The Wedding at Cana • The Proclamation of the Kingdom and the Call to Conversion • The Transfiguration • The Institution of the Eucharist
310			• The Agony in the Garden • The Scourging at the Pillar • The Crowning with Thorns • The Carrying of the Cross • The Crucifixion
311			• The Resurrection • The Ascension • The Descent of the Holy Spirit on Pentecost • The Assumption of Mary • The Coronation of Mary as Queen of Heaven and Earth

A Roadmap for This Journey   29

312			• The Annunciation • The Visitation • The Nativity • The Presentation of Jesus in the Temple • The Finding of Jesus in the Temple
313			• The Baptism of Jesus • The Wedding at Cana • The Proclamation of the Kingdom and the Call to Conversion • The Transfiguration • The Institution of the Eucharist
314			• The Agony in the Garden • The Scourging at the Pillar • The Crowning with Thorns • The Carrying of the Cross • The Crucifixion
315			• The Resurrection • The Ascension • The Descent of the Holy Spirit on Pentecost • The Assumption of Mary • The Coronation of Mary as Queen of Heaven and Earth
316	Phase 5: Building Up the Decades	5 Decades	• The Annunciation • The Visitation • The Nativity • The Presentation of Jesus in the Temple • The Finding of Jesus in the Temple
317			• The Baptism of Jesus • The Wedding at Cana • The Proclamation of the Kingdom and the Call to Conversion • The Transfiguration • The Institution of the Eucharist
318			• The Agony in the Garden • The Scourging at the Pillar • The Crowning with Thorns • The Carrying of the Cross • The Crucifixion
319			• The Resurrection • The Ascension • The Descent of the Holy Spirit on Pentecost • The Assumption of Mary • The Coronation of Mary as Queen of Heaven and Earth
320			• The Annunciation • The Visitation • The Nativity • The Presentation of Jesus in the Temple • The Finding of Jesus in the Temple
321			• The Baptism of Jesus • The Wedding at Cana • The Proclamation of the Kingdom and the Call to Conversion • The Transfiguration • The Institution of the Eucharist

322			• The Agony in the Garden • The Scourging at the Pillar • The Crowning with Thorns • The Carrying of the Cross • The Crucifixion
323			• The Resurrection • The Ascension • The Descent of the Holy Spirit on Pentecost • The Assumption of Mary • The Coronation of Mary as Queen of Heaven and Earth
324			• The Annunciation • The Visitation • The Nativity • The Presentation of Jesus in the Temple • The Finding of Jesus in the Temple
325			• The Baptism of Jesus • The Wedding at Cana • The Proclamation of the Kingdom and the Call to Conversion • The Transfiguration • The Institution of the Eucharist
326	Phase 5: Building Up the Decades	5 Decades	• The Agony in the Garden • The Scourging at the Pillar • The Crowning with Thorns • The Carrying of the Cross • The Crucifixion
327			• The Resurrection • The Ascension • The Descent of the Holy Spirit on Pentecost • The Assumption of Mary • The Coronation of Mary as Queen of Heaven and Earth
328			• The Annunciation • The Visitation • The Nativity • The Presentation of Jesus in the Temple • The Finding of Jesus in the Temple
329			• The Baptism of Jesus • The Wedding at Cana • The Proclamation of the Kingdom and the Call to Conversion • The Transfiguration • The Institution of the Eucharist
330			• The Agony in the Garden • The Scourging at the Pillar • The Crowning with Thorns • The Carrying of the Cross • The Crucifixion
331			• The Resurrection • The Ascension • The Descent of the Holy Spirit on Pentecost • The Assumption of Mary • The Coronation of Mary as Queen of Heaven and Earth

332	Phase 5: Building Up the Decades	5 Decades	• The Annunciation • The Visitation • The Nativity • The Presentation of Jesus in the Temple • The Finding of Jesus in the Temple
333			• The Baptism of Jesus • The Wedding at Cana • The Proclamation of the Kingdom and the Call to Conversion • The Transfiguration • The Institution of the Eucharist
334			• The Agony in the Garden • The Scourging at the Pillar • The Crowning with Thorns • The Carrying of the Cross • The Crucifixion
335			• The Resurrection • The Ascension • The Descent of the Holy Spirit on Pentecost • The Assumption of Mary • The Coronation of Mary as Queen of Heaven and Earth
336	Phase 6: Praying Together	5-decade Rosary (including beginning and ending prayers) on the specified day of the week	• The Agony in the Garden • The Scourging at the Pillar • The Crowning with Thorns • The Carrying of the Cross • The Crucifixion
337			• The Resurrection • The Ascension • The Descent of the Holy Spirit on Pentecost • The Assumption of Mary • The Coronation of Mary as Queen of Heaven and Earth
338			• The Baptism of Jesus • The Wedding at Cana • The Proclamation of the Kingdom and the Call to Conversion • The Transfiguration • The Institution of the Eucharist
339			• The Agony in the Garden • The Scourging at the Pillar • The Crowning with Thorns • The Carrying of the Cross • The Crucifixion
340			• The Annunciation • The Visitation • The Nativity • The Presentation of Jesus in the Temple • The Finding of Jesus in the Temple
341			• The Resurrection • The Ascension • The Descent of the Holy Spirit on Pentecost • The Assumption of Mary • The Coronation of Mary as Queen of Heaven and Earth

342	Phase 6: Praying Together	5-decade Rosary (including beginning and ending prayers) on the specified day of the week	• The Annunciation • The Visitation • The Nativity • The Presentation of Jesus in the Temple • The Finding of Jesus in the Temple
343			• The Agony in the Garden • The Scourging at the Pillar • The Crowning with Thorns • The Carrying of the Cross • The Crucifixion
344			• The Resurrection • The Ascension • The Descent of the Holy Spirit on Pentecost • The Assumption of Mary • The Coronation of Mary as Queen of Heaven and Earth
345			• The Baptism of Jesus • The Wedding at Cana • The Proclamation of the Kingdom and the Call to Conversion • The Transfiguration • The Institution of the Eucharist
346			• The Agony in the Garden • The Scourging at the Pillar • The Crowning with Thorns • The Carrying of the Cross • The Crucifixion
347			• The Annunciation • The Visitation • The Nativity • The Presentation of Jesus in the Temple • The Finding of Jesus in the Temple
348			• The Resurrection • The Ascension • The Descent of the Holy Spirit on Pentecost • The Assumption of Mary • The Coronation of Mary as Queen of Heaven and Earth
349			• The Annunciation • The Visitation • The Nativity • The Presentation of Jesus in the Temple • The Finding of Jesus in the Temple
350			• The Agony in the Garden • The Scourging at the Pillar • The Crowning with Thorns • The Carrying of the Cross • The Crucifixion
351			• The Resurrection • The Ascension • The Descent of the Holy Spirit on Pentecost • The Assumption of Mary • The Coronation of Mary as Queen of Heaven and Earth

A Roadmap for This Journey   33

352			• The Baptism of Jesus • The Wedding at Cana • The Proclamation of the Kingdom and the Call to Conversion • The Transfiguration • The Institution of the Eucharist
353			• The Agony in the Garden • The Scourging at the Pillar • The Crowning with Thorns • The Carrying of the Cross • The Crucifixion
354			• The Annunciation • The Visitation • The Nativity • The Presentation of Jesus in the Temple • The Finding of Jesus in the Temple
355			• The Resurrection • The Ascension • The Descent of the Holy Spirit on Pentecost • The Assumption of Mary • The Coronation of Mary as Queen of Heaven and Earth
356	Phase 6: Praying Together	5-decade Rosary (including beginning and ending prayers) on the specified day of the week	• The Annunciation • The Visitation • The Nativity • The Presentation of Jesus in the Temple • The Finding of Jesus in the Temple
357			• The Agony in the Garden • The Scourging at the Pillar • The Crowning with Thorns • The Carrying of the Cross • The Crucifixion
358			• The Resurrection • The Ascension • The Descent of the Holy Spirit on Pentecost • The Assumption of Mary • The Coronation of Mary as Queen of Heaven and Earth
359			• The Baptism of Jesus • The Wedding at Cana • The Proclamation of the Kingdom and the Call to Conversion • The Transfiguration • The Institution of the Eucharist
360			• The Agony in the Garden • The Scourging at the Pillar • The Crowning with Thorns • The Carrying of the Cross • The Crucifixion
361			• The Annunciation • The Visitation • The Nativity • The Presentation of Jesus in the Temple • The Finding of Jesus in the Temple

362	Phase 6: Praying Together	5-decade Rosary (including beginning and ending prayers) on the specified day of the week	• The Resurrection • The Ascension • The Descent of the Holy Spirit on Pentecost • The Assumption of Mary • The Coronation of Mary as Queen of Heaven and Earth
363			• The Annunciation • The Visitation • The Nativity • The Presentation of Jesus in the Temple • The Finding of Jesus in the Temple
364			• The Agony in the Garden • The Scourging at the Pillar • The Crowning with Thorns • The Carrying of the Cross • The Crucifixion
365			• The Resurrection • The Ascension • The Descent of the Holy Spirit on Pentecost • The Assumption of Mary • The Coronation of Mary as Queen of Heaven and Earth

THE BASIC PRAYERS OF THE ROSARY

These are the basic prayers of the Rosary. All the prayers of the Rosary can be found on page 367; you will not be asked to pray the introductory and concluding prayers until Day 336 of the podcast.

Our Father

Our Father, who art in heaven,
hallowed be thy name.
Thy kingdom come.
Thy will be done on earth, as it is in heaven.
Give us this day our daily bread,
and forgive us our trespasses,
as we forgive those who trespass
against us,
and lead us not into temptation,
but deliver us from evil.
Amen.

Hail Mary

Hail Mary, full of grace, the Lord is with you;
blessed are you among women,
and blessed is the fruit of your womb, Jesus.
Holy Mary, Mother of God,
pray for us sinners
now and at the hour of our death.
Amen.

Glory Be

Glory be to the Father, the Son, and the Holy Spirit;
as it was in the beginning, is now, and ever shall be,
world without end.
Amen.

THE MYSTERIES OF THE ROSARY

These are the mysteries that we meditate upon as we pray the Rosary. Each set of mysteries is traditionally prayed on a certain day of the week, explained on page 361. You will not be asked to pray the mysteries on their traditional days of the week until Day 336 of the podcast.

JOYFUL MYSTERIES

1. **The Annunciation (see Luke 1:26–38)**
   We pray for a humble heart.
   Mary is visited by the archangel Gabriel, who tells her God's plan for her to become the mother of our Savior, Jesus Christ, and she says yes with all her heart.
2. **The Visitation (see Luke 1:39–56)**
   We pray for a charitable heart.
   Filled with the Holy Spirit, Mary travels to see her cousin Elizabeth, who joyfully acknowledges Mary as blessed, affirming the divinity of the unborn Jesus.
3. **The Nativity (see Luke 2:1–20)**
   We pray for a heart poor in spirit.
   Mary gives birth to Jesus, the Son of God made man, laying him in a simple manger in Bethlehem as angels and shepherds glorify God.
4. **The Presentation of Jesus in the Temple (see Luke 2:22–39)**
   We pray for a pure heart.
   Mary and Joseph present the infant Jesus in the Temple, where Simeon proclaims that Jesus is the long-awaited Messiah.
5. **The Finding of Jesus in the Temple (see Luke 2:41–52)**
   We pray for conversion of heart.
   After searching for Jesus for three days, Mary and Joseph find him in the Temple, his Father's house, where he is talking with great understanding to the teachers.

LUMINOUS MYSTERIES

1. **The Baptism of Jesus (see Matthew 3:13–17)**
   We pray for a heart faithful to our baptismal vows.
   As Jesus begins his ministry, baptized by John the Baptist, the Holy Spirit descends upon him with the appearance of a dove, and the voice of the heavenly Father declares him beloved.

2. **The Wedding at Cana (see John 2:1–12)**
   We pray for a heart ready to do God's will.
   Mary asks Jesus to perform his first miracle, turning water into wine, which reveals Jesus' power and the importance of Mary's role in leading others to her son.

3. **The Proclamation of the Kingdom and the Call to Conversion (see Mark 1:14–15)**
   We pray for a heart filled with faith.
   Calling all to repent and believe in the Gospel, Jesus announces the arrival of God's Kingdom, as his teachings and miracles demonstrate God's mercy and love for all of us.

4. **The Transfiguration (see Matthew 17:1–13)**
   We pray for a heart filled with hope.
   Jesus takes Peter, James, and John up a mountain, where he is transfigured, shining with heavenly glory as he talks to Moses and Elijah, affirming his divinity and fulfillment of the Law and the Prophets.

5. **The Institution of the Eucharist (see Luke 22:14–23)**
   We pray for a heart filled with gratitude for the Holy Eucharist.
   On the night before his Crucifixion, Jesus shares the Last Supper with his Apostles, changing bread and wine into his Body, Blood, Soul, and Divinity as he institutes the Sacrament of the Holy Eucharist.

SORROWFUL MYSTERIES

1. **The Agony in the Garden (see Matthew 26:36–46)**
    We pray for a contrite and obedient heart.
    Jesus prays in the garden of Gethsemane before his arrest, demonstrating his profound obedience to the Father's will and revealing the depth of his human suffering.
2. **The Scourging at the Pillar (see Matthew 27:26)**
    We pray for a disciplined heart.
    Jesus is brutally scourged and humiliated as he bears the weight of humanity's sins, proving his unconditional and sacrificial love for us.
3. **The Crowning with Thorns (see Matthew 27:27–31)**
    We pray for a detached heart.
    Mocked and tortured by Roman soldiers, Jesus is crowned with thorns, and those who see him call for his crucifixion.
4. **The Carrying of the Cross (see Matthew 27:32)**
    We pray for a patient heart.
    Jesus carries the heavy Cross, showing his commitment to doing the Father's will as he endures suffering and humiliation on the path to Calvary.
5. **The Crucifixion (see Luke 23:33–46)**
    We pray for a holy heart.
    Jesus, the Savior of the world, is nailed to the Cross and dies, offering himself with unconditional love and mercy for us as the ultimate sacrifice for our sins, while forgiving his persecutors and entrusting Mary and John to each other.

GLORIOUS MYSTERIES

1. **The Resurrection (see Matthew 28:1–10)**
   We pray for a faithful heart.
   Jesus rises from the dead; he has defeated sin and death, offering hope and eternal life to all who believe in him.
2. **The Ascension (see Luke 24:50–53)**
   We pray for a heart ready for heaven.
   Telling his disciples to spread the Gospel and to baptize, Jesus ascends into heaven forty days after his Resurrection, returning to the Father.
3. **The Descent of the Holy Spirit on Pentecost (see Acts 2:1–13)**
   We pray for a wise heart.
   As the Apostles are gathered in prayer with Mary, the Holy Spirit comes down upon them, strengthening them with gifts to proclaim the Gospel.
4. **The Assumption of Mary (see Luke 1:46–56)**
   We pray for a heart devoted to Mary.
   Mary is taken body and soul into heaven by God's grace, affirming her unique role as the immaculate Mother of God and anticipating the resurrection of all believers at the end of time.
5. **The Coronation of Mary as Queen of Heaven and Earth (see Revelation 12:1–5)**
   We pray for final perseverance of heart.
   Mary is crowned Queen of Heaven and Earth by her son, Jesus Christ, as the exalted mother of the King.

PHASE 1
FORMING THE RELATIONSHIP

Days 1 – 7

INTRODUCTION

About This Phase

As Jesus said in Matthew 7:24, those who are wise build on solid foundations, not rock or sand. This first phase of *The Rosary in a Year* will focus on building a good foundation for your prayerful Rosary habit through achieving two main goals.

First, we will deepen our relationships with Jesus and Mary, the two persons we primarily meditate on in the mysteries of the Rosary. To accomplish this, we will practice awareness of the fact that we truly are praying in the presence of Jesus and Mary. Then, we will reflect on some of the titles of Mary and Jesus found in the Litany of the Blessed Virgin (the Litany of Loreto) and the Litany of the Sacred Heart. There's no need to pray the litanies in full right now—we will just select one or two titles to reflect on.

Second, we will begin to incorporate the prayers of the Rosary into our daily lives. To accomplish this goal, we will pray a short, manageable set of prayers each day: 1 Our Father, 3 Hail Marys, and 1 Glory Be.

By the end of this phase, we will have begun building the mental muscle of focus needed for prayer by praying a short selection of the prayers of the Rosary daily, and you will have a new way to deepen your relationships with Jesus and Mary!

> **PRAY** — Every day of this phase, we will pray 1 Our Father, 3 Hail Marys, and 1 Glory Be.

Tips for this phase
- Try out different times of day. Even if you think you know what time is best for you, this phase is a great opportunity to experiment and ask the Holy Spirit to show you the best time of day to form your Rosary habit.

- Remember that starting slow can be humbling, but it will set you up for long-lasting success.
- Use the litanies as guides for meditating on the persons of Jesus and Mary whenever you like! Throughout the podcast, if you find yourself needing a refresher, turn back to the litanies and pray with a title of Jesus or Mary as Fr. Mark-Mary teaches.
- Let the Holy Spirit guide you through this first phase. If you have questions about the Rosary and need more guidance, find a trusted book or other resource and dive in!

LITANIES

Litany of the Blessed Virgin (Litany of Loreto)

Lord, have mercy on us.
Christ, have mercy on us.
Lord, have mercy on us.
Christ, hear us.
Christ, graciously hear us.
God, the Father of heaven, have mercy on us.
God, the Son, Redeemer of the world, have mercy on us.
God, the Holy Spirit, have mercy on us.
Holy Trinity, one God, have mercy on us.
Holy Mary, pray for us.
Holy Mother of God, pray for us.
Holy Virgin of virgins, pray for us.
Mother of Christ, pray for us.
Mother of the Church, pray for us.
Mother of Mercy, pray for us.
Mother of divine grace, pray for us.
Mother most pure, pray for us.
Mother most chaste, pray for us.
Mother inviolate, pray for us.

Mother undefiled, pray for us.
Mother most amiable, pray for us.
Mother admirable, pray for us.
Mother of good counsel, pray for us.
Mother of our Creator, pray for us.
Mother of our Saviour, pray for us.
Virgin most prudent, pray for us.
Virgin most venerable, pray for us.
Virgin most renowned, pray for us.
Virgin most powerful, pray for us.
Virgin most merciful, pray for us.
Virgin most faithful, pray for us.
Mirror of justice, pray for us.
Seat of wisdom, pray for us.
Cause of our joy, pray for us.
Spiritual vessel, pray for us.
Vessel of honour, pray for us.
Singular vessel of devotion, pray for us.
Mystical rose, pray for us.
Tower of David, pray for us.
Tower of ivory, pray for us.
House of gold, pray for us.
Ark of the covenant, pray for us.
Gate of heaven, pray for us.
Morning star, pray for us.
Health of the sick, pray for us.
Refuge of sinners, pray for us.
Solace of Migrants, pray for us.
Comfort of the afflicted, pray for us.
Help of Christians, pray for us.
Queen of Angels, pray for us.
Queen of Patriarchs, pray for us.
Queen of Prophets, pray for us.
Queen of Apostles, pray for us.

Queen of Martyrs, pray for us.
Queen of Confessors, pray for us.
Queen of Virgins, pray for us.
Queen of all Saints, pray for us.
Queen conceived without original sin, pray for us.
Queen assumed into heaven, pray for us.
Queen of the most holy Rosary, pray for us.
Queen of families, pray for us.
Queen of peace, pray for us.
Lamb of God, Who takes away the sins of the world, spare us, O Lord.
Lamb of God, Who takes away the sins of the world, graciously hear us, O Lord.
Lamb of God, Who takes away the sins of the world, have mercy on us.
Pray for us, O holy Mother of God.
That we may be made worthy of the promises of Christ.
Let us pray.
Grant, we beseech thee,
O Lord God,
That we, your servants,
May enjoy perpetual health of mind and body;
And by the glorious intercession of the Blessed Mary, ever Virgin,
may be delivered from present sorrow,
and obtain eternal joy.
Through Christ our Lord.
Amen.

Litany of the Holy Name of Jesus

Lord, have mercy on us.
Christ, have mercy on us.
Lord, have mercy on us.
Jesus, hear us.
Jesus, graciously hear us.
God, the Father of heaven, have mercy on us.
God, the Son, Redeemer of the world, have mercy on us.

God, the Holy Spirit, have mercy on us.
Holy Trinity, one God, have mercy on us.
Jesus, Son of the living God, have mercy on us.
Jesus, splendor of the Father, have mercy on us.
Jesus, brightness of eternal Light, have mercy on us.
Jesus, king of glory, have mercy on us.
Jesus, sun of justice, have mercy on us.
Jesus, Son of the Virgin Mary, have mercy on us.
Jesus, most amiable, have mercy on us.
Jesus, most admirable, have mercy on us.
Jesus, the mighty God, have mercy on us.
Jesus, father of the world to come, have mercy on us.
Jesus, angel of the great council, have mercy on us.
Jesus, most powerful, have mercy on us.
Jesus, most patient, have mercy on us.
Jesus, most obedient, have mercy on us.
Jesus, meek and humble of heart, have mercy on us.
Jesus, lover of chastity, have mercy on us.
Jesus, lover of us, have mercy on us.
Jesus, God of peace, have mercy on us.
Jesus, author of life, have mercy on us.
Jesus, example of virtues, have mercy on us.
Jesus, zealous lover of souls, have mercy on us.
Jesus, our God, have mercy on us.
Jesus, our refuge, have mercy on us.
Jesus, father of the poor, have mercy on us.
Jesus, treasure of the faithful, have mercy on us.
Jesus, good shepherd, have mercy on us.
Jesus, true light, have mercy on us.
Jesus, eternal wisdom, have mercy on us.
Jesus, infinite goodness, have mercy on us.
Jesus, our way and our life, have mercy on us.
Jesus, joy of angels, have mercy on us.
Jesus, king of the Patriarchs, have mercy on us.

Jesus, master of Apostles, have mercy on us.
Jesus, teacher of Evangelists, have mercy on us.
Jesus, strength of Martyrs, have mercy on us.
Jesus, light of Confessors, have mercy on us.
Jesus, purity of Virgins, have mercy on us.
Jesus, crown of all Saints, have mercy on us.
Be merciful, spare us, O Jesus.
Be merciful, hear us, O Jesus.
From all evil, Jesus, deliver us.
From all sin, Jesus, deliver us.
From Thy wrath, Jesus, deliver us.
From the snares of the devil, Jesus, deliver us.
From the spirit of fornication, Jesus, deliver us.
From everlasting death, Jesus, deliver us.
Front the neglect of Thine inspirations, Jesus, deliver us.
Through the mystery of Thy holy Incarnation, Jesus, deliver us.
Through Thy nativity, Jesus, deliver us.
Through Thine infancy, Jesus, deliver us.
Through Thy most divine life, Jesus, deliver us.
Through Thy labors, Jesus, deliver us.
Through Thine agony and passion, Jesus, deliver us.
Through Thy cross and dereliction, Jesus, deliver us.
Through Thy sufferings, Jesus, deliver us.
Through Thy death and burial, Jesus, deliver us.
Through Thy resurrection, Jesus, deliver us.
Through Thy ascension, Jesus, deliver us.
Through the institution of Thy most holy Eucharist, Jesus, deliver us.
Through Thy joys, Jesus, deliver us.
Through Thy glory, Jesus, deliver us.
Lamb of God, Who takest away the sins of the world, Jesus, spare us.
Lamb of God, Who takest away the sins of the world, Jesus, graciously hear us.
Lamb of God, Who takest away the sins of the world, Jesus, have mercy on us.

Jesus hear us. Jesus, graciously hear us.

Let us pray:
O Lord Jesus Christ, Who hast said: "Ask, and ye shall receive; seek, and ye shall find; knock, and it shall be opened unto you"; grant, we beseech Thee, unto us who ask the gift of Thy most divine love, that we may ever love Thee with our whole hearts, words and works, and never cease from Thy praise.

Make us, O Lord, to have a perpetual fear as well as love of Thy holy Name, for Thou never ceases to govern those whom Thou foundest upon the solidity of Thy love. Who livest and reignest forever and ever. Amen.

Litany of the Sacred Heart

Lord, have mercy on us.
Christ, have mercy on us.
Lord, have mercy on us.
Christ, hear us.
Christ, graciously hear us.
God, the Father of Heaven, have mercy on us.
God, the Son, Redeemer of the world, have mercy on us.
God, the Holy Spirit, have mercy on us.
Holy Trinity, one God, have mercy on us.
Heart of Jesus, Son of the Eternal Father, have mercy on us.
Heart of Jesus, formed by the Holy Spirit in the womb of the Virgin Mother, have mercy on us.
Heart of Jesus, substantially united to the Word of God, have mercy on us.
Heart of Jesus, of infinite majesty, have mercy on us.
Heart of Jesus, sacred temple of God, have mercy on us.
Heart of Jesus, tabernacle of the Most High, have mercy on us.
Heart of Jesus, house of God and gate of heaven, have mercy on us.
Heart of Jesus, burning furnace of charity, have mercy on us.
Heart of Jesus, abode of justice and love, have mercy on us.

Heart of Jesus, full of goodness and love, have mercy on us.
Heart of Jesus, abyss of all virtues, have mercy on us.
Heart of Jesus, most worthy of all praise, have mercy on us.
Heart of Jesus, king and centre of all hearts, have mercy on us.
Heart of Jesus, in Whom are all the treasures of wisdom and knowledge, have mercy on us.
Heart of Jesus, in Whom dwells the fullness of divinity, have mercy on us.
Heart of Jesus, in Whom the Father was well pleased, have mercy on us.
Heart of Jesus, of Whose fullness we have all received, have mercy on us.
Heart of Jesus, desire of the everlasting hills, have mercy on us.
Heart of Jesus, patient and most merciful, have mercy on us.
Heart of Jesus, enriching all who invoke Thee, have mercy on us.
Heart of Jesus, fountain of life and holiness, have mercy on us.
Heart of Jesus, propitiation for our sins, have mercy on us.
Heart of Jesus, loaded down with opprobrium, have mercy on us.
Heart of Jesus, bruised for our offenses, have mercy on us.
Heart of Jesus, obedient unto death, have mercy on us.
Heart of Jesus, pierced with a lance, have mercy on us.
Heart of Jesus, source of all consolation, have mercy on us.
Heart of Jesus, our life and resurrection, have mercy on us.
Heart of Jesus, our peace and reconciliation, have mercy on us.
Heart of Jesus, vicitim for sin, have mercy on us.
Heart of Jesus, salvation of those who trust in Thee, have mercy on us.
Heart of Jesus, hope of those who die in Thee, have mercy on us.
Heart of Jesus, delight of all the saints, have mercy on us.
Lamb of God, Who takest away the sins of the world, spare us, O Lord.
Lamb of God, Who takest away the sins of the world, graciously hear us, O Lord.
Lamb of God, Who takest away the sins of the world, have mercy on us.

V. Jesus, meek and humble of Heart.
R. Make our hearts like unto Thine.

Let us pray:
O Almighty and eternal God, look upon the Heart of Thy dearly beloved Son, and upon the praise and satisfaction He offers Thee in the name of sinners and for those who seek Thy mercy; be Thou appeased, and grant us pardon in the name of the same Jesus Christ, Thy Son, Who liveth and reigneth with Thee, in the unity of the Holy Spirit forever and ever. Amen.

DAYS 1–7

DAY 1

"The Rosary is a priceless treasure which is inspired by God."
–St. Louis de Montfort

Before you pray, ask God to grant you the grace he wants to bestow on you through this *Rosary in a Year* journey.

Think carefully about the words of the prayers as you pray them, as if it were the first time you heard them.

Remember, you are starting small to lay a deep foundation, just like a weight lifter will start with lighter weights to master good "form" and build up well. Today, place your trust in God, and give him this small offering.

Today's Prayer: Pray 1 Our Father, 3 Hail Marys, and 1 Glory Be.

DAY 2

Today, focus on making yourself aware of the presence of Jesus as you pray. This isn't something you're manufacturing—this is something that is already a reality; you only need to remember and receive it. Jesus is looking upon you, right now, with love, care, attention, and encouragement. If it helps you call the presence of Jesus to mind, try looking at a piece of sacred art. Try envisioning yourself with him— where does your mind set the scene? What is Jesus wearing? What are some of the sights and sounds around you? As you pray for this short period of time today, ask the Holy Spirit for the grace to be aware of the reality of the presence of Jesus.

Today's Prayer: Pray 1 Our Father, 3 Hail Marys, and 1 Glory Be.

DAY 3

Today, we reflect on the person of Jesus using the Litany of the Sacred Heart, which can be found on page 48. Using one of Jesus' many titles in this litany, which was first approved for the faithful by the pope in 1899, we can contemplate who Jesus is, how he sees us, and how we should understand his role in our lives. You can use the title Fr. Mark-Mary reflects on in the podcast, or select a title of Jesus to reflect on yourself. No need to pray the entire litany—simply choose one of the titles the Church provides us for Jesus and reflect on it for the short time of prayer you have today.

Today's Prayer: Pray 1 Our Father, 3 Hail Marys, and 1 Glory Be.

DAY 4

Today, focus on making yourself aware of Mary's presence as you pray. When a loved one is in the room with you, you have a sense of that person's presence, even if you aren't speaking with him or her. Call this feeling to mind when you think of Mary present with you now as you pray. If it is helpful, use a piece of sacred art to remember that Mary is a real person, who is alive right now and is gazing with affection on you as you pray. As you pray today, simply ask the Lord for the grace to be aware of how Mary is with you—how she looks upon you, sees you, hears you, loves you.

Today's Prayer: Pray 1 Our Father, 3 Hail Marys, and 1 Glory Be.

DAY 5

Today, we reflect on the person of Mary using the Litany of the Blessed Virgin (the Litany of Loreto), which can be found on page 43. Using one of Mary's many titles in this litany, which was first approved for the faithful by the pope in 1587, we can contemplate who Mary is, how she looks at us, and how we should understand her role in our lives. You can use the title Fr. Mark-Mary reflects on in the podcast, or select a title of Mary to reflect on yourself. No need to pray the entire litany—simply choose one of the titles the Church provides us for Mary and reflect on it for the short time of prayer you have today.

Today's Prayer: Pray 1 Our Father, 3 Hail Marys, and 1 Glory Be.

DAY 6

"Love our Lady and make her loved. Recite the Rosary … And recite it as much as you can."
–St. Padre Pio

Today, ask for the grace to persevere in prayer even when difficulties come up.

Today's Prayer: Pray 1 Our Father, 3 Hail Marys, and 1 Glory Be.

DAY 7

As we start to learn to pray the Rosary in a deep way, we trust that we will not only obtain graces for ourselves but that we can be filled to overflowing and become a source of grace for the entire world in ways we do not even fully understand. As Pope Benedict XVI said, "May Mary help us to welcome within ourselves the grace emanating from these mysteries, so that through us we can 'water' society, beginning with our daily relationships, and purifying them from so many negative forces, thus opening them to the newness of God."

Today's Prayer: Pray 1 Our Father, 3 Hail Marys, and 1 Glory Be.

PHASE 2
BIBLICAL ROOTS OF THE ROSARY

Days 8 – 68

INTRODUCTION

About This Phase

Understanding the deep spiritual meaning of the Rosary is essential if we are going to still ourselves and drink deeply of the truth of the life and love of God through this prayer. In this second phase of *The Rosary in a Year*, the focus will be on understanding the biblical basis of the prayers and mysteries of the Rosary.

First, on Days 8–28, we will delve into the biblical roots of the prayers of the Rosary. The Our Father is found in Scripture word for word, while other prayers like the Hail Mary and Hail, Holy Queen are not. But every single prayer of the Rosary has biblical roots that we will uncover in the coming days.

Second, on Days 29–68, we will discover the biblical roots of the mysteries of the Rosary. Each mystery of the Rosary is a chance to meditate on a significant event in the lives of Jesus and Mary. In this phase, we will read, and re-read, a Scripture passage related to each of these events.

By the end of this phase, you will understand the biblical foundations of each prayer of the Rosary, as well as each of the twenty mysteries of the Rosary. This is a chance to make the basic elements of the Rosary, the prayers and the mysteries, more full of meaning in your prayer life!

READ	On some days, we will read a Scripture passage related to that day's mystery. Turn to the day to see what to read.

PRAY	Every day of this phase, we will pray 1 Our Father, 3 Hail Marys, and 1 Glory Be.

Tips for this phase

- Don't forget where we have been—if you find yourself forgetting to pray, remember the encouragement of Phase 1. Find a time of day that is best for you and set reminders if necessary!
- Remember that we are doing a "slow build," beginning with a just a few prayers a day, in order to strengthen our prayer "muscles" well.
- Any time we are reading the Bible, we are encountering the Word of God. If you find yourself wondering about the meaning of any passage of Scripture in this phase, turn to a trusted Catholic study Bible or other resource to learn from the Church how to understand what you read in Scripture.
- Some mysteries are described in more than one passage of Scripture. While we will be focusing our meditations on one Scripture passage per mystery, there is more to read for many mysteries. If any mysteries stand out to you, search the other Gospels for more to contemplate!

THE BIBLICAL FOUNDATION OF THE PRAYERS OF THE ROSARY

The prayers of the Rosary are truly steeped in the Scriptures. The Our Father is found verbatim in the Gospel of Matthew, while the other prayers of the Rosary include many direct quotations and indirect allusions from both the Old and New Testaments.

In the pages that follow, the prayers of the Rosary are placed side by side with words of Scripture. You will see that some Scripture verses give us the words we pray, while other verses form the foundation for the prayers.

HAIL MARY

Words of the prayer	Words of Scripture
Hail Mary, full of grace, the Lord is with thee.	Luke 1:28: "And he [the angel Gabriel] came to her and said, 'Hail, full of grace, the Lord is with you!'"
Blessed are you among women, and blessed is the fruit of your womb, Jesus.	Luke 1:42: "And she [Elizabeth] exclaimed with a loud cry, 'Blessed are you among women, and blessed is the fruit of your womb!'" Luke 1:48: "For he has regarded the low estate of his handmaiden. For behold, henceforth all generations will call me blessed."
Holy Mary, Mother of God,	Luke 1:43: "And why is this granted me, that the mother of my Lord should come to me?" Matthew 1:23 (see Isaiah 7:14): "'Behold, a virgin shall conceive and bear a son, and his name shall be called Emmanuel' (which means, God with us)."
pray for us sinners, now and at the hour of our death. Amen.	John 19:26–27: "When Jesus saw his mother, and the disciple whom he loved standing near, he said to his mother, 'Woman, behold, your son!' Then he said to the disciple, 'Behold, your mother!' And from that hour the disciple took her to his own home."

Phase 2: Biblical Roots of the Rosary

OUR FATHER

Words of the prayer

Our Father who art in heaven, hallowed be thy name.

Thy kingdom come. Thy will be done on earth, as it is in heaven.

Give us this day our daily bread,

Words of Scripture

Matthew 6:9: "Pray then like this: Our Father who art in heaven, Hallowed be thy name."
Ezekiel 36:23: "And I will vindicate the holiness of my great name, which has been profaned among the nations, and which you have profaned among them; and the nations will know that I am the Lord, says the Lord God, when through you I vindicate my holiness before their eyes."

Matthew 6:10: "Thy kingdom come. Thy will be done On earth as it is in heaven."
Matthew 6:33: "But seek first his kingdom and his righteousness, and all these things shall be yours as well."

Matthew 6:11: "Give us this day our daily bread."
Matthew 6:25: "Therefore I tell you, do not be anxious about your life, what you shall eat or what you shall drink, nor about your body, what you shall put on. Is not life more than food, and the body more than clothing?"
John 6:51: "I am the living bread which

came down from heaven; if any one eats of this bread, he will live for ever; and the bread which I shall give for the life of the world is my flesh."

And forgive us our trespasses, as we forgive those who trespass against us,

Matthew 6:12: "And forgive us our trespasses
As we forgive those who trespass against us."
Matthew 6:14: "For if you forgive men their trespasses, your heavenly Father also will forgive you; but if you do not forgive men their trespasses, neither will your Father forgive your trespasses."

And lead us not into temptation, but deliver us from evil.

Matthew 6:13: "And lead us not into temptation,
But deliver us from evil."
James 1:13–14: "Let no one say when he is tempted, 'I am tempted by God'; for God cannot be tempted with evil and he himself tempts no one; but each person is tempted when he is lured and enticed by his own desire."

GLORY BE

Words of the prayer

Glory be to the Father, and to the Son, and to the Holy Spirit,

As it was in the beginning, is now, and ever shall be, world without end. Amen.

Words of Scripture

Romans 11:36: "For from him and through him and to him are all things. To him be glory for ever. Amen."

Revelation 1:8: "'I am the Alpha and the Omega,' says the Lord God, who is and who was and who is to come, the Almighty."

THE SIGN OF THE CROSS

Words of the prayer

In the name of the Father, and of the Son, and of the Holy Spirit. Amen.

Words of Scripture

Matthew 28:19: "Go therefore and make disciples of all nations, baptizing them in the name of the Father and of the Son and of the Holy Spirit."

Revelation 14:1: "Then I looked, and behold, on Mount Zion stood the Lamb, and with him a hundred and forty-four thousand who had his name and his Father's name written on their foreheads."

THE HAIL HOLY QUEEN

Words of the prayer

Hail Holy Queen, Mother of Mercy, our life, our sweetness and our hope!

To thee do we cry poor banished children of Eve;

To thee do we send up our sighs, mourning and weeping in this valley of tears.

Words of Scripture

Psalm 45:9: "At your right hand stands the queen in gold of Ophir."
1 Kings 2:19: "So Bathsheba went to King Solomon, to speak to him on behalf of Adonijah. And the king rose to meet her, and bowed down to her; then he sat on his throne, and had a seat brought for the king's mother; and she sat on his right."
Note: In the Old Testament, the queen was the mother of the Davidic king—the queen mother." Therefore, calling Jesus' mother "Queen" flows from biblical tradition, since she is the Mother of Christ the King. The queen mother also interceded on behalf of the people.

Genesis 3:20: "The man called his wife's name Eve, because she was the mother of all living."

Revelation 21:4: "He will wipe away every tear from their eyes, and death shall be no more, neither shall there be mourning nor crying nor pain any more, for the former things have passed away."

Turn then, O most gracious advocate, thine eyes of mercy towards us	John 2:3: "When the wine failed, the mother of Jesus said to him, 'They have no wine.'" *Note: This passage shows how Mary, in advocating for the married couple at the wedding feast at Cana, can advocate for us and ask Jesus to turn our "water" into "wine."*
And after this our exile show unto us the blessed fruit of thy womb, Jesus;	1 Peter 1:17: "And if you invoke as Father him who judges each one impartially according to his deeds, conduct yourselves with fear throughout the time of your exile." Luke 1:42: "And she [Elizabeth] exclaimed with a loud cry, 'Blessed are you among women, and blessed is the fruit of your womb!'"
O clement, O loving, O sweet Virgin Mary.	Matthew 1:23 (see Isaiah 7:14): "'Behold, a virgin shall conceive and bear a son, and his name shall be called Emmanuel' (which means, God with us)."

THE FATIMA PRAYER

Words of the prayer	**Words of Scripture**
Oh my Jesus, forgive us our sins,	Hebrews 8:12: "'For I will be merciful toward their iniquities, and I will remember their sins no more.'"

Save us from the fires of hell,

John 3:16: "For God so loved the world that he gave his only-begotten Son, that whoever believes in him should not perish but have eternal life."

Lead all souls to Heaven, especially those in most need of Thy mercy.

Matthew 9:13: "Go and learn what this means, 'I desire mercy, and not sacrifice.' For I came not to call the righteous, but sinners.'"

THE APOSTLES CREED

Words of the prayer

Words of Scripture

I believe in God, the Father almighty, creator of Heaven and Earth.

Genesis 1:1: "In the beginning God created the heavens and the earth."

I believe in Jesus Christ, His only Son, our Lord.

John 3:16: "For God so loved the world that he gave his only-begotten Son, that whoever believes in him should not perish but have eternal life."

He was conceived by the power of the Holy Spirit and born of the Virgin Mary.

Luke 1:35: "And the angel said to her, 'The Holy Spirit will come upon you, and the power of the Most High will overshadow you; therefore the child to be born will be called holy, the Son of God.'"

He suffered under Pontius Pilate, was crucified, died, and was buried.	Mark 15:15: "So Pilate, wishing to satisfy the crowd, released for them Barabbas; and having scourged Jesus, he delivered him to be crucified."
He descended to the dead. On the third day He rose again.	1 Corinthians 15:3–4: "For I delivered to you as of first importance what I also received, that Christ died for our sins in accordance with the Scriptures, that he was buried, that he was raised on the third day in accordance with the Scriptures."
He ascended into Heaven and is seated at the right hand of the Father.	Mark 16:19: "So then the Lord Jesus, after he had spoken to them, was taken up into heaven, and sat down at the right hand of God."
He will come again to judge the living and the dead.	Matthew 25:31–33: "When the Son of man comes in his glory, and all the angels with him, then he will sit on his glorious throne. Before him will be gathered all the nations, and he will separate them one from another as a shepherd separates the sheep from the goats, and he will place the sheep at his right hand, but the goats at the left."
I believe in the Holy Spirit,	Acts 1:8: "But you shall receive power when the Holy Spirit has come upon you; and you shall be my witnesses in Jerusalem and in all Judea and Samaria and to the end of the earth."

The Holy Catholic Church,	Matthew 16:18: "And I tell you, you are Peter, and on this rock I will build my Church, and the gates of Hades shall not prevail against it."
The communion of saints	Romans 1:7: "To all God's beloved in Rome, who are called to be saints …"
The forgiveness of sins,	John 20:23: "If you forgive the sins of any, they are forgiven; if you retain the sins of any, they are retained."
the resurrection of the body,	Romans 6:5: "For if we have been united with him in a death like his, we shall certainly be united with him in a resurrection like his."
And life everlasting. Amen.	John 11:25: "Jesus said to her, 'I am the resurrection and the life; he who believes in me, though he die, yet shall he live.'"

THE BIBLICAL FOUNDATION OF THE MYSTERIES OF THE ROSARY

The mysteries of the Rosary are twenty events in the lives of Jesus Christ and his Mother, Mary, that we meditate upon while praying the prayers of the Rosary. Like the prayers of the Rosary, the mysteries are deeply rooted in Scripture.

In the pages that follow, you will find a passage of Scripture for each mystery of the Rosary.

THE ANNUNCIATION
Luke 1:26–38

"In the sixth month the angel Gabriel was sent from God to a city of Galilee named Nazareth, to a virgin betrothed to a man whose name was Joseph, of the house of David; and the virgin's name was Mary. And he came to her and said, 'Hail, full of grace, the Lord is with you!' But she was greatly troubled at the saying, and considered in her mind what sort of greeting this might be. And the angel said to her, 'Do not be afraid, Mary, for you have found favor with God. And behold, you will conceive in your womb and bear a son, and you shall call his name Jesus.

He will be great, and will be called the Son of the Most High;
and the Lord God will give to him the throne of his father David,
and he will reign over the house of Jacob for ever;
and of his kingdom there will be no end.'

And Mary said to the angel, 'How can this be, since I have no husband?' And the angel said to her,

'The Holy Spirit will come upon you,
and the power of the Most High will overshadow you;

therefore the child to be born will be called holy,
the Son of God.

And behold, your kinswoman Elizabeth in her old age has also conceived a son; and this is the sixth month with her who was called barren. For with God nothing will be impossible.' And Mary said, 'Behold, I am the handmaid of the Lord; let it be to me according to your word.' And the angel departed from her."

THE VISITATION
Luke 1:39-56

"In those days Mary arose and went with haste into the hill country, to a city of Judah, and she entered the house of Zechariah and greeted Elizabeth. And when Elizabeth heard the greeting of Mary, the child leaped in her womb; and Elizabeth was filled with the Holy Spirit and she exclaimed with a loud cry, 'Blessed are you among women, and blessed is the fruit of your womb! And why is this granted me, that the mother of my Lord should come to me? For behold, when the voice of your greeting came to my ears, the child in my womb leaped for joy. And blessed is she who believed that there would be a fulfilment of what was spoken to her from the Lord.' And Mary said,

'My soul magnifies the Lord,
and my spirit rejoices in God my Savior,
for he has regarded the low estate of his handmaiden.
For behold, henceforth all generations will call me blessed;
for he who is mighty has done great things for me,
and holy is his name.
And his mercy is on those who fear him
from generation to generation.
He has shown strength with his arm,
he has scattered the proud in the imagination of their hearts,

he has put down the mighty from their thrones,
and exalted those of low degree;
he has filled the hungry with good things,
and the rich he has sent empty away.
He has helped his servant Israel,
in remembrance of his mercy,
as he spoke to our fathers,
to Abraham and to his posterity for ever.'

And Mary remained with her about three months, and returned to her home."

THE NATIVITY
Luke 2:1–20

"In those days a decree went out from Caesar Augustus that all the world should be enrolled. This was the first enrollment, when Quirinius was governor of Syria. And all went to be enrolled, each to his own city. And Joseph also went up from Galilee, from the city of Nazareth, to Judea, to the city of David, which is called Bethlehem, because he was of the house and lineage of David, to be enrolled with Mary his betrothed, who was with child. And while they were there, the time came for her to be delivered. And she gave birth to her first-born son and wrapped him in swaddling cloths, and laid him in a manger, because there was no place for them in the inn.

And in that region there were shepherds out in the field, keeping watch over their flock by night. And an angel of the Lord appeared to them, and the glory of the Lord shone around them, and they were filled with fear. And the angel said to them, 'Be not afraid; for behold, I bring you good news of a great joy which will come to all the people; for to you is born this day in the city of David a Savior, who is Christ the Lord. And this will be a sign for you: you will find a baby wrapped in swaddling cloths and lying in a manger.' And suddenly there was with the angel a multitude of the heavenly host praising God and saying,

'Glory to God in the highest,

and on earth peace among men with whom he is pleased!'

When the angels went away from them into heaven, the shepherds said to one another, 'Let us go over to Bethlehem and see this thing that has happened, which the Lord has made known to us.' And they went with haste, and found Mary and Joseph, and the baby lying in a manger. And when they saw it they made known the saying which had been told them concerning this child; and all who heard it wondered at what the shepherds told them. But Mary kept all these things, pondering them in her heart. And the shepherds returned, glorifying and praising God for all they had heard and seen, as it had been told them."

THE PRESENTATION OF JESUS IN THE TEMPLE
Luke 2:22-39

"And when the time came for their purification according to the law of Moses, they brought him up to Jerusalem to present him to the Lord (as it is written in the law of the Lord, 'Every male that opens the womb shall be called holy to the Lord') and to offer a sacrifice according to what is said in the law of the Lord, 'a pair of turtledoves, or two young pigeons.' Now there was a man in Jerusalem, whose name was Simeon, and this man was righteous and devout, looking for the consolation of Israel, and the Holy Spirit was upon him. And it had been revealed to him by the Holy Spirit that he should not see death before he had seen the Lord's Christ. And inspired by the Spirit he came into the temple; and when the parents brought in the child Jesus, to do for him according to the custom of the law, he took him up in his arms and blessed God and said,

'Lord, now let your servant depart in peace,
according to your word;
for my eyes have seen your salvation
which you have prepared in the presence of all peoples,
a light for revelation to the Gentiles,
and for glory to your people Israel.'

And his father and his mother marveled at what was said about him; and Simeon blessed them and said to Mary his mother,

'Behold, this child is set for the fall and rising of many in Israel,
and for a sign that is spoken against
(and a sword will pierce through your own soul also),
that thoughts out of many hearts may be revealed.'

And there was a prophetess, Anna, the daughter of Phanuel, of the tribe of Asher; she was of a great age, having lived with her husband seven years from her virginity, and as a widow till she was eighty-four. She did not depart from the temple, worshiping with fasting and prayer night and day. And coming up at that very hour she gave thanks to God, and spoke of him to all who were looking for the redemption of Jerusalem.

And when they had performed everything according to the law of the Lord, they returned into Galilee, to their own city, Nazareth. And the child grew and became strong, filled with wisdom; and the favor of God was upon him."

THE FINDING OF JESUS IN THE TEMPLE
Luke 2:41-52

"Now his parents went to Jerusalem every year at the feast of the Passover. And when he was twelve years old, they went up according to custom; and when the feast was ended, as they were returning, the boy Jesus stayed behind in Jerusalem. His parents did not know it, but supposing him to be in the company they went a day's journey, and they sought him among their kinsfolk and acquaintances; and when they did not find him, they returned to Jerusalem, seeking him. After three days they found him in the temple, sitting among the teachers, listening to them and asking them questions; and all who heard him were amazed at his understanding and his answers. And when they saw him they were astonished; and his mother said to him, 'Son, why have you treated us so? Behold, your father and I have been looking for you anxiously.' And he said to them, 'How is it that you sought me? Did you not know that I must be in my Father's house?' And they did not understand the saying which he spoke to them. And he went down with them and came to Nazareth, and was obedient to them; and his mother kept all these things in her heart.

And Jesus increased in wisdom and in stature, and in favor with God and man."

THE BAPTISM OF JESUS
Matthew 3:13-17

"Then Jesus came from Galilee to the Jordan to John, to be baptized by him. John would have prevented him, saying, 'I need to be baptized by you, and do you come to me?' But Jesus answered him, 'Let it be so now; for thus it is fitting for us to fulfil all righteousness.' Then he consented. And when Jesus was baptized, he went up immediately from the water, and behold, the heavens were opened and he saw the Spirit of God descending like a dove, and alighting on him; and behold, a voice from heaven, saying, 'This is my beloved Son, with whom I am well pleased.'"

THE WEDDING AT CANA
John 2:1-12

"On the third day there was a marriage at Cana in Galilee, and the mother of Jesus was there; Jesus also was invited to the marriage, with his disciples. When the wine failed, the mother of Jesus said to him, 'They have no wine.' And Jesus said to her, 'O woman, what have you to do with me? My hour has not yet come.' His mother said to the servants, 'Do whatever he tells you.' Now six stone jars were standing there, for the Jewish rites of purification, each holding twenty or thirty gallons. Jesus said to them, 'Fill the jars with water.' And they filled them up to the brim. He said to them, 'Now draw some out, and take it to the steward of the feast.' So they took it. When the steward of the feast tasted the water now become wine, and did not know where it came from (though the servants who had drawn the water knew), the steward of the feast called the bridegroom and said to him, 'Every man serves the good wine first; and when men have drunk freely, then the poor wine; but you have kept the good wine until now.' This, the first of his signs, Jesus did at Cana in Galilee, and manifested his glory; and his disciples believed in him.

After this he went down to Capernaum, with his mother and his brethren and his disciples; and there they stayed for a few days."

THE PROCLAMATION OF THE KINGDOM AND THE CALL TO CONVERSION
Mark 1:14-15

"Now after John was arrested, Jesus came into Galilee, preaching the gospel of God, and saying, 'The time is fulfilled, and the kingdom of God is at hand; repent, and believe in the gospel.'"

THE TRANSFIGURATION
Matthew 17:1-13

"And after six days Jesus took with him Peter and James and John his brother, and led them up a high mountain apart. And he was transfigured before them, and his face shone like the sun, and his garments became white as light. And behold, there appeared to them Moses and Elijah, talking with him. And Peter said to Jesus, 'Lord, it is well that we are here; if you wish, I will make three booths here, one for you and one for Moses and one for Elijah.' He was still speaking, when behold, a bright cloud overshadowed them, and a voice from the cloud said, 'This is my beloved Son, with whom I am well pleased; listen to him.' When the disciples heard this, they fell on their faces, and were filled with awe. But Jesus came and touched them, saying, 'Rise, and have no fear.' And when they lifted up their eyes, they saw no one but Jesus only.

And as they were coming down the mountain, Jesus commanded them, 'Tell no one the vision, until the Son of man is raised from the dead.' And the disciples asked him, 'Then why do the scribes say that first Elijah must come?' He replied, 'Elijah does come, and he is to restore all things; but I tell you that Elijah has already come, and they did not know him, but did to him whatever they pleased. So also the Son of man will suffer at their hands.' Then the disciples understood that he was speaking to them of John the Baptist."

THE INSTITUTION OF THE EUCHARIST
Luke 22:14-23

"And when the hour came, he sat at table, and the apostles with him. And he said to them, 'I have earnestly desired to eat this Passover with you before I suffer; for I tell you I shall not eat it until it is fulfilled in the kingdom of God.' And he took a chalice, and when he had given thanks he said, 'Take this, and divide it among yourselves; for I tell you that from now on I shall not drink of the fruit of the vine until the kingdom of God comes.' And he took bread, and when he had given thanks he broke it and gave it to them, saying, 'This is my body which is given for you. Do this in remembrance of me.' And likewise the chalice after supper, saying, 'This chalice which is poured out for you is the new covenant in my blood.' But behold the hand of him who betrays me is with me on the table. For the Son of man goes as it has been determined; but woe to that man by whom he is betrayed!' And they began to question one another, which of them it was that would do this."

THE AGONY IN THE GARDEN
Matthew 26:36-46

"Then Jesus went with them to a place called Gethsemane, and he said to his disciples, 'Sit here, while I go over there and pray.' And taking with him Peter and the two sons of Zebedee, he began to be sorrowful and troubled. Then he said to them, 'My soul is very sorrowful, even to death; remain here, and watch with me.' And going a little farther he fell on his face and prayed, 'My Father, if it be possible, let this chalice pass from me; nevertheless, not as I will, but as you will.' And he came to the disciples and found them sleeping; and he said to Peter, 'So, could you not watch with me one hour? Watch and pray that you may not enter into temptation; the spirit indeed is willing, but the flesh is weak.' Again, for the second time, he went away and prayed, 'My Father, if this cannot pass unless I drink it, your will be done.' And again he came and found them sleeping, for their eyes were heavy. So, leaving them again, he went away and prayed for the third time, saying the same words. Then he came to the disciples and said to them, 'Are you still sleeping and taking your rest? Behold, the hour is at hand, and the Son of man is betrayed into the hands of sinners. Rise, let us be going; see, my betrayer is at hand.'"

THE SCOURGING AT THE PILLAR
Matthew 27:26

"Then he released for them Barabbas, and having scourged Jesus, delivered him to be crucified."

THE CROWNING WITH THORNS
Matthew 27:27-31

"Then the soldiers of the governor took Jesus into the praetorium, and they gathered the whole battalion before him. And they stripped him and put a scarlet robe upon him, and plaiting a crown of thorns they put it on his head, and put a reed in his right hand. And kneeling before him they mocked him, saying, 'Hail, King of the Jews!' And they spat upon him, and took the reed and struck him on the head. And when they had mocked him, they stripped him of the robe, and put his own clothes on him, and led him away to crucify him."

THE CARRYING OF THE CROSS
Matthew 27:32

"As they were marching out, they came upon a man of Cyrene, Simon by name; this man they compelled to carry his cross."

THE CRUCIFIXION
Luke 23:33–46

"And when they came to the place which is called The Skull, there they crucified him, and the criminals, one on the right and one on the left. And Jesus said, 'Father, forgive them; for they know not what they do.' And they cast lots to divide his garments. And the people stood by, watching; but the rulers scoffed at him, saying, 'He saved others; let him save himself, if he is the Christ of God, his Chosen One!' The soldiers also mocked him, coming up and offering him vinegar, and saying, 'If you are the King of the Jews, save yourself!' There was also an inscription over him, 'This is the King of the Jews.'

One of the criminals who were hanged railed at him, saying, 'Are you not the Christ? Save yourself and us!' But the other rebuked him, saying, 'Do you not fear God, since you are under the same sentence of condemnation? And we indeed justly; for we are receiving the due reward of our deeds; but this man has done nothing wrong.' And he said, 'Jesus, remember me when you come in your kingly power.' And he said to him, 'Truly, I say to you, today you will be with me in Paradise.'

It was now about the sixth hour, and there was darkness over the whole land until the ninth hour, while the sun's light failed; and the curtain of the temple was torn in two. Then Jesus, crying with a loud voice, said, 'Father, into your hands I commit my spirit!' And having said this he breathed his last."

THE RESURRECTION
Matthew 28:1–10

"Now after the sabbath, toward the dawn of the first day of the week, Mary Magdalene and the other Mary went to see the tomb. And behold, there was a great earthquake; for an angel of the Lord descended from heaven and came and rolled back the stone, and sat upon it. His appearance was like lightning, and his clothing white as snow. And for fear of him the guards trembled and became like dead men. But the angel said to the women, 'Do not be afraid; for I know that you seek Jesus who was crucified. He is not here; for he has risen, as he said. Come, see the place where he lay. Then go quickly and tell his disciples that he has risen from the dead, and behold, he is going before you to Galilee; there you will see him. Behold, I have told you.' So they departed quickly from the tomb with fear and great joy, and ran to tell his disciples. And behold, Jesus met them and said, 'Hail!' And they came up and took hold of his feet and worshiped him. Then Jesus said to them, 'Do not be afraid; go and tell my brethren to go to Galilee, and there they will see me.'"

THE ASCENSION
Luke 24:50-53

"Then he led them out as far as Bethany, and lifting up his hands he blessed them. While he blessed them, he parted from them, and was carried up into heaven. And they worshiped him, and returned to Jerusalem with great joy, and were continually in the temple blessing God."

THE DESCENT OF THE HOLY SPIRIT ON PENTECOST
Acts 2:1-13

"When the day of Pentecost had come, they were all together in one place. And suddenly a sound came from heaven like the rush of a mighty wind, and it filled all the house where they were sitting. And there appeared to them tongues as of fire, distributed and resting on each one of them. And they were all filled with the Holy Spirit and began to speak in other tongues, as the Spirit gave them utterance. Now there were dwelling in Jerusalem Jews, devout men from every nation under heaven. And at this sound the multitude came together, and they were bewildered, because each one heard them speaking in his own language. And they were amazed and wondered, saying, "Are not all these who are speaking Galileans? And how is it that we hear, each of us in his own native language? Parthians and Medes and Elamites and residents of Mesopotamia, Judea and Cappadocia, Pontus and Asia, Phrygia and Pamphylia, Egypt and the parts of Libya belonging to Cyrene, and visitors from Rome, both Jews and proselytes, Cretans and Arabians, we hear them telling in our own tongues the mighty works of God." And all were amazed and perplexed, saying to one another, 'What does this mean?' But others mocking said, 'They are filled with new wine.'"

THE ASSUMPTION OF MARY
Luke 1:46-56

"And Mary said,
   'My soul magnifies the Lord,
   and my spirit rejoices in God my Savior,
   for he has regarded the low estate of his handmaiden.
   For behold, henceforth all generations will call me blessed;
   for he who is mighty has done great things for me,
   and holy is his name.
   And his mercy is on those who fear him
   from generation to generation.
   He has shown strength with his arm,
   he has scattered the proud in the imagination of their hearts,
   he has put down the mighty from their thrones,

and exalted those of low degree;
he has filled the hungry with good things,
and the rich he has sent empty away.
He has helped his servant Israel,
in remembrance of his mercy,
as he spoke to our fathers,
to Abraham and to his posterity for ever.'

And Mary remained with her about three months, and returned to her home."

THE CORONATION OF MARY AS QUEEN OF HEAVEN AND EARTH
Revelation 12:1-5

"And a great sign appeared in heaven, a woman clothed with the sun, with the moon under her feet, and on her head a crown of twelve stars; she was with child and she cried out in her pangs of birth, in anguish for delivery. And another sign appeared in heaven; behold, a great red dragon, with seven heads and ten horns, and seven diadems upon his heads. His tail swept down a third of the stars of heaven, and cast them to the earth. And the dragon stood before the woman who was about to bear a child, that he might devour her child when she brought it forth; she brought forth a male child, one who is to rule all the nations with a rod of iron, but her child was caught up to God and to his throne."

DAYS 8–68

DAYS 8–28

Refer to "The Biblical Foundation of the Prayers of the Rosary" on the preceding pages to deepen your understanding as you listen to the podcast during these days.

Today's Prayer: Pray 1 Our Father, 3 Hail Marys, and 1 Glory Be.

DAY 29

Today's Mystery: The Annunciation

Today's Prayer:
- Prayerfully read the Scripture passage for today's mystery (Luke 1:26–38) on page 67 or in your own Bible.
- Pray 1 Our Father, 3 Hail Marys, and 1 Glory Be.

DAY 30

Today's Mystery: The Visitation

Today's Prayer:
- Prayerfully read the Scripture passage for today's mystery (Luke 1:39–56) on page 68 or in your own Bible.
- Pray 1 Our Father, 3 Hail Marys, and 1 Glory Be.

DAY 31

Today's Mystery: The Nativity

Today's Prayer:
- Prayerfully read the Scripture passage for today's mystery (Luke 2:1–20) on page 69 or in your own Bible.
- Pray 1 Our Father, 3 Hail Marys, and 1 Glory Be.

DAY 32

Today's Mystery: The Presentation of Jesus in the Temple

Today's Prayer:
- Prayerfully read the Scripture passage for today's mystery (Luke 2:22–39) on page 70 or in your own Bible.
- Pray 1 Our Father, 3 Hail Marys, and 1 Glory Be.

DAY 33

Today's Mystery: The Finding of Jesus in the Temple

Today's Prayer:
- Prayerfully read the Scripture passage for today's mystery (Luke 2:41–52) on page 71 or in your own Bible.
- Pray 1 Our Father, 3 Hail Marys, and 1 Glory Be.

DAY 34

Today's Mystery: The Baptism of Jesus

Today's Prayer:
- Prayerfully read the Scripture passage for today's mystery (Matthew 3:13–17) on page 72 or in your own Bible.
- Pray 1 Our Father, 3 Hail Marys, and 1 Glory Be.

DAY 35

Today's Mystery: The Wedding at Cana

Today's Prayer:
- Prayerfully read the Scripture passage for today's mystery (John 2:1–12) on page 73 or in your own Bible.
- Pray 1 Our Father, 3 Hail Marys, and 1 Glory Be.

DAY 36

Today's Mystery: The Proclamation of the Kingdom and the Call to Conversion

Today's Prayer:
- Prayerfully read the Scripture passage for today's mystery (Mark 1:14–15) on page 73 or in your own Bible.
- Pray 1 Our Father, 3 Hail Marys, and 1 Glory Be.

DAY 37

Today's Mystery: The Transfiguration

Today's Prayer:
- Prayerfully read the Scripture passage for today's mystery (Matthew 17:1–13) on page 74 or in your own Bible.
- Pray 1 Our Father, 3 Hail Marys, and 1 Glory Be.

DAY 38

Today's Mystery: The Institution of the Eucharist

Today's Prayer:
- Prayerfully read the Scripture passage for today's mystery (Luke 22:14–23) on page 74 or in your own Bible.
- Pray 1 Our Father, 3 Hail Marys, and 1 Glory Be.

DAY 39

Today's Mystery: The Agony in the Garden

Today's Prayer:
- Prayerfully read the Scripture passage for today's mystery (Matthew 26:36–46) on page 75 or in your own Bible.
- Pray 1 Our Father, 3 Hail Marys, and 1 Glory Be.

DAY 40

Today's Mystery: The Scourging at the Pillar

Today's Prayer:
- Prayerfully read the Scripture passage for today's mystery (Matthew 27:26) on page 76 or in your own Bible.
- Pray 1 Our Father, 3 Hail Marys, and 1 Glory Be.

DAY 41

Today's Mystery: The Crowning with Thorns

Today's Prayer:
- Prayerfully read the Scripture passage for today's mystery (Matthew 27:27–31) on page 76 or in your own Bible.
- Pray 1 Our Father, 3 Hail Marys, and 1 Glory Be.

DAY 42

Today's Mystery: The Carrying of the Cross

Today's Prayer:
- Prayerfully read the Scripture passage for today's mystery (Matthew 27:32) on page 76 or in your own Bible.
- Pray 1 Our Father, 3 Hail Marys, and 1 Glory Be.

DAY 43

Today's Mystery: The Crucifixion

Today's Prayer:
- Prayerfully read the Scripture passage for today's mystery (Luke 23:33–46) on page 77 or in your own Bible.
- Pray 1 Our Father, 3 Hail Marys, and 1 Glory Be.

DAY 44

Today's Mystery: The Resurrection

Today's Prayer:
- Prayerfully read the Scripture passage for today's mystery (Matthew 28:1–10) on page 77 or in your own Bible.
- Pray 1 Our Father, 3 Hail Marys, and 1 Glory Be.

DAY 45

Today's Mystery: The Ascension

Today's Prayer:
- Prayerfully read the Scripture passage for today's mystery (Luke 24:50–53) on page 78 or in your own Bible.
- Pray 1 Our Father, 3 Hail Marys, and 1 Glory Be.

DAY 46

Today's Mystery: The Descent of the Holy Spirit on Pentecost

Today's Prayer:
- Prayerfully read the Scripture passage for today's mystery (Acts 2:1–13) on page 78 or in your own Bible.
- Pray 1 Our Father, 3 Hail Marys, and 1 Glory Be.

DAY 47

Today's Mystery: The Assumption of Mary

Today's Prayer:
- Prayerfully read the Scripture passage for today's mystery (Luke 1:46–56) on page 79 or in your own Bible.
- Pray 1 Our Father, 3 Hail Marys, and 1 Glory Be.

DAY 48

Today's Mystery: The Coronation of Mary as Queen of Heaven and Earth

Today's Prayer:
- Prayerfully read the Scripture passage for today's mystery (Revelation 12:1–5) on page 80 or in your own Bible.
- Pray 1 Our Father, 3 Hail Marys, and 1 Glory Be.

DAY 49

Today's Mystery: The Annunciation

Today's Prayer:
- Prayerfully read the Scripture passage for today's mystery (Luke 1:26–38) on page 67 or in your own Bible.
- Pray 1 Our Father, 3 Hail Marys, and 1 Glory Be.

DAY 50

Today's Mystery: The Visitation

Today's Prayer:
- Prayerfully read the Scripture passage for today's mystery (Luke 1:39–56) on page 68 or in your own Bible.
- Pray 1 Our Father, 3 Hail Marys, and 1 Glory Be.

DAY 51

Today's Mystery: The Nativity

Today's Prayer:
- Prayerfully read the Scripture passage for today's mystery (Luke 2:1–20) on page 69 or in your own Bible.
- Pray 1 Our Father, 3 Hail Marys, and 1 Glory Be.

DAY 52

Today's Mystery: The Presentation of Jesus in the Temple

Today's Prayer:
- Prayerfully read the Scripture passage for today's mystery (Luke 2:22–39) on page 70 or in your own Bible.
- Pray 1 Our Father, 3 Hail Marys, and 1 Glory Be.

DAY 53

Today's Mystery: The Finding of Jesus in the Temple

Today's Prayer:
- Prayerfully read the Scripture passage for today's mystery (Luke 2:41–52) on page 70 or in your own Bible.
- Pray 1 Our Father, 3 Hail Marys, and 1 Glory Be.

DAY 54

Today's Mystery: The Baptism of Jesus

Today's Prayer:
- Prayerfully read the Scripture passage for today's mystery (Matthew 3:13–17) on page 72 or in your own Bible.
- Pray 1 Our Father, 3 Hail Marys, and 1 Glory Be.

DAY 55

Today's Mystery: The Wedding at Cana

Today's Prayer:
- Prayerfully read the Scripture passage for today's mystery (John 2:1–12) on page 73 or in your own Bible.
- Pray 1 Our Father, 3 Hail Marys, and 1 Glory Be.

DAY 56

Today's Mystery: The Proclamation of the Kingdom and the Call to Conversion

Today's Prayer:
- Prayerfully read the Scripture passage for today's mystery (Mark 1:14–15) on page 73 or in your own Bible.
- Pray 1 Our Father, 3 Hail Marys, and 1 Glory Be.

DAY 57

Today's Mystery: The Transfiguration

Today's Prayer:
- Prayerfully read the Scripture passage for today's mystery (Matthew 17:1–13) on page 74 or in your own Bible.
- Pray 1 Our Father, 3 Hail Marys, and 1 Glory Be.

DAY 58

Today's Mystery: The Institution of the Eucharist

Today's Prayer:
- Prayerfully read the Scripture passage for today's mystery (Luke 22:14–23) on page 74 or in your own Bible.
- Pray 1 Our Father, 3 Hail Marys, and 1 Glory Be.

DAY 59

Today's Mystery: The Agony in the Garden

Today's Prayer:
- Prayerfully read the Scripture passage for today's mystery (Matthew 26:36–46) on page 75 or in your own Bible.
- Pray 1 Our Father, 3 Hail Marys, and 1 Glory Be.

DAY 60

Today's Mystery: The Scourging at the Pillar

Today's Prayer:
- Prayerfully read the Scripture passage for today's mystery (Matthew 27:26) on page 76 or in your own Bible.
- Pray 1 Our Father, 3 Hail Marys, and 1 Glory Be.

DAY 61

Today's Mystery: The Crowning with Thorns

Today's Prayer:
- Prayerfully read the Scripture passage for today's mystery (Matthew 27:27–31) on page 76 or in your own Bible.
- Pray 1 Our Father, 3 Hail Marys, and 1 Glory Be.

DAY 62

Today's Mystery: The Carrying of the Cross

Today's Prayer:
- Prayerfully read the Scripture passage for today's mystery (Matthew 27:32) on page 76 or in your own Bible.
- Pray 1 Our Father, 3 Hail Marys, and 1 Glory Be.

DAY 63

Today's Mystery: The Crucifixion

Today's Prayer:
- Prayerfully read the Scripture passage for today's mystery (Luke 23:33–46) on page 77 or in your own Bible.
- Pray 1 Our Father, 3 Hail Marys, and 1 Glory Be.

DAY 64

Today's Mystery: The Resurrection

Today's Prayer:
- Prayerfully read the Scripture passage for today's mystery (Matthew 28:1–10) on page 77 or in your own Bible.
- Pray 1 Our Father, 3 Hail Marys, and 1 Glory Be.

DAY 65

Today's Mystery: The Ascension

Today's Prayer:
- Prayerfully read the Scripture passage for today's mystery (Luke 24:50–53) on page 78 or in your own Bible.
- Pray 1 Our Father, 3 Hail Marys, and 1 Glory Be.

DAY 66

Today's Mystery: The Descent of the Holy Spirit on Pentecost

Today's Prayer:
- Prayerfully read the Scripture passage for today's mystery (Acts 2:1–13) on page 78 or in your own Bible.
- Pray 1 Our Father, 3 Hail Marys, and 1 Glory Be.

DAY 67

Today's Mystery: The Assumption of Mary

Today's Prayer:
- Prayerfully read the Scripture passage for today's mystery (Luke 1:46–56) on page 79 or in your own Bible.
- Pray 1 Our Father, 3 Hail Marys, and 1 Glory Be.

DAY 68

Today's Mystery: The Coronation of Mary as Queen of Heaven and Earth

Today's Prayer:
- Prayerfully read the Scripture passage for today's mystery (Revelation 12:1–5) on page 80 or in your own Bible.
- Pray 1 Our Father, 3 Hail Marys, and 1 Glory Be.

PHASE 3
MEDITATING ON THE MYSTERIES

Days 69 – 188

INTRODUCTION

About This Phase

There are many ways to meditate on the mysteries of the Rosary. In this phase, we will experience three:

- reading Scripture prayerfully (*lectio divina*),
- reading reflections from the saints and others, and
- viewing sacred art prayerfully (*"visio divina"*).

In addition to practicing meditation in these various ways, we will increase our time commitment by beginning to pray one decade of the Rosary each day.

First, on Days 69–88, we will meditate on each mystery of the Rosary by praying with the Scriptures associated with it. Unlike last time, when we were reading the Scriptures primarily to understand the *narrative* behind the mystery, this time we are praying with the Scriptures in order to meditate. This form of prayer is traditionally known as *lectio divina*.

Second, on Days 89–128, we will meditate on each mystery by prayerfully reading two reflections, mostly from the saints, on that mystery. There are so many riches and insights to glean from the great saints who came before us!

Third, on Days 129–188, we will meditate on each mystery by prayerfully contemplating three different images. Each of the images is a beautiful piece of sacred art that can lead the viewer into a deeper understanding of the mystery of the Rosary it depicts. This form of prayer is sometimes called *"visio divina."* Each day will include reflection questions to help you pray with the artwork. These questions are not meant as quizzes but as prompts to help you connect the art with the day's mystery and with your daily life in prayer. Some of the questions may be less impactful for you than others. Feel free to focus on one or two questions that you find fruitful or to use all of the questions to aid your prayer.

By the end of this phase, you will have meditated on the Scriptures, prayerfully read reflections from the saints, and prayed with sacred images depicting each mystery of the Rosary. You will have a true interior "library" or "archive" of phrases, insights, and imagery for each mystery of the Rosary!

READ	On some days, we will read a Scripture passage or a reflection related to that day's mystery. Turn to the day to see what to read.

PRAY	• On some days, we will spend 5 minutes in silent personal reflection meditating on the day's mystery with the material provided for that day. • Every day of this phase, we will pray 1 decade of the Rosary (1 Our Father, 10 Hail Marys, and 1 Glory Be).

Tips for this phase

- Remember that even though you read the Scriptures for each mystery during the last phase, you will be approaching these passages in a new way through meditative prayer during this phase. You can also refer to trusted Catholic prayer guides for more information about *lectio divina* if you are unfamiliar with this kind of prayer.
- In addition to the material provided in this prayer guide, you can make use of your own favorite sacred art or Catholic saints' reflections to help you meditate on the mysteries of the Rosary.
- Journaling is one way to stay focused and remember your

thoughts while meditating. If you have not begun keeping a journal of your insights on each mystery, now is a great time to begin! You may prefer to divide your journal into sections, with one section dedicated to each mystery, so that you can easily find your place.

DAYS 69–188

DAY 69

Today's Mystery: The Annunciation

Today's Prayer:
- Pray with the Scripture passage for today's mystery (Luke 1:26–38) in *lectio divina*. Turn to page 67 to read the passage or use your own Bible.
- Spend 5 minutes reflecting or journaling on today's mystery.
- Pray 1 decade of the Rosary (1 Our Father, 10 Hail Marys, and 1 Glory Be).

DAY 70

Today's Mystery: The Visitation

Today's Prayer:
- Pray with the Scripture passage for today's mystery (Luke 1:39–56) in *lectio divina*. Turn to page 68 to read the passage or use your own Bible.
- Spend 5 minutes reflecting or journaling on today's mystery.
- Pray 1 decade of the Rosary (1 Our Father, 10 Hail Marys, and 1 Glory Be).

DAY 71

Today's Mystery: The Nativity

Today's Prayer:
- Pray with the Scripture passage for today's mystery (Luke 2:1–20) in *lectio divina*. Turn to page 69 to read the passage or use your own Bible.
- Spend 5 minutes reflecting or journaling on today's mystery.
- Pray 1 decade of the Rosary (1 Our Father, 10 Hail Marys, and 1 Glory Be).

DAY 72

Today's Mystery: The Presentation of Jesus in the Temple

Today's Prayer:
- Pray with the Scripture passage for today's mystery (Luke 2:22–39) in *lectio divina*. Turn to page 70 to read the passage or use your own Bible.
- Spend 5 minutes reflecting or journaling on today's mystery.
- Pray 1 decade of the Rosary (1 Our Father, 10 Hail Marys, and 1 Glory Be).

DAY 73

Today's Mystery: The Finding of Jesus in the Temple

Today's Prayer:
- Pray with the Scripture passage for today's mystery (Luke 2:41–52) in *lectio divina*. Turn to page 71 to read the passage or use your own Bible.
- Spend 5 minutes reflecting or journaling on today's mystery.
- Pray 1 decade of the Rosary (1 Our Father, 10 Hail Marys, and 1 Glory Be).

DAY 74

Today's Mystery: The Baptism of Jesus

Today's Prayer:
- Pray with the Scripture passage for today's mystery (Matthew 3:13–17) in *lectio divina*. Turn to page 72 to read the passage or use your own Bible.
- Spend 5 minutes reflecting or journaling on today's mystery.
- Pray 1 decade of the Rosary (1 Our Father, 10 Hail Marys, and 1 Glory Be).

DAY 75

Today's Mystery: The Wedding at Cana

Today's Prayer:
- Pray with the Scripture passage for today's mystery (John 2:1–12) in *lectio divina*. Turn to page 73 to read the passage or use your own Bible.
- Spend 5 minutes reflecting or journaling on today's mystery.
- Pray 1 decade of the Rosary (1 Our Father, 10 Hail Marys, and 1 Glory Be).

DAY 76

Today's Mystery: The Proclamation of the Kingdom and the Call to Conversion

Today's Prayer:
- Pray with the Scripture passage for today's mystery (Mark 1:14–15) in *lectio divina*. Turn to page 73 to read the passage or use your own Bible.
- Spend 5 minutes reflecting or journaling on today's mystery.
- Pray 1 decade of the Rosary (1 Our Father, 10 Hail Marys, and 1 Glory Be).

DAY 77

Today's Mystery: The Transfiguration

Today's Prayer:
- Pray with the Scripture passage for today's mystery (Matthew 17:1–13) in *lectio divina*. Turn to page 74 to read the passage or use your own Bible.
- Spend 5 minutes reflecting or journaling on today's mystery.
- Pray 1 decade of the Rosary (1 Our Father, 10 Hail Marys, and 1 Glory Be).

DAY 78

Today's Mystery: The Institution of the Eucharist

Today's Prayer:
- Pray with the Scripture passage for today's mystery (Luke 22:14–23) in *lectio divina*. Turn to page 74 to read the passage or use your own Bible.
- Spend 5 minutes reflecting or journaling on today's mystery.
- Pray 1 decade of the Rosary (1 Our Father, 10 Hail Marys, and 1 Glory Be).

DAY 79

Today's Mystery: The Agony in the Garden

Today's Prayer:
- Pray with the Scripture passage for today's mystery (Matthew 26:36–46) in *lectio divina*. Turn to page 75 to read the passage or use your own Bible.
- Spend 5 minutes reflecting or journaling on today's mystery.
- Pray 1 decade of the Rosary (1 Our Father, 10 Hail Marys, and 1 Glory Be).

DAY 80

Today's Mystery: The Scourging at the Pillar

Today's Prayer:
- Pray with the Scripture passage for today's mystery (Matthew 27:26) in *lectio divina*. Turn to page 76 to read the passage or use your own Bible.
- Spend 5 minutes reflecting or journaling on today's mystery.
- Pray 1 decade of the Rosary (1 Our Father, 10 Hail Marys, and 1 Glory Be).

DAY 81

Today's Mystery: The Crowning with Thorns

Today's Prayer:
- Pray with the Scripture passage for today's mystery (Matthew 27:27–31) in *lectio divina*. Turn to page 76 to read the passage or use your own Bible.
- Spend 5 minutes reflecting or journaling on today's mystery.
- Pray 1 decade of the Rosary (1 Our Father, 10 Hail Marys, and 1 Glory Be).

DAY 82

Today's Mystery: The Carrying of the Cross

Today's Prayer:
- Pray with the Scripture passage for today's mystery (Matthew 27:32) in *lectio divina*. Turn to page 76 to read the passage or use your own Bible.
- Spend 5 minutes reflecting or journaling on today's mystery.
- Pray 1 decade of the Rosary (1 Our Father, 10 Hail Marys, and 1 Glory Be).

DAY 83

Today's Mystery: The Crucifixion

Today's Prayer:
- Pray with the Scripture passage for today's mystery (Luke 23:33–46) in *lectio divina*. Turn to page 77 to read the passage or use your own Bible.
- Spend 5 minutes reflecting or journaling on today's mystery.
- Pray 1 decade of the Rosary (1 Our Father, 10 Hail Marys, and 1 Glory Be).

DAY 84

Today's Mystery: The Resurrection

Today's Prayer:
- Pray with the Scripture passage for today's mystery (Matthew 28:1–10) in *lectio divina*. Turn to page 77 to read the passage or use your own Bible.
- Spend 5 minutes reflecting or journaling on today's mystery.
- Pray 1 decade of the Rosary (1 Our Father, 10 Hail Marys, and 1 Glory Be).

DAY 85

Today's Mystery: The Ascension

Today's Prayer:
- Pray with the Scripture passage for today's mystery (Luke 24:50–53) in *lectio divina*. Turn to page 78 to read the passage or use your own Bible.
- Spend 5 minutes reflecting or journaling on today's mystery.
- Pray 1 decade of the Rosary (1 Our Father, 10 Hail Marys, and 1 Glory Be).

DAY 86

Today's Mystery: The Descent of the Holy Spirit on Pentecost

Today's Prayer:
- Pray with the Scripture passage for today's mystery (Acts 2:1–13) in *lectio divina*. Turn to page 78 to read the passage or use your own Bible.
- Spend 5 minutes reflecting or journaling on today's mystery.
- Pray 1 decade of the Rosary (1 Our Father, 10 Hail Marys, and 1 Glory Be).

DAY 87

Today's Mystery: The Assumption of Mary

Today's Prayer:
- Pray with the Scripture passage for today's mystery (Luke 1:46–56) in *lectio divina*. Turn to page 79 to read the passage or use your own Bible.
- Spend 5 minutes reflecting or journaling on today's mystery.
- Pray 1 decade of the Rosary (1 Our Father, 10 Hail Marys, and 1 Glory Be).

DAY 88

Today's Mystery: The Coronation of Mary as Queen of Heaven and Earth

Today's Prayer:
- Pray with the Scripture passage for today's mystery (Revelation 12:1–5) in *lectio divina*. Turn to page 80 to read the passage or use your own Bible.
- Spend 5 minutes reflecting or journaling on today's mystery.
- Pray 1 decade of the Rosary (1 Our Father, 10 Hail Marys, and 1 Glory Be).

DAY 89

Today's Mystery: The Annunciation

Today's Prayer:
- Read today's reflection.
- Spend 5 minutes reflecting or journaling on today's mystery.
- Pray 1 decade of the Rosary (1 Our Father, 10 Hail Marys, and 1 Glory Be).

Read the Reflection:
"Virgin, you have heard ... that you will conceive and bear a son; you have heard that it will be by the Holy Spirit and not by a man. The angel is waiting for your reply. It is time for him to return to the One who sent him. We, too, are waiting for this merciful word, my lady, we who are miserably weighed down under a sentence of condemnation. The price of our salvation is being offered you. If you consent, we shall immediately be set free. We all have been made in the eternal Word of God, and look, we are dying. In your brief reply we shall be restored and so brought back to life. Doleful Adam and his unhappy offspring, exiled from Paradise, implore you, kind Virgin, to give this answer; David asks it, Abraham asks it; all the other holy patriarchs, your very own fathers beg it of you, as do those now dwelling in the region of the shadow of death. For it the whole world is waiting, bowed down at your feet. And rightly so, because on your answer depends the comfort of the afflicted, the redemption of captives, the deliverance of the damned; the salvation of all the sons of Adam, your whole race ... So, answer the angel quickly or rather, through the angel, answer God. Only say the word and receive the Word: give yours and conceive God's. Breathe one fleeting word and embrace the everlasting Word. Why do you delay? Why be afraid? Believe, give praise and receive. Let humility take courage and shyness confidence. This is not the moment for

virginal simplicity to forget prudence. In this circumstance, alone, O prudent Virgin, do not fear presumptuousness, for if your reserve pleased by its silence, now much more must your goodness speak. Blessed Virgin, open your heart to faith, your lips to consent and your womb to your Creator. Behold, the long-desired of all nations is standing at the door and knocking. Get up, run, open! Get up by faith, run by prayer, open by consent!

'Behold,' she says, 'I am the handmaiden of the Lord; let it be to me according to your word.'"

–St. Bernard of Clairvaux, *Four Homilies in Praise of the Virgin Mother*

DAY 90

Today's Mystery: The Visitation

Today's Prayer:
- Read today's reflection.
- Spend 5 minutes reflecting or journaling on today's mystery.
- Pray 1 decade of the Rosary (1 Our Father, 10 Hail Marys, and 1 Glory Be).

Read the Reflection:
"Mary set out from Nazareth to go to the city of Hebron, distant seventy miles, that is, at least seven days journey, over rugged mountains, and without any other companion but her spouse Joseph. The holy Virgin made haste, as the Evangelist records: 'Mary went into the hill country with haste.' St. Luke i. 39. Tell us, O Blessed Lady, why you undertake so long and painful a journey, and why you are in such haste on your way? I am going, she replies, to do my office of exercising charity, I am going to console a family. If then, O holy Mother of God, your office is to console us, and to

dispense favours to our souls, Oh come and visit and console my poor soul. Your visit sanctified the house of Elizabeth; come, O Mary, and sanctify me also.

The Holy Virgin arrived at the house of Elizabeth. She was already become Mother of God, but she was the first to salute her relation: '*She entered and saluted Elizabeth.*' Elizabeth, enlightened by the Holy Spirit, knew that the divine Word was already made flesh in the womb of Mary; and hence she called her blessed amongst women, and the fruit of her womb blessed also: '*Blessed art thou amongst women, and blessed is the fruit of thy womb.*' And full of holy confusion and joy she at the same time exclaimed: '*Whence is this to me, that the mother of my Lord should come to me?*' But what did the humble Mary answer to such words? she answered: '*My soul doth magnify the Lord.*' As though she had said: Elizabeth, thou praisest me, but I praise my God, for having exalted me to the dignity of becoming his mother: '*He hath regarded the humility of his handmaid.*' O most holy Mary, since you dispense so many favours to those who ask for them, I beseech you to impart to me your profound humility. You esteem yourself as nothing before God; but I am worse than nothing, for I am nothing and a sinner. You can make me humble. Make me such by your holy intercession, for the love of that God who made you his Mother."

–St. Alphonsus Liguori, *The Way of Salvation*

DAY 91

Today's Mystery: The Nativity

Today's Prayer:
- Read today's reflection.
- Spend 5 minutes reflecting or journaling on today's mystery.
- Pray 1 decade of the Rosary (1 Our Father, 10 Hail Marys, and 1 Glory Be).

Read the Reflection:
"Our Saviour, dearly-beloved, was born today: let us be glad. For there is no proper place for sadness, when we keep the birthday of the Life, which destroys the fear of mortality and brings to us the joy of promised eternity. No one is kept from sharing in this happiness. There is for all one common measure of joy, because as our Lord the destroyer of sin and death finds none free from charge, so is He come to free us all. Let the saint exult in that he draws near to victory. Let the sinner be glad in that he is invited to pardon. Let the gentile take courage in that he is called to life. For the Son of God in the fullness of time which the inscrutable depth of the Divine counsel has determined, has taken on him the nature of man, thereby to reconcile it to its Author: in order that the inventor of death, the devil, might be conquered through that (nature) which he had conquered …

Therefore the Word of God, Himself God, the Son of God who '*in the beginning was with God,*' through whom '*all things were made*' and '*without*' whom '*was nothing made*' … with the purpose of delivering man from eternal death, became man …

Such then beloved was the nativity which became the Power of God and the Wisdom of God even Christ, whereby He might be one with us in manhood and surpass us in Godhead. For unless He were true God, He would not bring us a remedy, unless He were true Man, He would not give us an example. Therefore the exulting angel's song when the Lord was born is this, '*Glory to God in the Highest*,' and their message, '*peace on earth to men of good will*' ... For they see that the heavenly Jerusalem is being built up out of all the nations of the world: and over that indescribable work of the Divine love how ought the humbleness of men to rejoice, when the joy of the lofty angels is so great?

Let us then, dearly beloved, give thanks to God the Father, through His Son, in the Holy Spirit, Who '*for His great mercy, wherewith He has loved us*,' has had pity on us: and '*when we were dead in sins, has quickened us together in Christ*' ... that we might be in Him a new creation and a new production. Let us put off then the old man with his deeds: and having obtained a share in the birth of Christ let us renounce the works of the flesh. Christian, acknowledge your dignity, and becoming a partner in the Divine nature, refuse to return to the old baseness by degenerate conduct. Remember the Head and Body of which you are a member. Recollect that you were rescued from the power of darkness and brought out into God's light and kingdom. By the mystery of Baptism you were made the temple of the Holy Spirit: do not put such a denizen to flight from you by base acts, and subject yourself once more to the devil's thraldom: because your purchase money is the blood of Christ, because He shall judge you in truth Who ransomed you in mercy, who with the Father and the Holy Spirit reigns for ever and ever. Amen."

–St. Leo the Great, *Sermon 21 (On the Feast of the Nativity, I)*

DAY 92

Today's Mystery: The Presentation of Jesus in the Temple

Today's Prayer:
- Read today's reflection.
- Spend 5 minutes reflecting or journaling on today's mystery.
- Pray 1 decade of the Rosary (1 Our Father, 10 Hail Marys, and 1 Glory Be).

Read the Reflection:
"Christ, therefore, was carried into the temple, being yet a little child at the breast; and the blessed Symeon being endowed with the grace of prophecy, takes him in his arms, and filled with the highest joy, blessed God, and said, *Lord, now lettest Thou Thy servant depart in peace according to Thy Word, for mine eyes have seen Thy Salvation, Which Thou has prepared before the face of all the nations, the Gentiles' light for revelation, and a glory of Thy people Israel.* For the mystery of Christ had been prepared even before the very foundation of the world, but was manifested in the last ages of time, and became a light for those who in darkness and error had fallen under the devil's hand …

And what does the prophet Symeon say of Christ? *Behold this child is set for the fall and rising again of many in Israel, and for a sign that shall be spoken against.* For the Emmanuel is set by God the Father for the foundations of Sion, *being a stone elect, chief of the corner, and honorable.* Those then that trusted in Him were not ashamed; but those who were unbelieving and ignorant, and unable to perceive the mystery regarding Him, fell, and were broken in pieces. For God the Father again has somewhere said, *Behold I lay in Sion a stone of stumbling and a rock of offence, and He that believeth on It shall not be ashamed; but on whomsoever It shall fall, It will winnow him.* But the prophet bade the Israelites be secure, saying, *Sanctify the Lord Himself, and He shall be thy fear: and if thou trust upon Him, He shall be thy sanctification, nor shall ye strike against Him as on a stone of stumbling, and a rock of offence.* Because, however, Israel did not sanctify the Emmanuel Who is Lord and God, nor was willing to trust in Him, having stumbled as upon a stone because of unbelief, it was broken in pieces and fell. But many rose again, those, namely, who embraced faith in Him. For they changed from a legal to a spiritual service; from having in them a slavish spirit, they were enriched with That Spirit Which maketh free, even the Holy Spirit; they were made partakers of the divine nature; they were counted worthy of the adoption of sons; and live in hope of gaining the city that is above, even the citizenship, to wit, the kingdom of heaven …"

–St. Cyril of Alexandria, *Commentary on the Gospel of Saint Luke*

DAY 93

Today's Mystery: The Finding of Jesus in the Temple

Today's Prayer:
- Read today's reflection.
- Spend 5 minutes reflecting or journaling on today's mystery.
- Pray 1 decade of the Rosary (1 Our Father, 10 Hail Marys, and 1 Glory Be).

Read the Reflection:
"Consider when this was. When the Lord Jesus, as to His Human Nature, was twelve years old (for as to His Divine Nature He is before all times, and without time), He tarried behind them in the temple, and disputed with the elders, and they wondered at His doctrine; and His parents who were returning from Jerusalem

sought Him among their company, among those, that is, who were journeying with them, and when they found Him not, they returned in trouble to Jerusalem, and found Him disputing in the temple with the elders, when He was, as I said, twelve years old. But what wonder? The Word of God is never silent, though it is not always heard. He is found then in the temple, and His mother says to Him, *'Why have You thus dealt with us? Your father and I have sought You sorrowing'*; and He said, *'Did you not know that I must be about My Father's service?'* This He said for that the Son of God was in the temple of God, for that temple was not Joseph's, but God's ...

You see then, brethren, that He did not say, *'I must needs be about My Father's service,'* in any such sense as that we should understand Him thereby to have said, *'You are not My parents.'* They were His parents in time, God was His Father eternally. They were the parents of the Son of Man—*'He,'* the Father of His Word, and Wisdom, and Power, by whom He made all things. But if all things were made by that Wisdom, *'which reaches from one end to another mightily, and sweetly orders all things,'* then were they also made by the Son of God to whom He Himself as Son of Man was afterwards to be subject; and the Apostle says that He is the Son of David, *'who was made of the seed of David according to the flesh.'* But yet the Lord Himself proposes a question to the Jews, which the Apostle solves in these very words; for when he said, *'who was made of the seed of David,'* he added, *'according to the flesh,'* that it might be understood that He is not the Son of David according to His Divinity, but that the Son of God is David's Lord; for thus in another place, when He is setting forth the privileges of the Jewish people, the Apostle says, *'Whose are the fathers, of whom as concerning the flesh Christ came, Who is over all, God blessed forever.'* As, *'according to the flesh,'* He is David's Son; but as being *'God over all, blessed for ever,'* He is David's Lord. The Lord then says to the Jews, *'Whose Son do you say that Christ is?'* They answered, *'The Son of David.'* For this they knew, as they had learned it easily from the preaching of the

Prophets; and in truth, He was of the seed of David, '*but according to the flesh*,' by the Virgin Mary, who was espoused to Joseph. When they answered then that Christ was David's Son, Jesus said to them, '*How then does David in spirit call Him Lord, saying, The Lord said to my Lord, Sit on My right hand, till I put Your enemies under Your feet. If David then in spirit call Him Lord, how is He his Son?*' And the Jews could not answer Him. So we have it in the Gospel. He did not deny that He was David's Son, so that they could not understand that He was also David's Lord. For they acknowledged in Christ that which He became in time, but they did not understand in Him what He was in all eternity. Wherefore wishing to teach them His Divinity, He proposed a question touching His Humanity; as though He would say, '*You know that Christ is David's Son, answer Me, how He is also David's Lord?*' And that they might not say, '*He is not David's Lord*,' He introduced the testimony of David himself. And what does he say? He says indeed the truth. For you find God in the Psalms saying to David, '*Of the fruit of your body will I set upon your seat.*' Here then He is the Son of David. But how is He the Lord of David, who is David's Son? '*The Lord said to my Lord, Sit on My right hand.*' Can you wonder that David's Son is his Lord, when you see that Mary was the mother of her Lord? He is David's Lord then as being God. David's Lord, as being Lord of all; and David's Son, as being the Son of Man. At once Lord and Son. David's Lord, '*who, being in the form of God, thought it not robbery to be equal with God*;' and David's Son, in that '*He emptied Himself, taking the form of a servant.*'"

–St. Augustine, *Sermons on Selected Lessons of the New Testament: Sermon 1*

DAY 94

Today's Mystery: The Baptism of Jesus

Today's Prayer:
- Read today's reflection.
- Spend 5 minutes reflecting or journaling on today's mystery.
- Pray 1 decade of the Rosary (1 Our Father, 10 Hail Marys, and 1 Glory Be).

Read the Reflection:
"Is there, then, here any room left for doubt, when the Father clearly calls from heaven in the Gospel narrative, and says: '*This is My beloved Son, in Whom I am well pleased*'? … When the Son also speaks, upon Whom the Holy Spirit showed Himself in the likeness of a dove? When the Holy Spirit also speaks, Who came down in the likeness of a dove? When David, too, speaks: '*The voice of the Lord is above the waters, the God of glory thundered, the Lord above many waters*'? When Scripture testifies that at the prayer of Jerubbaal, fire came down from heaven, … and again, when Elijah prayed, fire was sent forth and consecrated the sacrifice.

Do not consider the merits of individuals, but the office of the priests. Or, if you look at the merits, consider the priest as Elijah. Look upon the merits of Peter also, or of Paul, who handed down to us this mystery which they had received of the Lord Jesus. To those [of old] a visible fire was sent that they might believe; for us who believe, the Lord works invisibly; for them that happened for a figure, for us for warning. Believe, then, that the Lord Jesus is present at the invocation of the priest, Who said: '*Where two or three are, there am I also*' … How much where the Church is, and where His Mysteries are, does He vouchsafe to impart His presence!"

–St. Ambrose, *On the Mysteries*

DAY 95

Today's Mystery: The Wedding at Cana

Today's Prayer:
- Read today's reflection.
- Spend 5 minutes reflecting or journaling on today's mystery.
- Pray 1 decade of the Rosary (1 Our Father, 10 Hail Marys, and 1 Glory Be).

Read the Reflection:
"Even when she was living on this earth, the only thought of Mary, after the glory of God, was to relieve the wretched. And we know that then she enjoyed already the privilege of obtaining whatever she asked. This we know from what took place at the nuptials of Cana of Galilee, when the wine failed, and the blessed Virgin, compassionating the distress and mortification of that family, asked the Son to relieve them by a miracle, making known to him this want: They have no wine: 'Vinum non habent.' Jesus answered: 'Woman, what is that to thee and to me? my hour is not yet come.' Observe, that although the Lord appeared to refuse this favor to his mother, by saying: Of what importance is it, oh woman, to me and to thee that the wine has failed? It does not become me now to perform any miracle, as the time has not arrived, the time of my preaching, when with signs I must confirm my doctrine; yet notwithstanding this, Mary, as if the Son had already granted her the favor, said to the attendants, fill the water-pots with water: 'Imple hydrias aqua.' Come fill the water-pots, and you will be consoled; and Jesus Christ, indeed, to please his mother, changed that water into the best wine. But how is this? If the time appointed for miracles was the time of preaching, how could it be anticipated by the miracle of the wine, contrary to the divine decree? Nothing, it may be answered, was done contrary to the divine decrees;

for although, generally speaking, the time for signs had not come, yet from eternity God had established by another general decree, that nothing the divine mother could ask should be denied her; and therefore Mary, well acquainted with her privilege, although her Son seemed to have then set aside her petition, said notwithstanding, that the water-pots should be filled, as though the favor were already granted. This, St. John Chrysostom would express, when commenting on the passage of John above mentioned—'Oh woman, what is that to thee and to me?'—he says, that although Jesus had answered thus, yet, for the honor of his mother, he did not fail to comply with her demand. St. Thomas confirms the same, when he observes, that by these words—'My hour has not yet come'—Jesus Christ wished to show that he would have deferred the miracle, if another had asked him to perform it; but because his mother asked it, he immediately performed it. St. Cyril and St. Jerome confirm this, according to Barrada. And Jansenius of Ghent says, commenting on the same passage of St. John: That he might honor his mother, he anticipated the time of working miracles.

In a word, it is certain that no creature can obtain for us miserable sinners so many mercies as this good advocate, who is honored by God with this privilege, not only as his beloved handmaid, but also as his true mother ... And how does Mary obtain favors? It is enough that her Son hears her voice: Make me to hear thy voice: 'Fac me audire vocem tuam.' It is enough that she speaks, and her Son immediately hears her."

–St. Alphonsus Liguori, *The Glories of Mary*

DAY 96

Today's Mystery: The Proclamation of the Kingdom

Today's Prayer:
- Read today's reflection.
- Spend 5 minutes reflecting or journaling on today's mystery.
- Pray 1 decade of the Rosary (1 Our Father, 10 Hail Marys, and 1 Glory Be).

Read the Reflection:
"The beginning, then, of this sermon is introduced as follows: '*And when He saw the great multitudes, He went up into a mountain: and when He was set, His disciples came unto Him: and He opened His mouth, and taught them, saying.*' If it is asked what the '*mountain*' means, it may well be understood as meaning the greater precepts of righteousness; for there were lesser ones which were given to the Jews. Yet it is one God who, through His holy prophets and servants, according to a thoroughly arranged distribution of times, gave the lesser precepts to a people who as yet required to be bound by fear; and who, through His Son, gave the greater ones to a people whom it had now become suitable to set free by love. Moreover, when the lesser are given to the lesser, and the greater to the greater, they are given by Him who alone knows how to present to the human race the medicine suited to the occasion. Nor is it surprising that the greater precepts are given for the kingdom of heaven, and the lesser for an earthly kingdom, by that one and the same God, who made heaven and earth. With respect, therefore, to that righteousness which is the greater, it is said through the prophet, '*Your righteousness is like the mountains of God:*' and this may well mean that the one Master alone fit to teach matters of so great importance teaches on a mountain. Then He teaches sitting, as behooves the dignity of the instructor's office; and His

disciples come to Him, in order that they might be nearer in body for hearing His words, as they also approached in spirit to fulfil His precepts. '*And He opened His mouth, and taught them, saying.*' The circumlocution before us, which runs, '*And He opened His mouth,*' perhaps gracefully intimates by the mere pause that the sermon will be somewhat longer than usual, unless, perchance, it should not be without meaning, that now He is said to have opened His own mouth, whereas under the old law He was accustomed to open the mouths of the prophets."

–St. Augustine, *On the Sermon on the Mount*

DAY 97

Today's Mystery: The Transfiguration

Today's Prayer:
- Read today's reflection.
- Spend 5 minutes reflecting or journaling on today's mystery.
- Pray 1 decade of the Rosary (1 Our Father, 10 Hail Marys, and 1 Glory Be).

Read the Reflection
"This mountain is the place of mysteries … this summit is the summit of the heavens. Here the signs of the Kingdom are shown beforehand, here the mysteries of the crucifixion are communicated in advance; here the beauty of the Kingdom is revealed, here the descent of the glorified Christ's second coming is anticipated. On this mountain, the brilliant radiance of the just is shown in shadows; on this mountain, the good things to come are presented in image, as if they were here. This mountain … shapes today, without any deception, the process of our own being shaped and conformed to the image of Christ …

[R]econciliation with God and the forgiveness of the charges against us came to belong to human nature through Jesus; the co-eternal Word of God the Father wanted to show that humanity had been cleansed of the serpent's venom, which had been emptied against him, and he revealed this Mystery to his disciples on Mount Thabor. For when, wishing to put before them his words about the Kingdom and his second, glorious coming, he spoke words of prophecy (and perhaps they were imperfectly disposed towards what had first been said to them about the Kingdom, and were exclusively focused on the things they idly considered in their own minds), he wanted to convince them from present experience of what was to happen, he mysteriously worked a revelation for them on Mount Thabor, as in an image. [It was] a prophetic preview of the Kingdom of heaven, as if he were saying to them: 'So that the passage of time may not, perhaps, create unbelief in your hearts, "Amen, I say to you"—quickly, immediately—"there are some of those standing here and listening to me who will not taste death before they see the Son of Man coming in the glory of his Father."' And revealing once again that action is for him simultaneous with his willing, the Evangelist says that 'After six days, Jesus took Peter and James and John and led them up a high mountain by themselves and was transfigured before their eyes, and his face shone like the sun, his garments became white as light, and behold, Moses and Elijah appeared to them, speaking with him.'

These are the divine prodigies behind the present festival; what we celebrate here, on this mountain now, is for us, too, a saving Mystery. This sacred initiation into the Mystery of Christ, this public solemnity, gathers us together. So that we might come inside the ineffable sanctuary, and might enter the place of Mysteries along with those chosen ones who were inspired to speak God's words, let us listen to a divine, most sacred voice, as it seems to invite us from the peak of the mountain above us, inviting us with strong words of persuasion and saying, 'Come, let us go up to the mountain of the Lord, on the day of the Lord—in the place of the Lord in the house of our God.' [Our hope is] that, bathed in a vision of him, flooded with light, we might be changed for the better and joined together as one; and that, grasping hold of the light in light, we might cry out: 'How fearful is this place! This is nothing other than the house of God, this is the gate of heaven!' This is the place towards which we must hasten, I make bold to say, since Jesus, who dwells there and who has gone up to heaven before us, is our guide on the way. With him, let us also flash like lightning before spiritual eyes, renewed in the shape of our souls and made divine, transformed along with him in order to be like him ...

Let us run forward boldly and brightly, then, let us enter into the cloud ... Be lifted up like Peter, to a vision, a mental image, of God; be changed by a good and holy transformation, leave the world behind, depart from the earth, abandon the flesh. Let go of this creation, and go over to the Creator, to whom Peter, in his ecstasy, says, 'Lord, it is good for us to be here.' How right you are, Peter! Truly it is good for us to be here with Jesus, to remain with him for endless ages! What could be more blessed, more lofty, or more precious than this, to be with God and to be like God in form—to be in the light? So then, let each of us, who has received God in his heart, and who has been transfigured into that divine form, say in our joy: 'It is good for us to be here, where everything is full of light, where there is joy and good spirits and exultation, where everything in our hearts is peaceful and calm and free from conflict, where God is to be seen. Here, in the heart, he makes his dwelling with the Father, here he comes close to us and says, "Today salvation has come to this house; here all the treasures of eternal blessing are gathered along with Christ and stored away; here the first-fruits of all the coming ages are stored, their images sketched out as in a mirror."'

–St. Anastasius of Sinai, *Homily on the Transfiguration*

DAY 98

Today's Mystery: The Institution of the Eucharist

Today's Prayer:
- Read today's reflection.
- Spend 5 minutes reflecting or journaling on today's mystery.
- Pray 1 decade of the Rosary (1 Our Father, 10 Hail Marys, and 1 Glory Be).

Read the Reflection:
"See, dearest daughter, in what an excellent state is the soul who receives, as she should, this Bread of Life, this Food of the Angels. By receiving this Sacrament she dwells in Me and I in her, as the fish in the sea, and the sea in the fish—thus do I dwell in the soul, and the soul in Me—the Sea Pacific. In that soul grace dwells, for, since she has received this Bread of Life in a state of grace, My grace remains in her, after the accidents of bread have been consumed. I leave you the imprint of grace, as does a seal, which, when lifted from the hot wax upon which it has been impressed, leaves behind its imprint, so the virtue of this Sacrament remains in the soul, that is to say, the heat of My Divine charity, and the clemency of the Holy Spirit. There also remains to you the wisdom of My only-begotten Son, by which the eye of your intellect has been illuminated to see and to know the doctrine of My Truth, and, together with this wisdom, you participate in My strength and power, which strengthen the soul against her sensual self-love, against the Devil, and against the world. Thou seest then that the imprint remains, when the seal has been taken away, that is, when the material accidents of the bread, having been consumed, this True Sun has returned to Its Centre, not that it was ever really separated from It, but constantly united to Me. The Abyss of My loving desire for your salvation has given you, through My dispensation and Divine

Providence, coming to the help of your needs, the sweet Truth as Food in this life, where you are pilgrims and travellers, so that you may have refreshment, and not forget the benefit of the Blood. See then how straitly you are constrained and obliged to render Me love, because I love you so much, and, being the Supreme and Eternal Goodness, deserve your love."

–St. Catherine of Siena, *Dialogue*

DAY 99

Today's Mystery: The Agony in the Garden

Today's Prayer:
- Read today's reflection.
- Spend 5 minutes reflecting or journaling on today's mystery.
- Pray 1 decade of the Rosary (1 Our Father, 10 Hail Marys, and 1 Glory Be).

Read the Reflection:
"Behold, our most loving Saviour, having come to the Garden of Gethsemani, did of his own accord make a beginning of his bitter Passion by giving full liberty to the passions of fear, of weariness, and of sorrow to come and afflict him with all their torments: *He began to fear; and to be heavy, to grow sorrowful, and to be sad.*

    He began, then, first to feel a great fear of death, and of the sufferings he would have soon to endure. *He began to fear;* but how? Was it not he himself that had offered himself spontaneously to endure all these torments? *He was offered because He willed it.* Was it not he who had so much desired this hour of his Passion, and who had said shortly before, *With desire have I desired to eat this Pasch with you?* And yet how is it that he was seized with such a fear of death, that he even prayed his Father to deliver him from it? *My Fa-*

ther, if it be possible, let this chalice pass from Me. The Venerable Bede answers this, and says, 'He prays that the chalice may pass from him, in order to show that he was truly man.' He, our loving Saviour, chose indeed to die for us in order by his death to prove to us the love that he bore us; but in order that men might not suppose that he had assumed a fantastic body (as some heretics have blasphemously asserted), or that by virtue of his divinity he had died without suffering any pain, He therefore made this prayer to his heavenly Father, not indeed with a view of being heard, but to give us to understand that he died as man, and afflicted with a great fear of death and of the sufferings which should accompany his death.

O most amiable Jesus! Thou wouldst, then, take upon Thee our fearfulness in order to give us Thy courage in suffering the trials of this life. Oh, be Thou forever blessed for Thy great mercy and love! Oh, may all our hearts love Thee as much as Thou desirest, and as much as Thou deservest!"

–St. Alphonsus Liguori, *The Passion and the Death of Jesus Christ*

DAY 100

Today's Mystery: The Scourging at the Pillar

Today's Prayer:
- Read today's reflection.
- Spend 5 minutes reflecting or journaling on today's mystery.
- Pray 1 decade of the Rosary (1 Our Father, 10 Hail Marys, and 1 Glory Be).

Read the Reflection:
The Blessed Virgin Speaks
"When the time of my Son's Passion arrived, his enemies seized him, striking him on his cheek and neck; and spitting upon him,

they mocked him. Then, led to the pillar, he stripped himself, and himself stretched his hands to the pillar, which his enemies pitiless bound. Now, while tied there he had no clothing, but stood as he was born, and suffered the shame of his nakedness. Then his enemies rose up, for they stood on all sides, his friends having fled, and they scourged his body, pure from all spot or sin. At the first blow, I, who stood nearest, fell as if dead, and on recovering my senses, I beheld his body bruised and beaten to the very ribs, so that his ribs could be seen; and what was still more bitter, when the scourge was raised, his very flesh was furrowed by the thongs. And when my Son stood thus, all bloody, all torn, so that no soundness could be found in him, nor any spot to scourge, then one, his spirit roused within him, asked: 'Will you slay him thus unjudged?' and he immediately cut his bonds. Then my Son put on his clothes, and I beheld the spot where my Son's feet stood all full of blood, and I knew my Son's course by his footprints, for wherever he went, the earth seemed stained with blood; nor did they suffer him to clothe himself, but they compelled and urged him to hasten."

–St. Bridget, *Revelations*

DAY 101

Today's Mystery: The Crowning with Thorns

Today's Prayer:
- Read today's reflection.
- Spend 5 minutes reflecting or journaling on today's mystery.
- Pray 1 decade of the Rosary (1 Our Father, 10 Hail Marys, and 1 Glory Be).

Read the Reflection:
"*And plaiting a crown of thorns, they put it on his head.* Hence instead of a crown of glory, they imposed on him a crown of indignity; *he will crown you with a crown of tribulation* (Isa 22:18). These thorns signify the prickles of sinners, which prick their consciences: and Christ received these for us, for he died for our sins (1 Cor 15:3). Or it can be referred to Adam's curse, where it was said: *thorns and thistles will it bring forth to you* (Gen 3:18). Hence it signified that this curse was undone."

–St. Thomas Aquinas, *Commentary on the Gospel of Matthew*

DAY 102

Today's Mystery: The Carrying of the Cross

Today's Prayer:
- Read today's reflection.
- Spend 5 minutes reflecting or journaling on today's mystery.
- Pray 1 decade of the Rosary (1 Our Father, 10 Hail Marys, and 1 Glory Be).

Read the Reflection:
"Outside the city, to the northwest of Jerusalem, there is a little hill: Golgotha is its name in Aramaic; *locus Calvariae*, in Latin: the place of skulls or Calvary.

Offering no resistance, Jesus gives himself up to the execution of the sentence. He is to be spared nothing, and upon his shoulders falls the weight of the ignominious cross. But, through love, the Cross is to become the throne from which he reigns.

The people of Jerusalem and those from abroad who have come for the Passover push their way through the city streets, to catch a passing glimpse of Jesus of Nazareth, the King of the Jews. There is a tumult of voices, and, now and then, short silences: perhaps when Jesus fixes his eyes on someone:

If anyone wishes to come after me, let him take up his cross daily and follow me (Lk 9:23).

How lovingly Jesus embraces the wood which is to bring him to death!

Is it not true that as soon as you cease to be afraid of the Cross, of what people call the cross, when you set your will to accept the Will of God, then you find happiness, and all your worries, all your sufferings, physical or moral, pass away?

Truly the Cross of Jesus is gentle and lovable. There, sorrows cease to count; there is only the joy of knowing that we are co-redeemers with Him."

–St. Josemaria Escriva, *The Way of the Cross*

DAY 103

Today's Mystery: The Crucifixion

Today's Prayer:
- Read today's reflection.
- Spend 5 minutes reflecting or journaling on today's mystery.
- Pray 1 decade of the Rosary (1 Our Father, 10 Hail Marys, and 1 Glory Be)

Read the Reflection:
"We have now to witness a new kind of martyrdom—a Mother condemned to see an innocent Son, and one whom she loves with the whole affection of her soul, cruelly tormented and put to death before her own eyes: 'There stood by the cross of Jesus His Mother.'

Saint John believed that in these words he had said enough of Mary's martyrdom. Consider her at the foot of the cross in the presence of her dying Son, and then see if there be sorrow like unto her sorrow. Let us remain for awhile this day on Calvary, and consider the fifth sword which, in the death of Jesus, transfixed the heart of Mary.

As soon as our agonized Redeemer had reached the Mount of Calvary, the executioners stripped Him of His clothes, and piercing His hands and feet 'not with sharp but with blunt nails,' as Saint Bernard says, to torment Him more, they fastened Him on the cross. Having crucified Him, they planted the cross, and thus left Him to die. The executioners left Him; but not so Mary. She then drew nearer to the cross, to be present at His death: 'I did not leave Him' (thus the Blessed Virgin revealed to Saint Bridget), 'but stood nearer to the cross.'

'But what did it avail thee, O Lady,' says Saint Bonaventure, 'to go to Calvary, and see this Son expire? Shame should have prevented thee; for His disgrace was thine, since thou wert His Mother. At least, horror of witnessing such a crime as the crucifixion of a God by His own creatures, should have prevented thee from going there.' But the same Saint answers, 'Ah, thy heart did not then think of its own sorrows, but of the sufferings and death of thy dear Son,' and therefore thou wouldst thyself be present, at least to compassionate Him. 'Ah, true Mother,' says the Abbot William, 'most loving Mother, whom not even the fear of death could separate from thy beloved Son' …

'All,' says Simon of Cassia, 'who then saw this Mother silent, and not uttering a complaint in the midst of such great suffering, were filled with astonishment.' But if Mary's lips were silent, her heart was not so, for she incessantly offered the life of her Son to the Divine Justice for our salvation. Therefore, we know that by the merits of her dolours she cooperated in our birth to the life of grace; and hence we are the children of her sorrows. 'Christ,' says Lanspergius, 'was pleased that she, the coöperatress in our redemption, and whom He had determined to give us for our Mother, should be there present; for it was at the foot of the cross that she was to bring us, her children, forth.' If any consolation entered that sea of bitterness, the heart of Mary, the only one was this, that she knew that by her sorrows she was leading us to eternal salvation, as Jesus Himself revealed to Saint Bridget: 'My Mother Mary, on account of her compassion and love, was made the Mother of all in heaven and on earth.' And indeed these were the last words with which Jesus bid her farewell before His death: this was His last recommendation, leaving us to her for her children in the person of Saint John: 'Woman, behold thy son.' From that time Mary began to perform this good office of a mother for us ... and this same office the Blessed Virgin has ever continued, and still continues, to perform."

–St. Alphonsus Liguori, *The Glories of Mary*

DAY 104

Today's Mystery: The Resurrection

Today's Prayer:
- Read today's reflection.
- Spend 5 minutes reflecting or journaling on today's mystery.
- Pray 1 decade of the Rosary (1 Our Father, 10 Hail Marys, and 1 Glory Be).

Read the Reflection:
"Let all who are devout and lovers of God rejoice in this feast; let the wise servant enter into the joy of his Lord; let those who have toiled during Lent now receive their pay; let those who have worked

from the first hour receive now their just wage; let those who came after the third hour be thankful to join the feast; let even those who came after the sixth hour doubt nothing, for they do not suffer loss, even if they delay until the ninth hour; for our Lord is gracious and receives the last even as the first. He gives satisfaction to him who comes at the eleventh hour as he does to him who came at the first. He comforts the first and has mercy on the last; he is generous with the one and likewise with the other.

Come all and enter into the joy of your Lord. First and last, receive your reward; rich and poor, dance together; the industrious and the sluggish, tend to this day; those fasting and those not fasting, be joyful today. The table is set and rich with food, enjoy the banquet; the calf is fatted and aplenty, let no one go away hungry. All of you together enjoy the banquet of faith; all of you indulge in the riches of his goodness. Let no one lament his poverty, for the universal kingdom has been revealed; let no one mourn his sins, for forgiveness has shone from the grave. Let no one be terrified of death, for the death of our Savior has liberated us: He destroyed death by enduring it, he has despoiled hell by descending into it. He angered hell by allowing it to taste his flesh ... Where, O death, is your sting? O hell, where is your victory? Christ is risen, and the demons are destroyed. Christ is risen, and the angels rejoice. Christ is risen, and life is restored. Christ is risen, and no dead person remains in the tomb: for Christ in rising from the dead became the firstborn of the dead. To him be glory and power forever and ever. Amen."

–St. John Chrysostom (attr.), Easter homily

DAY 105

Today's Mystery: The Ascension

Today's Prayer:
- Read today's reflection.
- Spend 5 minutes reflecting or journaling on today's mystery.
- Pray 1 decade of the Rosary (1 Our Father, 10 Hail Marys, and 1 Glory Be).

Read the Reflection:
"Although Christ's bodily presence was withdrawn from the faithful by the Ascension, still the presence of His Godhead is ever with the faithful, as He Himself says (Matthew 28:20): 'Behold, I am with you all days, even to the consummation of the world.' For, 'by ascending into heaven He did not abandon those whom He adopted,' as Pope Leo says (De Resurrec., Serm. ii). But Christ's Ascension into heaven, whereby He withdrew His bodily presence from us, was more profitable for us than His bodily presence would have been.

First of all, in order to increase our faith, which is of things unseen. Hence our Lord said (John 16) that the Holy Spirit shall come and 'convince the world ... of justice,' that is, of the justice 'of those that believe,' as Augustine says (Tract. xcv super Joan.): 'For even to put the faithful beside the unbeliever is to put the unbeliever to shame'; wherefore he goes on to say (10): 'Because I go to the Father; and you shall see Me no longer'—'For "blessed are they that see not, yet believe." Hence it is of our justice that the world is reproved: because "you will believe in Me whom you shall not see."'

Secondly, to uplift our hope: hence He says (John 14:3): 'If I shall go, and prepare a place for you, I will come again, and will take you to Myself; that where I am, you also may be.' For by placing in heaven the human nature which He assumed, Christ gave us the hope of going thither; since 'wheresoever the body shall be, there shall the eagles also be gathered together,' as is written in Matthew 24:28. Hence it is written likewise (Micah 2:13): 'He shall go up that shall open the way before them.'

Thirdly, in order to direct the fervor of our charity to heavenly things. Hence the Apostle says (Colossians 3:1-2): 'Seek the things that are above, where Christ is sitting at the right hand of God. Mind the things that are above, not the things that are upon the earth': for as is said (Matthew 6:21): 'Where thy treasure is, there is thy heart also.' And since the Holy Spirit is love drawing us up to heavenly things, therefore our Lord said to His disciples (John 16:7): 'It is expedient to you that I go; for if I go not, the Paraclete will not come to you; but if I go, I will send Him to you.' On which words Augustine says (Tract. xciv super Joan.): 'Ye cannot receive the Spirit, so long as ye persist in knowing Christ according to the flesh. But when Christ withdrew in body, not only the Holy Spirit, but both Father and Son were present with them spiritually.'"

–St. Thomas Aquinas, *Summa Theologiae*

DAY 106

Today's Mystery: The Descent of the Holy Spirit on Pentecost

Today's Prayer:
- Read today's reflection.
- Spend 5 minutes reflecting or journaling on today's mystery.
- Pray 1 decade of the Rosary (1 Our Father, 10 Hail Marys, and 1 Glory Be).

Read the Reflection:
"Who, then, can doubt of the Godhead of the Holy Spirit, since where the grace of the Spirit is, there the manifestation of the

Godhead appears. By which evidence we infer not a diversity but the unity of the divine power. For how can there be a severance of power, where the effect of the working in all is one?

What, then, is that fire? Not certainly one made up of common twigs, or roaring with the burning of the reeds of the woods, but that fire which improves good deeds like gold, and consumes sins like stubble. This is undoubtedly the Holy Spirit, Who is called both the fire and light of the countenance of God; light as we said above: '*The light of Your countenance has been sealed upon us, O Lord.*' What is, then, the light that is sealed, but that of the seal of the Spirit, believing in Whom, '*you were sealed,*' he says, '*with the Holy Spirit of promise.*'

And as there is a light of the divine countenance, so, too, does fire shine forth from the countenance of God, for it is written: '*A fire shall burn in His sight.*' For the grace of the day of judgment shines beforehand, that forgiveness may follow to reward the service of the saints. O the great fullness of the Scriptures, which no one can comprehend with human genius! O greatest proof of the Divine Unity!"

–St. Ambrose, *On the Holy Spirit*

DAY 107

Today's Mystery: **The Assumption of Mary**

Today's Prayer:
- Read today's reflection.
- Spend 5 minutes reflecting or journaling on today's mystery.
- Pray 1 decade of the Rosary (1 Our Father, 10 Hail Marys, and 1 Glory Be).

Read the Reflection:

"What the Ascension was to our Lord, that the Assumption is to our Lady. Certainly she, the new Garden of Paradise, in which grew the Lily of divine sinlessness and the red Rose of the Church, should not be delivered over and forgotten by the heavenly Gardener. She, in whose womb was celebrated the nuptials of eternity and time is more of eternity than time. If husband and wife in marriage are made two in one flesh, then shall not she; who is the new Eve of the new Adam, be also made two in one spirit with Him?

As Christ ascended into heaven to the unity of the divine nature, so Mary is assumed into heaven in the unity of Christ's human nature. Her mystical flight is the event to which our whole generation moves.

Our age of carnalities, which loves the 'body beautiful,' is lifted out of its despair by the Assumption, to honor a body that is beautiful because it is a temple of God, a gate through which the Word of heaven passed to earth, a Tower of Ivory which the Word of heaven passed to earth, a Tower of Ivory up which climbed divine Love to kiss upon the lips of His Mother a mystic rose."

–Venerable Fulton J. Sheen, *Meditations on the Fifteen Mysteries of the Rosary*

DAY 108

Today's Mystery: The Coronation of Mary as Queen of Heaven and Earth

Today's Prayer:
- Read today's reflection.
- Spend 5 minutes reflecting or journaling on today's mystery.
- Pray 1 decade of the Rosary (1 Our Father, 10 Hail Marys, and 1 Glory Be).

Read the Reflection:
"We, too, approach thee to-day, O Queen; and again, I say, O Queen, O Virgin Mother of God, staying our souls with our trust in thee, as with a strong anchor. Lifting up mind, soul and body, and all ourselves to thee, rejoicing in psalms and hymns and spiritual canticles, we reach through thee One who is beyond our reach on account of His Majesty. If, as the divine Word made flesh taught us[,] honour shown to servants is honour shown to our common Lord, how can honour shown to thee, His Mother, be slighted? How is it not most desirable? Art thou not honoured as the very breath of life? Thus shall we best show our service to our Lord Himself. What do I say to our Lord? It is sufficient that those who think of Thee should recall the memory of Thy most precious gift as the cause of our lasting joy. How it fills us with gladness! How the mind that dwells on this holy treasury of Thy grace enriches itself.

This is our thank-offering to thee, the first fruits of our discourses, the best homage of my poor mind, whilst I am moved by desire of thee, and full of my own misery. But do thou graciously receive my desire, knowing that it exceeds my power. Watch over us, O Queen, the dwelling-place of our Lord. Lead and govern all our ways as thou wilt. Save us from our sins. Lead us into the calm harbour of the divine will. Make us worthy of future happiness through the sweet and face-to-face vision of the Word made flesh through thee. With Him, glory, praise, power, and majesty be to the Father and to the holy and life-giving Spirit, now and for ever. Amen."

–St. John Damascene, *Sermon 1: On the Assumption*

DAY 109

Today's Mystery: The Annunciation

Today's Prayer:
- Read today's reflection.
- Spend 5 minutes reflecting or journaling on today's mystery.
- Pray 1 decade of the Rosary (1 Our Father, 10 Hail Marys, and 1 Glory Be).

Read the Reflection:
"Today are strains of praise sung joyfully by the choir of angels, and the light of the advent of Christ shines brightly upon the faithful. Today is the glad spring-time to us, and Christ the Sun of righteousness has beamed with clear light around us, and has illumined the minds of the faithful. Today is Adam made anew, and moves in the choir of angels, having winged his way to heaven. Today is the whole circle of the earth filled with joy, since the sojourn of the Holy Spirit has been realized to men. Today the grace of God and the hope of the unseen shine through all wonders transcending imagination, and make the mystery that was kept hidden from eternity plainly discernible to us. Today are woven the chaplets of never-fading virtue. Today, God, willing to crown the sacred heads of those whose pleasure is to hearken to Him, and who delight in His festivals, invites the lovers of unswerving faith as His called and His heirs; and the heavenly kingdom is urgent to summon those who mind celestial things to join the divine service of the incorporeal choirs. ... Today is the illustrious and ineffable mystery of Christians, who have willingly set their hope like a seal upon Christ, plainly declared to us. Today did Gabriel, who stands by God, come to the pure virgin, bearing to her the glad annunciation, '*Hail, thou that art highly favoured! And she cast in her mind what manner of salutation this might be. And the*

angel immediately proceeded to say, The Lord is with you: fear not, Mary; for you have found favour with God. Behold, you shall conceive in your womb, and bring forth a son, and shall call His name Jesus. He shall be great, and shall be called the Son of the Highest; and the Lord God shall give unto Him the throne of His father David, and He shall reign over the house of Jacob for ever: and of His kingdom there shall be no end. Then said Mary unto the angel, How shall this be, seeing I know not a man?'* Shall I still remain a virgin? Is the honour of virginity not then lost by me? And while she was yet in perplexity as to these things, the angel placed shortly before her the summary of his whole message, and said to the pure virgin, *'The Holy Spirit shall come upon you, and the power of the Highest shall overshadow you; therefore also that holy thing which shall be born of you shall be called the Son of God.'* For what it is, that also shall it be called by all means … *'Therefore also that holy thing which shall be born of you shall be called the Son of God.'* And if He is the Son of God, then is He also God, of one form with the Father, and co-eternal; in Him the Father possesses all manifestation; He is His image in the person, and through His reflection the (Father's) glory shines forth. And as from the ever-flowing fountain the streams proceed, so also from this ever-flowing and ever-living fountain does the light of the world proceed, the perennial and the true, namely Christ our God. For it is of this that the prophets have preached: *'The streams of the river make glad the city of God.'* And not one city only, but all cities; for even as it makes glad one city, so does it also the whole world."

–St. Gregory Thaumaturgus, *The First Homily: On the Annunciation to the Holy Virgin Mary*

DAY 110

Today's Mystery: The Visitation

Today's Prayer:
- Read today's reflection.
- Spend 5 minutes reflecting or journaling on today's mystery.
- Pray 1 decade of the Rosary (1 Our Father, 10 Hail Marys, and 1 Glory Be).

Read the Reflection:
"Now in those days Mary arose and departed in haste to the hill country, into a town in Judah, and entered into the house of Zachariah and greeted Elizabeth. It is customary that all those who believe provide reasons for their faith. And thus the angel who announced the mysteries, that her faith might be bolstered by an example, announced to the Virgin Mary the pregnancy of an old and barren woman, showing that God can do anything pleasing to him. When Mary heard this, not for lack of faith in the prophecy, nor uncertainty about the message, nor out of doubt for the example provided, but in the eagerness of her desire, to fulfill a pious duty, in the hastiness of joy, she went to the hill country. For, now filled with God, to where would she strive with haste except to the heights? Sluggish efforts are foreign to the grace of the Holy Spirit … [L]earn humility. She comes as a relative to her relative, as a junior to her senior; and not only does she come, but she is even the first to greet … [T]he superior comes to the inferior, in order to help the inferior, Mary to Elizabeth, Christ to John; and later, to sanctify John's baptism, the Lord came to this baptism. The benefits of Mary's arrival and the Lord's presence are immediately apparent; for *as soon as Elizabeth heard Mary's greeting, the infant in her womb leapt for joy, and she was filled with the Holy Spirit.* Observe the distinction and choice of words. Elizabeth hears the voice first, but John is the first to be aware of grace. Elizabeth hears with bodily ears, but John leaps for joy at the meaning of the mystery. She is

aware of Mary's presence, but he is aware of the Lord's: a woman aware of a woman's presence, the infant that of the infant. The women speak about grace; the children are working within to unfold the mystery of love to the benefit of their mothers, who prophesy by the spirit of their sons. The infant leaps for joy, the mother is filled [with the Holy Spirit]. The mother is not filled before her son, but with her son is filled with the Holy Spirit. John exults, and the spirit of Mary exults likewise. Elizabeth is filled when John exults. Mary, however, is not to be filled, yet we know that her spirit exults—for the incomprehensible one was working incomprehensibly in his mother—and Elizabeth is filled after she conceived, Mary before she conceived ...

For behold, when the voice of your greeting came to my ears, the babe in my womb leaped for joy. And blessed is she who believed (Luke 1:44–45). You see that Mary did not doubt, but believed, and by her belief obtained the fruit of her faith ... But you who have heard and believed are also blessed. For any soul that believes both conceives and generates the Word of God and acknowledges his works. May the soul of Mary reside in each of you, that you may magnify the Lord, may her spirit be in each of you, that you may exult in God. If according to the flesh Christ has but one mother, according to faith everyone's fruit is Christ."

–St. Ambrose, *Commentary on the Gospel of St. Luke*

DAY 111

Today's Mystery: The Nativity

Today's Prayer:
- Read today's reflection.
- Spend 5 minutes reflecting or journaling on today's mystery.
- Pray 1 decade of the Rosary (1 Our Father, 10 Hail Marys, and 1 Glory Be).

Read the Reflection:

"He Who is the delight and glory of the angels is become the salvation and the consolation of all who suffer. He Who is glorious and transcendent in His own city, and beatifies its citizens by His presence, became little and humble, when in exile, that He might rejoice the exiles. He Who in the highest heavens is the glory of the Father became, as a Child on earth, 'peace to men of good will.'

A Little One is given to little ones, that the Great One may be given to the great, and that those whom the Little One justifies, the Great and Mighty One may afterwards magnify and render glorious. Hence, without doubt, St. Paul, the vessel of election, pours out to us the treasures which he had received from the fullness of this Child. For Christ, though a Child, is full of grace and truth. 'In Him dwelleth all the fullness of the Godhead corporally.' Hence, I repeat, St. Paul utters that good word which you have heard so often during these past days: 'Rejoice in the Lord always: again I say, Rejoice.' Of the showing forth of the mystery, he says 'Rejoice'; of the promise of it he adds: 'Again I say, Rejoice.' For both the mystery and its promise are causes of great joy. Rejoice that you have received the gifts of the left hand; rejoice in the expectation of the rewards of the right. 'His left hand is under my head, and his right hand shall embrace me.' For the left hand raises, the right receives. The left hand heals and justifies; the right embraces and blesses. In the left hand are contained His merits, in the right His rewards. In the right are delights, in the left are remedies.

But see how gentle the Physician is! behold how wise! Consider diligently the novelty of these remedies that He brings. See how they are not merely precious, but beautiful as well. They are fruits beneficial for our healing, and at the same time they are charming to the spiritual eye, sweet to the spiritual taste."

–St. Bernard, *On the Miraculous Nature of the Nativity*

DAY 112

Today's Mystery: **The Presentation of Jesus in the Temple**

Today's Prayer:
- Read today's reflection.
- Spend 5 minutes reflecting or journaling on today's mystery.
- Pray 1 decade of the Rosary (1 Our Father, 10 Hail Marys, and 1 Glory Be).

Read the Reflection:
"The eternal Father had already determined to save man, who was lost through sin, and free him from eternal death. But because he wished that, at the same time, his divine justice should not be defrauded of a full and due satisfaction, he did not spare the life of his own Son, already made man in order to redeem man; but he required that he should pay, to its most rigorous extent, the penalty merited by men: 'He that spared not even his own Son,' says the apostle, 'but delivered him up for us all.' He sent him therefore on the earth to become man, destined for him a mother, and chose the Virgin Mary; but as he did not wish his divine Word to become her Son before she accepted him by her express consent, so he did not wish that Jesus should sacrifice his life for the salvation of men without the concurrence of the consent of Mary, that together with the sacrifice of the life of the Son, the heart of the mother might be sacrificed also. St. Thomas teaches, that the relation of mother gives an especial right over her children; hence Jesus, being innocent in himself and not deserving any punishment for his own sins, it seemed fitting that he should not be destined to the cross as the victim for the sins of the world without the consent of his mother, by which she should voluntarily offer him to death.

But although Mary, from the moment she was made mother of Jesus, gave her consent to his death, yet the Lord wished her, on this day, to make, in the temple, a solemn sacrifice of herself, by offering solemnly her Son, and sacrificing to the divine justice his precious life. Hence St. Epiphanius called her a priest: 'Virginem appello velut sacerdotem.' Now we begin to see how much this sacrifice cost her, and what heroic virtue she was obliged to practice when she had herself to sign the sentence of condemnation of her dear Jesus to death.

Now behold Mary actually on her way to Jerusalem to offer her Son; she hastens her steps towards the place of sacrifice, and she herself carries her beloved victim in her arms. She enters the temple, approaches the altar, and there, filled with modesty, humility, and devotion, she presents her Son to the Most High. At this moment St. Simeon, who had received the promise from God that he should not die before seeing the expected Messias, takes the divine child from the hands of the Virgin, and, enlightened by the Holy Spirit, announces to her how much sorrow this sacrifice must cause her, this sacrifice which she was about to make of her Son, with whom must her blessed soul also be sacrificed. Here St. Thomas of Villanova contemplates the holy old man, who, when he had to announce the fatal prophecy to this poor mother, is agitated and silent. Then the saint considers Mary, who asks: Why, oh Simeon, in the time of so great consolation, are you thus disturbed? 'Unde tanta turbatio?' To whom he answers: Oh, noble and holy Virgin, I wished not to announce to thee such bitter tidings, but since the Lord wishes it thus, for thy greater merit, hear what I say to thee. This infant who now causes thee, and with reason, so much joy, oh God, shall one day bring thee the most cruel suffering that any creature has ever experienced in the world; and this will be when thou shalt see him persecuted by men of every sort, and placed on the earth as the mark of their sneers and derision, even until he is put to death before thy eyes. Know that after his death there will be many martyrs who, for love of this thy Son, will be tormented and slain; but if their martyrdom will be of the body, thy martyrdom, oh divine mother, will be of the heart."

Yes, of the heart, for nothing but compassion for the sufferings of this Son so dear could be meant by the sword of sorrow that St. Simeon predicted was to pierce the heart of the mother: 'And thy own soul a sword shall pierce.' Already the most holy Virgin, as St. Jerome says, had been enlightened through the divine Scriptures to know the sufferings which the Redeemer was to endure in his life, and still more at the time of his death …

She consented to all with a firmness which made the angels wonder, and pronounced the sentence that her Son should die … Oh, charity without measure! oh, constancy without example! oh, victory that merits the eternal admiration of heaven and of earth!"

–St. Alphonsus Liguori, *The Glories of Mary*

DAY 113

Today's Mystery: **The Finding of Jesus in the Temple**

Today's Prayer:
- Read today's reflection.
- Spend 5 minutes reflecting or journaling on today's mystery.
- Pray 1 decade of the Rosary (1 Our Father, 10 Hail Marys, and 1 Glory Be).

Read the Reflection:
"And when He was twelve years old, they went up to Jerusalem according to the custom of the feast.

After the Evangelist had said that Jesus advanced in wisdom and grace with God and men, he next shows that what he says is true; for he carries Him to Jerusalem in company with the holy Virgin, upon the summons of the feast; and then he says that He remained behind, and was afterwards found in the temple sitting in the midst of the doctors both asking and answering questions regarding those things, as we may feel sure, which were spoken of old by the law; and that He was wondered at by all for His questions and answers. Thou seest Him advancing in wisdom and grace, by reason of His becoming known unto many as being what He was.

Thy father and I have sought Thee sorrowing.

His mother certainly knew that He was not the child of Joseph, but she so speaks to avoid the suspicions of the Jews. And upon her saying, that *Thy father and I have sought Thee sorrowing*, the Savior answers:

Did ye not know that I must be at My Father's?

Here then first He makes more open mention of Him Who is truly His Father, and lays bare His own divinity."

–St. Cyril of Alexandria, *Commentary on the Gospel of Saint Luke*

DAY 114

Today's Mystery: The Baptism of Jesus

Today's Prayer:
- Read today's reflection.
- Spend 5 minutes reflecting or journaling on today's mystery.
- Pray 1 decade of the Rosary (1 Our Father, 10 Hail Marys, and 1 Glory Be).

Read the Reflection:
"Christ is illumined, let us shine forth with Him. Christ is baptized, let us descend with Him that we may also ascend with Him. …

But John baptizes, Jesus comes to Him … perhaps to sanctify the Baptist himself, but certainly to bury the whole of the old Adam in the water; and before this and for the sake of this, to sanctify Jordan; for as He is Spirit and Flesh, so He consecrates us by Spirit and water ... '*I have need to be baptized by You*' ... says the Voice to the Word, the Friend to the Bridegroom; ... he that is above all among them that are born of women, ... to Him Who is the Firstborn of every creature; ... he who was and is to be the Forerunner to Him Who was and is to be manifested. '*I have need to be baptized by You*'; add to this '*and for You*'; for he knew that he would be baptized by Martyrdom, ... But what says Jesus? '*Allow it to be so now,*' for this is the time of His Incarnation; for He knew that yet a little while and He should baptize the Baptist ... And what is the '*Fire?*' The consuming of the chaff, and the heat of the Spirit ...

Jesus goes up out of the water ... for with Himself He carries up the world ... and sees the heaven opened which Adam had shut against himself and all his posterity ... as the gates of Paradise by the flaming sword. And the Spirit bears witness to His Godhead, for he descends upon One that is like Him, as does the Voice from Heaven (for He to Whom the witness is borne came from thence), and like a Dove, for He honours the Body (for this also was God, through its union with God) by being seen in a bodily form; and moreover, the Dove has from distant ages been wont to proclaim the end of the Deluge ...

But let us venerate today the Baptism of Christ; and let us keep the feast well ... [B]e purified, and you shall be clean (for God rejoices in nothing so much as in the amendment and salvation of man, on whose behalf is every discourse and every Sacrament), that you may be like lights in the world, a quickening force to all other men; that you may stand as perfect lights beside That great Light, and may learn the mystery of the illumination of Heaven, enlightened by the Trinity more purely and clearly, of Which even now you are receiving in a measure the One Ray from the One Godhead in Christ Jesus our Lord; to Whom be the glory and the might for ever and ever. Amen."

–St. Gregory of Nazianzus, *Oration 39*

DAY 115

Today's Mystery: **The Wedding at Cana**

Today's Prayer:
- Read today's reflection.
- Spend 5 minutes reflecting or journaling on today's mystery.
- Pray 1 decade of the Rosary (1 Our Father, 10 Hail Marys, and 1 Glory Be).

Read the Reflection:
"Nay, may we not say that our Lord Himself had commenced His ministry, that is, bade farewell to His earthly home, at a feast? for it was at the marriage entertainment at Cana of Galilee that He did His first miracle, and manifested forth His glory. He was in the house of friends, He was surrounded by intimates and followers, and He took a familiar interest in the exigences of the feast. He supplied a principal want which was interfering with their festivity. It was His contribution to it. By supplying it miraculously He showed that He was beginning a new life, the life of a Messenger from God, and that that feast was the last scene of the old life. And, moreover, He made use of one remarkable expression, which seems to imply that this change of condition really was in His thoughts, if we may dare so to speak of them, or at all to interpret them. For when His Mother said unto Him, 'They have no wine,' He answered, 'What have I to do with thee?' He had had to do with her for thirty years. She had borne Him, she had nursed Him, she had taught Him. And when He had reached twelve years old, at the age when the young may expect to be separated from their parents, He had only become more intimately one with them, for we are told that 'He went down with them, and came to Nazareth, and was subject unto them.' Eighteen years had passed away since this occurred. St. Joseph (as it seems) had been taken to his rest.

Mary remained; but from Mary, His Mother, He must now part, for the three years of His ministry. He had gently intimated this to her at the very time of His becoming subject to her, intimated that His heavenly Father's work was a higher call than any earthly duty. 'Wist ye not,' He said, when found in the Temple, 'that I must be about My Father's business?' The time was now come when this was to be fulfilled, and, therefore, when His Mother addressed Him at the marriage feast, He answered, 'What have I to do with thee?' What is between Me and thee, My Mother, any longer? 'The time is fulfilled, and the Kingdom of God is at hand.'

And hence the words which I have quoted were but the introduction to others like them, in which He seemed to put His Mother from His thoughts, as being called to the work of a divine ministry."

–John Henry Newman, *Sermons Bearing on Subjects of the Day*

DAY 116

Today's Mystery: **The Proclamation of the Kingdom**

Today's Prayer:
- Read today's reflection.
- Spend 5 minutes reflecting or journaling on today's mystery.
- Pray 1 decade of the Rosary (1 Our Father, 10 Hail Marys, and 1 Glory Be).

Read the Reflection:
"To begin with, I shall show that, since your duty is to continue and fulfil in yourselves the life, virtues and actions of Jesus Christ on earth, so must you also prolong and fulfil, in yourself, the states and mysteries of Jesus, and frequently implore Jesus Himself to consummate and accomplish them in you and in His whole Church.

You cannot too often realize and reflect on the truth that the mysteries of the life of Christ have not yet reached their full perfection and completeness. Although they are perfect and complete in Christ's own Person, they are not yet completed in you who are His members, nor in Holy Mother Church, which is His Mystical Body. It is the plan of the Son of God that His whole Church should participate in and actually be, as it were, the continuation and extension of the mystery of His Incarnation, birth, Childhood, hidden life, public life of teaching and of labor, His Passion and His death, by the graces He desires to impart to you, and by the effects He wishes to accomplish in you through these same mysteries. By this means, He desires to fulfil His mysteries in you.

Therefore, St. Paul says that Jesus Christ is fulfilled in His Church (Eph. 1, 22–23) and that we all come together in His perfection and His maturity (Eph. 4, 13), which means, as I have said, His mystical Body, which is the Church—a maturity which will not be complete until the Day of Judgment. And St. Paul again speaks elsewhere of the same fulness of God which is accomplished in you, and of the growth and increase of God in you (Eph. 3, 19). And in another place he says that [h]e fills up in [h]is body the Passion of Jesus Christ (Col. 1, 24). Now what he says of the fulfilment of the mystery of the Passion may also be said of the other mysteries of the life of Jesus Christ.

So the Son of God plans to perfect and complete in you all His states and mysteries. He intends to fulfil in you the divine life which has been His for all eternity in the bosom of His Father, imparting a participation in that life, and making you live, with Him, a life entirely pure and holy.

It is His design to complete in you the mystery of His Incarnation, birth and hidden life, by taking flesh in you and being born in your souls, as it were, through the Sacraments of Holy Baptism and the Blessed Eucharist, causing you to live by a spiritual and inward life, a life hidden with Him in God.

It is His design to perfect in you the mystery of His Passion, death and Resurrection, by causing you to suffer, to die and to rise again with Him and in Him. It is His design to fulfil His glorious immortal life in heaven, by causing you to live, in Him and with Him, a glorious and immortal life after death. He likewise intends to perfect and accomplish in you and in His Church all the other mysteries of His life by the communication and participation granted to you by His holy Will, through the continuation and extension of these mysteries operating in you.

This universal plan of the Son of God will not be completed until the Day of Judgment. The ranks of the saints will not be filled up until the consummation of the time God has allotted to men for their sanctification. Therefore, the mysteries of Jesus will not be complete until the end of the time determined by Jesus Christ Himself for their consummation in you and in His Church, that is, until the end of the world.

Now the life you have here on earth was given to you only for the accomplishment of the infinite designs of Jesus Christ for mankind. Hence, you should employ all your time, your days, your years, in cooperating with Jesus Christ in the divine task of consummating His mysteries in yourself. You must cooperate in this by good works and prayer, by frequent application of mind and heart to the contemplation, adoration and veneration of the sacred mysteries of His life according to the different seasons of the year, so that, by these very mysteries, He may work in you all He desires to accomplish for His pure glory. This is the first reason why you must have a special devotion to all the infinitely precious details and aspects of the life of Jesus."

–St. John Eudes, *The Life and the Kingdom of Jesus*

DAY 117

Today's Mystery: The Transfiguration

Today's Prayer:
- Read today's reflection.
- Spend 5 minutes reflecting or journaling on today's mystery.
- Pray 1 decade of the Rosary (1 Our Father, 10 Hail Marys, and 1 Glory Be).

Read the Reflection:
"The Lord Jesus Himself shone bright as the sun; His raiment became white as the snow; and Moses and Elias talked with Him. Jesus Himself indeed shone as the sun, signifying that '*He is the light which lights every man that comes into the world.*' What this sun is to the eyes of the flesh, that is He to the eyes of the heart; and what that is to the flesh of men, that is He to their hearts. Now His raiment is His Church. For if the raiment be not held together by him who puts it on, it will fall off. Of this raiment, Paul was as it were a sort of last border. For he says himself, '*I am the least of the Apostles.*' And in another place, '*I am the last of the Apostles.*' Now in a garment the border is the last and least part. Wherefore as that woman which suffered from an issue of blood, when she had touched the Lord's border was made whole, so the Church which came from out of the Gentiles, was made whole by the preaching of Paul. What wonder if the Church is signified by white raiment, when you hear the Prophet Isaiah saying, '*Though your sins be as scarlet, I will make them white as snow*'? Moses and Elias, that is, the Law and the Prophets, what avail they, except they converse with the Lord? Except they give witness to the Lord, who would read the Law or the Prophets? Mark how briefly the Apostle expresses this; '*For by the Law is the knowledge of sin; but now the righteousness of God without the Law is manifested.*'

behold the sun; *'being witnessed by the Law and the Prophets,'* behold the shining of the Sun.

Peter sees this, and as a man savouring the things of men says, *'Lord, it is good for us to be here.'* He had been wearied with the multitude, he had found now the mountain's solitude; there he had Christ the Bread of the soul. What! should he depart thence again to travail and pains, possessed of a holy love to Godward, and thereby of a good conversation? He wished well for himself; and so he added, *'If You will, let us make here three tabernacles; one for You, and one for Moses, and one for Elias.'* To this the Lord made no answer; but notwithstanding Peter was answered. *'For while he yet spoke, a bright cloud came, and overshadowed them.'* He desired three tabernacles; the heavenly answer showed him that we have One, which human judgment desired to divide. Christ, the Word of God, the Word of God in the Law, the Word in the Prophets. Why, Peter, do you seek to divide them? It were more fitting for you to join them. You seek three; understand that they are but One ...

Come down, Peter: you were desiring to rest on the mount; come down, *'preach the word, be instant in season, out of season, reprove, rebuke, exhort with all longsuffering and doctrine.'* Endure, labour hard, bear your measure of torture; that you may possess what is meant by the white raiment of the Lord, through the brightness and the beauty of an upright labouring in charity ... *'The Life came down, that He might be slain; the Bread came down, that He might hunger; the Way came down, that life might be wearied in the way; the Fountain came down, that He might thirst;* and do you refuse to labour? "Seek not your own." Have charity, preach the truth; so shall you come to eternity, where you shall find security.'"

–St. Augustine, *Sermons on Selected Lessons of the New Testament: Sermon 28*

DAY 118

Today's Mystery: The Institution of the Eucharist

Today's Prayer:
- Read today's reflection.
- Spend 5 minutes reflecting or journaling on today's mystery.
- Pray 1 decade of the Rosary (1 Our Father, 10 Hail Marys, and 1 Glory Be).

Read the Reflection:
"For you have just heard him say distinctly, *That our Lord Jesus Christ in the night in which He was betrayed, took bread, and when He had given thanks He broke it, and gave to His disciples, saying, Take, eat, this is My Body: and having taken the cup and given thanks, He said, Take, drink, this is My Blood.* Since then He Himself declared and said of the Bread, *This is My Body*, who shall dare to doubt any longer? And since He has Himself affirmed and said, *This is My Blood*, who shall ever hesitate, saying, that it is not His blood?

He once in Cana of Galilee, turned the water into wine, akin to blood, and is it incredible that He should have turned wine into blood? When called to a bodily marriage, He miraculously wrought that wonderful work; and *on the children of the bride-chamber* ... shall He not much rather be acknowledged to have bestowed the fruition of His Body and Blood?

Wherefore with full assurance let us partake as of the Body and Blood of Christ: for in the figure of Bread is given to you His Body, and in the figure of Wine His Blood; that you by partaking of the Body and Blood of Christ, may be made of the same body and the same blood with Him. For thus we come to bear Christ in us, because His Body and Blood are distributed through our members; thus it is that, according to the blessed Peter, *we become partakers of the divine nature* ...

Christ on a certain occasion discoursing with the Jews said, *Unless you eat My flesh and drink My blood, you have no life in you* ... They not having heard His saying in a spiritual sense were offended, and went back, supposing that He was inviting them to eat flesh.

In the Old Testament also there was show-bread; but this, as it belonged to the Old Testament, has come to an end; but in the New Testament there is Bread of heaven, and a Cup of salvation, sanctifying soul and body; for as the Bread corresponds to our body, so is the Word appropriate to our soul.

Consider therefore the Bread and the Wine not as bare elements, for they are, according to the Lord's declaration, the Body and Blood of Christ; for even though sense suggests this to you, yet let faith establish you. Judge not the matter from the taste, but from faith be fully assured without misgiving, that the Body and Blood of Christ have been vouchsafed to you.

Having learned these things, and been fully assured that the seeming bread is not bread, though sensible to taste, but the Body of Christ; and that the seeming wine is not wine, though the taste will have it so, but the Blood of Christ; and that of this David sung of old, saying, *And bread strengthens man's heart, to make his face to shine with oil,* 'strengthen your heart,' by partaking thereof as spiritual, and '*make the face of your soul to shine.*' And so having it unveiled with a pure conscience, may you reflect as a mirror the glory of the Lord ... and proceed from glory to glory, in Christ Jesus our Lord:— To whom be honour, and might, and glory, for ever and ever. Amen."

–St. Cyril of Jerusalem, *Catechetical Lecture 22*

DAY 119

Today's Mystery: The Agony in the Garden

Today's Prayer:
- Read today's reflection.
- Spend 5 minutes reflecting or journaling on today's mystery.
- Pray 1 decade of the Rosary (1 Our Father, 10 Hail Marys, and 1 Glory Be).

Read the Reflection:
"The Gospels mutually complement one another, since some are understood through others because they all are the teaching of the one Spirit. John, who was pre-eminently a teacher of spiritual ideals, acquaints us with this petition of the Lord that all the others pass over in silence, when he says that the Lord prayed as follows: 'Holy Father, keep them in thy name. While I was with them I kept them in thy name. Those whom thou hast given me I guarded.' Hence, that prayer was not for Himself but for the Apostles, nor is He sad on His own account who warns them to pray that they may not be tempted, nor is the angel sent to Him who, if He wished, could bring down twelve thousand legions from heaven, nor is He who is troubled unto death afraid because of death, nor does He pray that the cup may pass over Him; He prays that the cup may pass away from Him, but it cannot pass away unless He drinks it. To pass away does not mean to depart from its place, but not to exist at all. And this is indeed the very meaning that the statements in the Gospels and from the Apostles point out when they declare: 'Heaven and earth will pass away, but my words will not pass away.' The Apostle also says: 'Behold the former things have passed away and have been made new,' as He likewise does in the words: 'And the figure of this world will pass away.'

Hence, the cup for which He prays to the Father that it may

pass away cannot pass away unless He drinks it, and that for which the Lord prays He assuredly prays for these men whom He Himself has saved as long as He remained with them, and whom He has also entrusted to the Father that they may be saved. But now, since He is about to accomplish the mystery of the death, He prays that the Father may be their protector. Supposing, indeed, that the incident is true, the presence of the angel who has been sent to Him is not open to question, and the assurance that His prayer has been granted is unmistakable, since at the conclusion of the prayer He exhorts them to sleep. The Evangelist now makes known the result of the prayer that was heard, as well as the confidence with which He exhorted them to sleep in the work of the passion itself, when He says to the Apostles who would escape from the hands of His persecutors: 'That the word which he had said might be fulfilled, "Of those whom thou hast given I have not lost one."' The request in the prayer is fulfilled by Himself, and all are saved. He begs the Father to save in His own name those whom He has saved. And so surely did He save them that, even though the faith of Peter was filled with terror, it did not fail, because of the repentance that immediately followed."

–St. Hilary of Poitiers, *The Trinity*

DAY 120

Today's Mystery: The Scourging at the Pillar

Today's Prayer:
- Read today's reflection.
- Spend 5 minutes reflecting or journaling on today's mystery.
- Pray 1 decade of the Rosary (1 Our Father, 10 Hail Marys, and 1 Glory Be).

Read the Reflection:

"When I came for adoration, an inner recollection took hold of me immediately, and I saw the Lord Jesus tied to a pillar, stripped of His clothes, and the scourging began immediately. I saw four men who took turns at striking the Lord with scourges. My heart almost stopped at the sight of these tortures. The Lord said to me, I suffer even greater pain than that which you see. And Jesus gave me to know for what sins He subjected himself to the scourging: these are sins of impurity. Oh, how dreadful was Jesus' moral suffering during the scourging! Then Jesus said to me, Look and see the human race in its present condition. In an instant, I saw horrible things: the executioners left Jesus, and other people started scourging Him; they seized the scourges and struck the Lord mercilessly. These were priests, religious men and women; and high dignitaries of the Church, which surprised me greatly. There were lay people of all ages and walks of life. All vented their malice on the innocent Jesus. Seeing this, my heart fell as if into a mortal agony. And while the executioners had been scourging Him, Jesus had been silent and looking into the distance; but when those other souls I mentioned scourged Him, Jesus closed His eyes, and a soft, but most painful moan escaped from His Heart. And Jesus gave me to know in detail the gravity of the malice of these ungrateful souls: You see, this is a torture greater than My death. Then my lips too fell silent, and I began to experience the agony of death, and I felt that no one would comfort me or snatch me from that state but the One who had put me into it. Then the Lord said to me, I see the sincere pain of your heart which brought great solace to My Heart. See and take comfort."

–St. Faustina, *Diary* 445

DAY 121

Today's Mystery: The Crowning with Thorns

Today's Prayer:
- Read today's reflection.
- Spend 5 minutes reflecting or journaling on today's mystery.
- Pray 1 decade of the Rosary (1 Our Father, 10 Hail Marys, and 1 Glory Be).

Read the Reflection:
"Pilate tried to strike a balance between satisfying the Sanhedrin and his own conscience. But Pilate was wrong in thinking that the drawing of blood would calm their passions and melt them to pity. Such compromises in the face of justice rarely achieve their ends. If guilty, Pilate should have condemned Him to death; if innocent, he should have released Him.

Our Lord looked forward to giving His life as a ransom for sin; He had described Himself as having a baptism wherewith He was to be baptized. John gave Him the baptism of water, but the Roman soldiers now gave Him His baptism of blood. After opening His sacred flesh with violent stripes, they now put on Him a purple robe which adhered to His bleeding body. Then they plaited a crown of thorns which they placed on His head. How the soldiers cursed when one thorn plucked their fingers, but how they sneered when the crown of thorns crowned His brow! They then mocked Him and put a reed in His hand after beating Him on the head. Then they knelt down before Him in feigned adoration."

–Venerable Fulton J. Sheen, *Life of Christ*

DAY 122

Today's Mystery: The Carrying of the Cross

Today's Prayer:
- Read today's reflection.
- Spend 5 minutes reflecting or journaling on today's mystery.
- Pray 1 decade of the Rosary (1 Our Father, 10 Hail Marys, and 1 Glory Be).

Read the Reflection:
"The way Christ was brought to his crucifixion was a dishonor, *bearing his own cross*, for death on a cross was a disgrace: *a hanged man is accursed by God* (Deut 21:23). And thus, avoiding the cross as something unholy, and fearing even to touch it, they laid the cross on the condemned Jesus. Thus, it says that he went out, *bearing his own cross* ...

Christ bore his cross as a king does his scepter; his cross is the sign of his glory, which is his universal dominion over all things: *the Lord will reign from the wood* (Ps 95:9); *the government will be upon his shoulder, and his name will be called: Wonderful, Counselor, Mighty God, Everlasting Father, Prince of Peace* (Isa 9:6). He carried his cross as a victor carries the trophy of his victory: *he disarmed the principalities and powers and made a public example of them, triumphing over them in himself* (Col 2:15). Again, he carried his cross as a teacher his candelabrum, as a support for the light of his teaching, because for believers the message of the cross is the power of God: *no one after lighting a lamp puts it in a cellar or under a bushel but on a stand, that those who enter may see the light* (Luke 11:33)."

–St. Thomas Aquinas, *Commentary on the Gospel of John*

DAY 123

Today's Mystery: **The Crucifixion**

Today's Prayer:
- Read today's reflection.
- Spend 5 minutes reflecting or journaling on today's mystery.
- Pray 1 decade of the Rosary (1 Our Father, 10 Hail Marys, and 1 Glory Be).

Read the Reflection:
"Now, as my Son was led away like a robber, he wiped away the blood from his eyes. And when he was condemned, they gave him his cross to bear. When he had carried it a short way, one came up and assumed it. Meanwhile, as my Son was going to the place of his Passion, some smote him on the back, others struck him in the face. And so violently and rudely was he struck, that though I did not see the person striking, I distinctly heard the sound of the blow. And when I came with him to the place of the Passion, I there beheld all the instruments prepared for his death. And my Son himself coming thither, divested himself of his clothes, the attendants saying to each other: 'These vestments are ours, nor can he have them again, that is condemned to death.' Now, while my Son stood as naked as when he was born, one running up, handed him a cloth, with which, exulting inwardly, he covered him. Then his cruel executioners seized him, and stretched him on the cross. First they fixed his right hand to the beam, which was pierced for nails, and they transfixed his hand in the part where the bone was firmest. Then drawing his other hand with a rope, they affixed it in like manner to the cross. Then they crucified his right foot, and over it the left, with two nails, so that all the nerves and veins were extended and broken. This done, they fitted a crown of thorns to his head, which so acutely wounded the venerable head of my Son, that his eyes were filled, his ears stopped up, with the blood that streamed

down, and his whole beard matted with the gore. And as he stood thus pierced and bloody, condoling with me as I stood mourning, he looked with blood-stained eyes to John, my kinsman, and commended me to him. At that time, I heard some saying that my Son was a robber, others that he was a liar, others that none better deserved death than my Son, and these words renewed my grief. But, as has been said, when the first nail was driven into him, horrified at the first blow, I fell as though dead, my eyes darkened, my hands trembling, my feet quivering, nor for bitterness could I look again before he was nailed fast. On rising, I beheld my Son hanging miserably, and I, his most wretched mother, filled with terror on all sides, could scarcely stand for grief. But my Son, seeing me and his friends weeping disconsolately, in a loud and tearful voice cried out to his Father, saying: 'Father, why hast thou forsaken me?' Then his eyes appeared half dead, his cheeks hollow, and his countenance mournful, his mouth open and his tongue bloodstained, his body collapsed as though he had nothing within, the humors being all drained; his whole body pale and languid from the loss and flow of blood. His hands and feet were stretched out most rigidly, drawn and shaped to the form of the cross, his beard and hair all clotted with blood … Then in his great anguish of body, he cried in his humanity to his Father: 'Father, into thy hands I commend my spirit.' When I, his most afflicted mother, heard these words, all my limbs trembled in my bitter grief of heart. And as often as I thought of this word, it was present and fresh in my ears. And as death came on, when his heart was breaking from excessive pain, then all his members quivered, and his head, rising slightly, inclined. His mouth was seen to open, disclosing his tongue all covered with blood. His hands shrunk a little from the holes of the nails, and the feet bore more of the weight of the body. His fingers and arms extended in a manner, and his back was pressed back on the cross. Then some said to me: 'Mary, thy Son is dead.' Others said: 'He is dead, but he will rise again.'"

–St. Bridget, *Revelations*

DAY 124

Today's Mystery: The Resurrection

Today's Prayer:
- Read today's reflection.
- Spend 5 minutes reflecting or journaling on today's mystery.
- Pray 1 decade of the Rosary (1 Our Father, 10 Hail Marys, and 1 Glory Be).

Read the Reflection:
"I am speaking to you, newly-born infants, little children in Christ, new sons and daughters of the Church, grace of the Father, fruitfulness of Mother Church, a holy branch, a new swarm [of bees], the flower of our ministry, and the fruit of our labor, my joy and crown, all who stand in Christ, I address you with apostolic words: *The night is far gone, the day is at hand. Let us then cast off the works of darkness and put on the armor of light; let us conduct ourselves becomingly as in the day, not in reveling and drunkenness, not in debauchery and licentiousness, not in quarreling and jealousy. But put on the Lord Jesus Christ, and make no provision for the flesh, to gratify its desires* (Romans 13:12–14), that you may put on the life of him whom you have put on in this sacrament. *For as many of you as were baptized into Christ have put on Christ. There is neither Jew nor Greek, there is neither slave nor free, there is neither male nor female; for you are all one in Christ Jesus* (Galatians 3:27–28). Such is the power this sacrament holds. For it is a sacrament of new life, a life which begins in this world by the remission of past sins, and which will be perfected in the resurrection of the dead. *We were buried therefore with him by baptism into death, so that as Christ was raised from the dead by the glory of the Father, we too might walk in newness of life* (Romans 6:4). But you are now walking by faith, still sojourning in this mortal body away from the Lord; but he to whom your steps are ordered

is himself the certain way: Jesus Christ, who for our sake deigned to become man. For he has stored up abundant sweetness for those who fear him, which he will reveal and fulfill when we have attained the reality which even now we attain in hope …

[Y]ou have at the same time received the unity of the spirit in the bond of peace, if you both, as I wish, as I hope, as I exhort and implore, keep intact what you have received and go on to accomplish greater things … [T]he Lord himself, having purified himself of the mortality of the flesh, and not indeed a different flesh but raising up a body which would no longer die, marked the Sunday by his Resurrection, which is the third day after the day of his Passion, and the eighth day, the day after the Sabbath, and this same day is the first day. Wherefore you also do not yet know the reality, but at present are certain in hope, since you will have the sacrament of this reality and have received the pledge of the Spirit. *If then you have been raised with Christ, seek the things that are above, where Christ is, seated at the right hand of God. Set your minds on things that are above, not on things that are on earth. For you have died, and your life is hid with Christ in God. When Christ who is our life appears, then you also will appear with him in glory (Colossians 3:1–4)."*

–St. Augustine, *Sermon 8*

DAY 125

Today's Mystery: The Ascension

Today's Prayer
- Read today's reflection.
- Spend 5 minutes reflecting or journaling on today's mystery.
- Pray 1 decade of the Rosary (1 Our Father, 10 Hail Marys, and 1 Glory Be).

Read the Reflection:

"Run with the heart's affection, journey on with love, ascend by charity. Why do you seek for the way? Cleave unto Christ, who by Descending and Ascending has made Himself the Way. Do you wish to ascend? Hold fast to Him that ascends. For by your own self you can not rise. *For no man has ascended up to heaven, but He that came down from heaven, even the Son of Man which is in heaven.* If no one ascends but He that descended, that is, the Son of Man, our Lord Jesus, do you wish to ascend also? Be then a member of Him who Only has ascended. For He the Head, with all the members, is but One Man. And since no one can ascend, but he who in His Body is made a member of Him; that is fulfilled, *'that no man has ascended, but He that descended.'* For you can not say, *'Lo, why has Peter, for instance, ascended, why has Paul ascended, why have the Apostles ascended, if no one has ascended, but He that descended?'* The answer to this is, *'What do Peter, and Paul, and the rest of the Apostles, and all the faithful, what do they hear from the Apostle? "Now you are the Body of Christ, and members in particular." If then the Body of Christ and His members belong to One, do not make two of them ...'*

[A]ccording to His Divinity we cannot be what He is; seeing that He is the Creator, we the creature; He the Maker, we His work; He the Framer, we framed by Him; but in order that we might be one with Him in Him, He vouchsafed to be our Head, by taking of us flesh wherein to die for us ...

Seeing then that we are of His members, in order that we may understand this mystery as I have said, Brethren, let us live holily, let us love God for His Own sake. Now He who shows to us while in our pilgrimage the form of a servant, reserves for those that reach their country the form of God. With the form of a servant has He laid down the way, with the form of God He has prepared the home. Seeing then that it is a hard matter for us to comprehend this, but no hard matter to believe it; for Isaiah says, *'Unless ye believe you shall not understand;'* let us *'walk by faith as long as we are in pilgrimage from the Lord, till we come to sight where we shall see face to face.'* As walking by faith, let us do good works. In these good works, let there be a free love of God for His Own sake, and an active love of our neighbour. For we have nothing we can do for God; but because we have something we may do for our neighbour, we shall by our good offices to the needy, gain His favour who is the source of all abundance. Let every one then do what he can for others; let him freely bestow upon the needy of his superfluity. One has money; let him feed the poor, let him clothe the naked, let him build a church, let him do with his money all the good he can. Another has good counsel; let him guide his neighbour, let him by the light of holiness drive away the darkness of doubting. Another has learning; let him draw out of this store of the Lord, let him minister food to his fellow-servants, strengthen the faithful, recall the wandering, seek the lost, do all the good he can. Something there is, which even the poor may deal out to one another; let one lend feet to the lame, another give his own eyes to guide the blind; another visit the sick, another bury the dead. These are things which all may do, so that in a word it would be hard to find one who has not some means of doing good to others. And last of all comes that important duty which the Apostle speaks of; '*Bear ye one another's burdens, and so shall you fulfil the law of Christ.*'"

–St. Augustine, *Sermons on Selected Lessons of the New Testament: Sermon 41*

DAY 126

Today's Mystery: The Descent of the Holy Spirit on Pentecost

Today's Prayer:
- Read today's reflection.
- Spend 5 minutes reflecting or journaling on today's mystery.
- Pray 1 decade of the Rosary (1 Our Father, 10 Hail Marys, and 1 Glory Be).

Read the Reflection:

"We well know by our faith, that the Holy Spirit proceeds from the Father and the Son, through their mutual love for each other, and therefore that the gift of love which the Lord infuses into our souls, and which is the greatest of all gifts, is particularly attributed to the Holy Spirit, as St. Paul speaks: *The charity of God is poured abroad in our hearts, by the Holy Spirit, who is given to us, Rom. v. 5* ... God ordained in the old law, that fire should be kept continually burning upon his altar: *The fire on the altar shall always burn. Lev. vi. 12.* St. Gregory says that the altars of God are our hearts, in which he desires that the fire of his love should always burn. And hence the Eternal Father, not satisfied with having given us his Son Jesus Christ, to save us by his death, would also give us the Holy Spirit, to dwell in our hearts, and keep them continually inflamed with his love. And Jesus himself declared, that it was in order to influence our hearts with this holy love, that he came into the world, and that he desired nothing more than to see it kindled: *I am come to send fire upon the earth: and what will I but that it be kindled? St. Luke, xii. 49.* Hence, forgetting the injuries and ingratitude he received from men in this world, when he had ascended into heaven, he sent down upon us the Holy Spirit ... Hence it was that the Holy Spirit chose to appear in the form of fiery tongues: *And there appeared to them parted tongues, as it were of fire. Acts, ii. 3.* And hence, the Church instructs us to pray: 'May the Holy Spirit, we beseech thee, O Lord, inflame us with that fire which our Lord Jesus Christ came to cast upon the earth, and which he ardently desired should be enkindled.' This was the holy fire which has inspired the saints to do such great things for God, to love their enemies, to desire contempt, to renounce all worldly goods, and to embrace with cheerfulness, even torments and death. Love cannot remain idle, and never says: 'It is enough.' The soul that loves God, the more she does for her beloved, desires the more to do for him, in order to please him the more, and to draw down his love the more. This holy love is enkindled in mental prayer: *In my meditation a fire shall flame out. Ps.* xxxviii. 4. If therefore we desire to be on fire with the love of God, we must delight in prayer; this is the blessed furnace in which this divine ardour is enkindled."

–St. Alphonsus Liguori, *The Way of Salvation*

DAY 127

Today's Mystery: The Assumption of Mary

Today's Prayer:
- Read today's reflection.
- Spend 5 minutes reflecting or journaling on today's mystery.
- Pray 1 decade of the Rosary (1 Our Father, 10 Hail Marys, and 1 Glory Be)

Read the Reflection:
1. "The glorious Virgin who mounts to the heavens today has without a doubt heaped joy upon joy for the citizens of the world above. For it is she whose voice of greeting makes those whom the maternal womb still encloses leap with joy! And if the soul of an unborn child melted when Mary spoke, how great do you think was the joy of the citizens of heaven when they succeeded in hearing her voice, seeing her face, and enjoying her blessed presence?

    But what, dearly beloved, does this solemnity of her assumption hold for us? What is there for us to be happy about? What is the reason for our displays of joy? The whole world has been made bright by the presence of Mary, so that the heavenly country itself shines more brightly by the radiant light of the virginal torch. *Thanksgiving and the voice of praise* rightly resound in the heavens. Doesn't it seem better for us, though, to beat our breasts than clap our hands? For as much as heaven exults at her presence, does it not follow that our world below should mourn her absence just as much?

But enough of this sad contrariness! Truly, here we have no abiding city! Instead, we seek that to which blessed Mary has come today. If we are true citizens of that city, it is fitting that we should remember it even by the rivers of Babylon, that we should join in its pleasures and share its joy, especially that which so fully makes glad the city of God, and should feel the showers that water the earth. Our queen has gone before us; she has gone before and has been caught up in glory, so that we may follow her as servants follow their mistress, crying, *draw us after you: we shall run in the odor of your ointments.* Someone to plead our cause has been sent before us in our journey, she who is the mother of the judge, the mother of pity! She will transact the business of our salvation effectively and with prayer.

2. Our earth has today sent to heaven a precious gift, that by giving and receiving a happy bond of friendship human affairs should be joined to the divine; the earthly should be joined to the heavenly and the highest to the lowest. For the exalted fruit of the earth has gone up to the place from where all good and perfect gifts come down. Therefore the Blessed Virgin, when she goes up on high, will give gifts to humans. Why should she not? At least she will not lack the opportunity, nor the will. She is the Queen of Heaven, she is merciful; she is the Mother of the only-begotten Son of God. Nothing can so commend the greatness of her power and holiness ..."

–St. Bernard of Clairvaux, *On the Solemnity of the Assumption of the Blessed Virgin Mary: Sermon One*

DAY 128

Today's Mystery: The Coronation of Mary as Queen of Heaven and Earth

Today's Prayer:
- Read today's reflection.
- Spend 5 minutes reflecting or journaling on today's mystery.
- Pray 1 decade of the Rosary (1 Our Father, 10 Hail Marys, and 1 Glory Be).

Read the Reflection:
"This great title ['*Regina Angelorum,*' or 'Queen of Angels'] may be fitly connected with the Maternity of Mary, that is, with the coming upon her of the Holy Ghost at Nazareth after the Angel Gabriel's annunciation to her, and with the consequent birth of our Lord at Bethlehem. She, as the Mother of our Lord, comes nearer to Him than any angel; nearer even than the Seraphim who surround Him, and cry continually, 'Holy, Holy, Holy.'

The two Archangels who have a special office in the Gospel are St. Michael and St. Gabriel—and they both of them are associated in the history of the Incarnation with Mary: St. Gabriel, when the Holy Ghost came down upon her; and St. Michael, when the Divine Child was born.

St. Gabriel hailed her as 'Full of grace,' and as 'Blessed among women,' and announced to her that the Holy Ghost would come down upon her, and that she would bear a Son who would be the Son of the Highest.

Of St. Michael's ministry to her, on the birth of that Divine Son, we learn in the Apocalypse, written by the Apostle St. John. We know our Lord came to set up the Kingdom of Heaven among men; and hardly was He born when He was assaulted by the powers of the world who wished to destroy Him. Herod sought to take His life, but he was defeated by St. Joseph's carrying His Mother and Him off into Egypt. But St. John in the Apocalypse tells us that Michael and his angels were the real guardians of Mother and Child, then and on other occasions.

First, St. John saw in vision 'a great sign in heaven' (meaning by 'heaven' the Church, or Kingdom of God), 'a woman clothed with the sun, and with the moon under her feet, and on her head a crown of twelve stars'; and when she was about to be delivered of her Child there appeared 'a great red dragon,' that is, the evil spirit, ready 'to devour her son' when He should be born. The Son was preserved by His own Divine power, but next the evil spirit persecuted her; St. Michael, however, and his angels came to the rescue and prevailed against him.

'There was a great battle,' says the sacred writer; 'Michael and his Angels fought with the dragon, and the dragon fought and his angels; and that great dragon was cast out, the old serpent, who is called the devil.' Now, as then, the Blessed Mother of God has hosts of angels who do her service; and she is their Queen."

–St. John Henry Newman, "Mary Is the *Regina Angelorum,*' the Queen of Angels"

DAY 129

Today's Mystery: **The Annunciation**

Today's Prayer:
- Pray with today's sacred art in "*visio divina.*" The reflection questions that are provided can help you focus on different aspects of the art and connect them to the mystery. You may find all of the prompts fruitful, or you may prefer to read and reflect on just one or two.
- Pray 1 decade of the Rosary (1 Our Father, 10 Hail Marys, and 1 Glory Be).

View Sacred Art: *The Annunciation*, Fra Angelico

Reflect:
- Our Lady is depicted here in this painting like a queen sitting on her throne. How is she a queen? How does she exercise her queenship? How is meditating on Mary's royalty helpful for us?
- Notice the ray of light shining down on Our Lady and the dove, which represents the Holy Spirit, descending on her. What significant moment does this painting capture?
- There is a book open on Our Lady's lap. What do you think she was reading or praying when the angel Gabriel came to her?
- Notice that Our Lady's hands and Gabriel's hands look the same and they are bowing to each other. Why do you think they greet each other in this way?
- On the left, we can see Adam and Eve being expelled from the garden of Eden. How does Our Lady undo what Eve did in the garden of Eden? How were Mary and the Incarnation already promised in the garden of Eden?
- Contrast the faces of Adam and Eve with the serene face of Mary. What does sin do to us and to our countenance?

DAY 130

Today's Mystery: The Visitation

Today's Prayer:
- Pray with today's sacred art in "*visio divina*," using as many or as few of the reflection questions as you find fruitful.
- Pray 1 decade of the Rosary (1 Our Father, 10 Hail Marys, and 1 Glory Be)

View Sacred Art: *The Visitation*, Rembrandt

Reflect:
- Notice the light in this painting radiating from Our Lady. How is she bringing the light to Elizabeth and Zechariah?
- There is a peacock with a brood of chicks in the bottom left corner of the painting. A peacock can be used to symbolize divinity and immortality. Why then might the artist have included a peacock with her brood?
- Notice that the advanced age of Zechariah and Elizabeth is clearly depicted. How does this help us to meditate on how great a miracle the birth of John the Baptist truly was?
- Elizabeth's eyes are gazing up toward heaven, as if heaven is revealing something to her. What does she know about Mary and the child in her womb, even before Mary has a chance to tell her?
- We see that Elizabeth embraces Mary while her cloak is still being removed by an attendant. It seems like Elizabeth cannot wait to embrace her cousin. Who are some of the "Elizabeths" in your life who cannot wait to see you and share in your joy? How can you be an "Elizabeth" for others?
- Mary is holding a handkerchief in this depiction of the Visitation. What does this add to the painting? Do you think Mary was moved to tears of joy in seeing Elizabeth and hearing her words? Or perhaps she was moved to tears while contemplating the Annunciation on her journey?

DAY 131

Today's Mystery: The Nativity

Today's Prayer:
- Pray with today's sacred art in "*visio divina,*" using as many or as few of the reflection questions as you find fruitful.
- Pray 1 decade of the Rosary (1 Our Father, 10 Hail Marys, and 1 Glory Be).

View Sacred Art: The Nativity

Reflect:
- It looks like Jesus is reaching for St. Joseph. Why do you think Jesus chose St. Joseph to be his father on earth? What was his mission as the father in the Holy Family?
- Notice Joseph's bare feet, representing his poverty. Although he was not wealthy, Joseph is a model for workers since he worked to provide in the very best way for Mary and for Jesus. How can his example inspire us in our work?
- Notice the angels in the painting. One angel seems to resemble Mary and the other resembles Joseph. Even the colors they are wearing are similar. Do you think these angels could be the guardian angels of Mary and Joseph?
- Behind and above Jesus are clouds that look like an entrance to heaven above. How is this scene heaven on earth?
- Notice how Mary and Jesus both have their hands on their hearts. How will these hearts suffer greatly but also change the world through their suffering?
- Mary has three fingers on her heart. What do you think these three fingers represent?
- Mary is not holding Jesus. Rather, she places him in a manger, which Caryll Houselander in her book *The Reed of God* calls "the first Calvary" (see pages 59-60). How does Mary not keep Jesus for herself, but gives Him to all of us, even if this involves great suffering?

DAY 132

Today's Mystery: The Presentation of Jesus in the Temple

Today's Prayer:
- Pray with today's sacred art in "*visio divina*," using as many or as few of the reflection questions as you find fruitful.
- Pray 1 decade of the Rosary (1 Our Father, 10 Hail Marys, and 1 Glory Be).
-

View Sacred Art: The Presentation

Reflect:
- Notice the two doves in the center of the painting. The Holy Family sacrificed two turtledoves because Mary and Joseph were poor. How can our small sacrifices out of our poverty be most pleasing to God?
- The old man in the center of the painting is most likely Simeon. He has been waiting for this moment for years, knowing that he would see the Messiah before his death (see Luke 2:25–26). What is important for those who are about to die? How can Simeon's example help us set priorities in our own lives now so that we are prepared for the hour of our death?
- While there are several people around her, Mary just looks at Jesus and seems to be consumed with him. How can we be better at just looking to Jesus, not being distracted with other things or people?
- Notice the elderly woman on the right pointing to the child. This woman is most likely the prophetess Anna. Anna had been praying and fasting in the Temple for years (see Luke 2:37). Upon seeing Jesus, Anna "spoke of him to all who were looking for the redemption of Jerusalem" (Luke 2:38). How can we be better at speaking of Jesus to all those looking for redemption?
- St. Joseph stands to the left in the painting. What do you think he might have felt upon hearing Simeon tell Mary that Jesus would be "a sign that is spoken against" and that "a sword will pierce" her heart? (Luk 2:34–35). How do you feel upon hearing that those you love most are in pain or will experience great pain? How can meditating on the Presentation help us in these moments?
- Notice how beautiful and grand the Temple in the background of this scene is. And yet the Temple is simply a "type" or a foreshadowing of Christ's body. How is this little baby so much grander than the Temple?

DAY 133

Today's Mystery: The Finding of Jesus in the Temple

Today's Prayer:
- Pray with today's sacred art in "*visio divina*," using as many or as few of the reflection questions as you find fruitful.
- Pray 1 decade of the Rosary (1 Our Father, 10 Hail Marys, and 1 Glory Be).

View Sacred Art: The Finding in the Temple

Reflect:
- The words on the sheet that Jesus is pointing to are from Luke 4:18: "The Spirit of the Lord is upon me." This is taken from Isaiah 61:1. Jesus reads this verse at the synagogue in Nazareth in the beginning of his public ministry. How is this joyful mystery of the Finding of Jesus in the Temple a foretaste of Jesus' public ministry and his teaching? How is Jesus fulfilling this mission by first teaching the teachers in the Temple?
- Notice how Jesus has his foot on the stool. This seems to represent how he is teaching and preaching with authority. How is his authority different from the authority of the teachers in the Temple?
- Luke writes in his Gospel that Jesus was also "listening to" the teachers "and asking them questions" (Luke 2:46). Why was Jesus asking the teachers questions? What do you think he was asking them?
- Luke writes in his Gospel that the teachers are "amazed" by Jesus' words (Luke 2:47). Notice the faces of the elders in this mosaic. Some seem receptive; others seem annoyed or perplexed. Does Jesus' teaching have the same effect today?
- The city of Jerusalem is visible in the background. During Jesus' public ministry, he will often be at odds with the teachers in Jerusalem. Why do you think there is such a difference between the way the teachers react to him when he is twelve years old and the way they will react to him later?
- Jesus was missing for three days after his family had been in Jerusalem for the Passover. How does this mystery foreshadow his Passion?

DAY 134

Today's Mystery: The Baptism of Jesus

Today's Prayer:
- Pray with today's sacred art in "*visio divina,*" using as many or as few of the reflection questions as you find fruitful.
- Pray 1 decade of the Rosary (1 Our Father, 10 Hail Marys, and 1 Glory Be).

View Sacred Art: The Baptism of Our Lord

Reflect:
- A dove, representing the Holy Spirit, hovers over Christ in a glow of light while angels surround him. The artist seems to be emphasizing the words of the Gospel: "the heavens were opened" (Matthew 4:16). How does Christ open heaven for us?
- John the Baptist is depicted carrying a staff that looks like a cross, even though Jesus at this point has yet not died on the Cross. St. Paul says in Romans 6:3, "Do you not know that all of us who have been baptized in Christ Jesus were baptized into his death?" How do we, too, take on Jesus' death in our Baptism, in order to rise with him again into new life?
- There are several items in this painting that will appear in the Passion. Angels are holding the Cross, the hammer and nails, the crown of thorns, and the chalice from the Agony in the Garden. They seem to hold these items triumphantly. How does the Passion and death of Jesus lead to his glory and the promise of life for us?
- After Jesus was baptized, there was "a voice from heaven, saying, 'This is my beloved Son, with whom I am well pleased'" (Matthew 3:17). Why did the Father allow his beloved Son to experience the tremendous suffering and gruesome death of the Cross? How can meditating on this mystery help us to reconcile our own suffering and the Father's love for us?
- Jesus is stepping into the same river where many people have been baptized by John. St. Paul says in Scripture, "For our sake he made him to be sin who knew no sin, so that in him we might become the righteousness of God" (2 Corinthians 5:21). What is Jesus taking on by going into the water?
- Notice John's face. He looks concerned or even in pain. The Gospel of Matthew tells us that John was aware of his own unworthiness but was still obedient to Jesus' request for his baptism. In what ways can we be obedient to Jesus even though we are unworthy?

DAY 135

Today's Mystery: The Wedding at Cana

Today's Prayer:
- Pray with today's sacred art in "*visio divina*," using as many or as few of the reflection questions as you find fruitful.
- Pray 1 decade of the Rosary (1 Our Father, 10 Hail Marys, and 1 Glory Be).

View Sacred Art: Wedding at Cana, Carl Bloch

Reflect:
- This depiction of the Wedding at Cana focuses on the moment the steward tries the water that has been turned into wine by Jesus. Why do you think the artist focused on this moment?
- John 2:9 says that before drinking the wine, the steward was unaware of its source. The servants who obeyed Our Lord and Our Lady's directions, however, saw the miracle take place. How can obedience to Our Lord, as Our Lady urges us, lead to blessings within our lives?
- One servant is shown pointing toward Jesus, indicating where he got the wine. Notice another servant, dressed in blue, staring in awe at the wine the steward has in his hand. He is amazed by the miracle that Jesus just did. How would you react if you were one of the servants?
- Look at the steward. His body and his face seem to express how good the wine is. How is this wine a sign of the goodness of the New Covenant?
- After the Holy Spirit fell upon the disciples at Pentecost, some people ridiculed them by saying, "They are filled with new wine" (Acts 2:13). While this comment was meant to be derisive, there is a deeper sense in which it is true. Why is being filled with the Holy Spirit sometimes compared to being filled with wine?
- The Gospel of John tells us that the changing of water to wine at this wedding feast was the first miracle of Jesus, leading his followers to have faith in him. How can the miracles of Christ strengthen our faith?

DAY 136

Today's Mystery: The Proclamation of the Kingdom and the Call to Conversion

Today's Prayer:
- Pray with today's sacred art in "*visio divina,*" using as many or as few of the reflection questions as you find fruitful.
- Pray 1 decade of the Rosary (1 Our Father, 10 Hail Marys, and 1 Glory Be).

View Sacred Art: *Healing of the Lepers at Capernaum*, James Tissot

Reflect:
- This painting depicts the leper who came to thank Jesus after being healed of his disease. Notice how the leper's hands are outstretched and how grateful he seems to be free of his leprosy. Have you experienced being set free from sin?
- This is the only leper to come back to thank Jesus, but ten lepers were healed. What do you think the other nine who were healed are doing at this moment instead of thanking Jesus? This leper still has his bandages on. He does not even take time to remove them before going to thank Jesus. How can we be like this man, who makes it his first priority to thank Jesus?
- The man in yellow is looking at the leper who is praising and thanking God. The leper is now healed but the man in yellow might not yet know that. Do we sometimes criticize others, not being fully aware of how Jesus is working in their lives?
- The leper does not seem to notice or care that other people are looking at him. How can we be less concerned with people's opinions and be more concerned with our relationship with the Lord?
- Because leprosy was contagious, the leper had been banished from his home and forced to live in a leper colony. Have you ever felt left out or unwanted? How can you invite Jesus into these places within your heart?
- We can think about this miracle when we meditate on the proclamation of the Kingdom. How does this miracle proclaim that "the kingdom of heaven is at hand" (Matthew 4:17)?

DAY 137

Today's Mystery: The Transfiguration

Today's Prayer:
- Pray with today's sacred art in "*visio divina*," using as many or as few of the reflection questions as you find fruitful.
- Pray 1 decade of the Rosary (1 Our Father, 10 Hail Marys, and 1 Glory Be).

View Sacred Art: The Transfiguration

Reflect:
- Notice Moses on the left, holding the tablets of the Ten Commandments, with light coming from his face. Exodus 34:29–30 tells us that Moses' face shone after he came down from Mount Sinai. How is Moses a foreshadowing of Jesus?
- Jesus is holding a scroll, although Scripture does not say that he held a scroll at the Transfiguration. Why do you think the artist included a scroll here? Do you think the scroll could be related to the tablets in Moses' hands?
- Angels are shown in the top corners of the image. As the *Catechism of the Catholic Church* says, "Angels have been present since creation and throughout the history of salvation, announcing this salvation from afar or near and serving the accomplishment of the divine plan: they ... announced births and callings; and assisted the prophets, just to cite a few examples" (CCC 332). Why do you think the artist included angels in this image of the Transfiguration?
- Notice Jesus' garments are white. This is a stained-glass window, so the image must be dazzling when the sun shines through it. What do these white garments represent?
- See the rainbow around Jesus. After the Flood, God sent a rainbow to represent the covenant he made (see Genesis 9:8–17). Why do you think the artist included a rainbow in this depiction of the Transfiguration?
- Notice the greenery and flowers on the mountain. Why do you think the artist used garden imagery for this mystery?

DAY 138

Today's Mystery: The Institution of the Eucharist

Today's Prayer:
- Pray with today's sacred art in "*visio divina*," using as many or as few of the reflection questions as you find fruitful.
- Pray 1 decade of the Rosary (1 Our Father, 10 Hail Marys, and 1 Glory Be).

View Sacred Art: The Last Supper

Reflect:
- This image, based on Leonardo da Vinci's painting of the Last Supper, is depicting the moment when Jesus says to his Apostles at the Last Supper, "Truly, truly, I say to you, one of you will betray me" (John 13:21). Why do you think the artist chose to depict this scene?
- Notice the different reactions of the Apostles to these words of Jesus. How would you react if you were one of the Apostles?
- Look at Jesus' face. John's Gospel says Jesus "was troubled in spirit" (John 13:21). What does Jesus' face say? Is he accusatory?
- St. John the Apostle is shown sitting at Jesus' right hand. John is referred to in the Gospel as the one "whom Jesus loved" (John 13:23). How can we be more like John, fully embracing Jesus' love for us in the Eucharist?
- St. Peter is shown talking to St. John. The Gospel tells us that he asked him, "Tell us who it is of whom he speaks" (John 13:24). Why do you think Peter asked John this question? Why did Peter not ask Jesus himself?
- Notice that Jesus is reaching for a dish with his right hand. Judas is also reaching for the dish. Sometimes the ones closest to Jesus can betray him and cause him great sorrow. How should we respond when we hear of scandals in the Church? How can we be quick to turn to Jesus, knowing he is ultimately in control?

DAY 139

Today's Mystery: The Agony in the Garden

Today's Prayer:
- Pray with today's sacred art in "*visio divina*," using as many or as few of the reflection questions as you find fruitful.
- Pray 1 decade of the Rosary (1 Our Father, 10 Hail Marys, and 1 Glory Be).

View Sacred Art: The Agony in the Garden

Reflect:
- In the center of the painting, Jesus is kneeling in prayer. He seems upright and strong. How does Jesus show his strength in these sorrowful mysteries?
- Notice the angel bringing the Cross to Jesus, almost as if it is a gift. How are our crosses gifts?
- This painting actually depicts two events. The foreground shows the Agony in the Garden, and the background shows soldiers dressed in Medieval clothing, who may be fighting in the Spanish effort to reunite under Catholic rule in the Reconquista. What do you think the artist is saying by showing a more contemporary event within a painting that depicts the Agony in the Garden?
- If you look closely, it seems that Jesus is shown leading the soldiers on the left side of the background image. Where is Jesus leading them? How does God intervene in battles, in history or in our personal lives?
- On the left, Peter is sleeping while holding a book. Why do you think the artist depicted him with a book?
- One can see a lot of gold in this painting. Notice the frame around the painting, which gives it a majestic appearance. How does God conquer through the Cross? How does he show himself as King in his Passion, death, and Resurrection? How can we give appropriate honor to Jesus Christ, as King of the Universe?

DAY 140

Today's Mystery: The Scourging at the Pillar

Today's Prayer:
- Pray with today's sacred art in "*visio divina*" using as many or as few of the reflection questions as you find fruitful.
- Pray 1 decade of the Rosary (1 Our Father, 10 Hail Marys, and 1 Glory Be).

View Sacred Art: The Scourging

Reflect:
- Jesus' face is sorrowful yet at peace. He does not shrink from the blows that are about to fall on him. How is he "like a lamb that is led to the slaughter" (Isaiah 53:7), as Isaiah the prophet foretold?
- Notice the face of the man behind Jesus dressed in blue. He seems to have satisfaction while whipping Jesus. Why do you think he has this satisfied look about him? Has the suffering of others ever satisfied us?
- See the man standing in front of Jesus about to whip him. He is looking in Jesus' eyes. When have we perhaps willingly caused Jesus to suffer by committing sin, knowing that this sin will grieve him?
- There are two men speaking to each other in the background. They do not seem to be watching what is taking place and perhaps they do not care. Have we ever reacted this way to those suffering around us?
- Notice the guard on the left of the painting. He is sitting in a nonchalant way and looking away from Jesus. When have we been indifferent in the sins we have committed against God?
- The church of Santa Prassede, or St. Praxedes, in Rome, holds a pillar that has been venerated for hundreds of years as a relic of the pillar where Jesus was flogged (although this relic may not be the actual historical pillar). The pillar depicted in this image looks like the relic in the church of Santa Prassede. How can this resemblance to the relic be a reminder of the reality of Christ's Passion?

DAY 141

Today's Mystery: The Crowning with Thorns

Today's Prayer:
- Pray with today's sacred art in "*visio divina*," using as many or as few of the reflection questions as you find fruitful.
- Pray 1 decade of the Rosary (1 Our Father, 10 Hail Marys, and 1 Glory Be).

View Sacred Art: *Christ Crowned with Thorns*, Titian

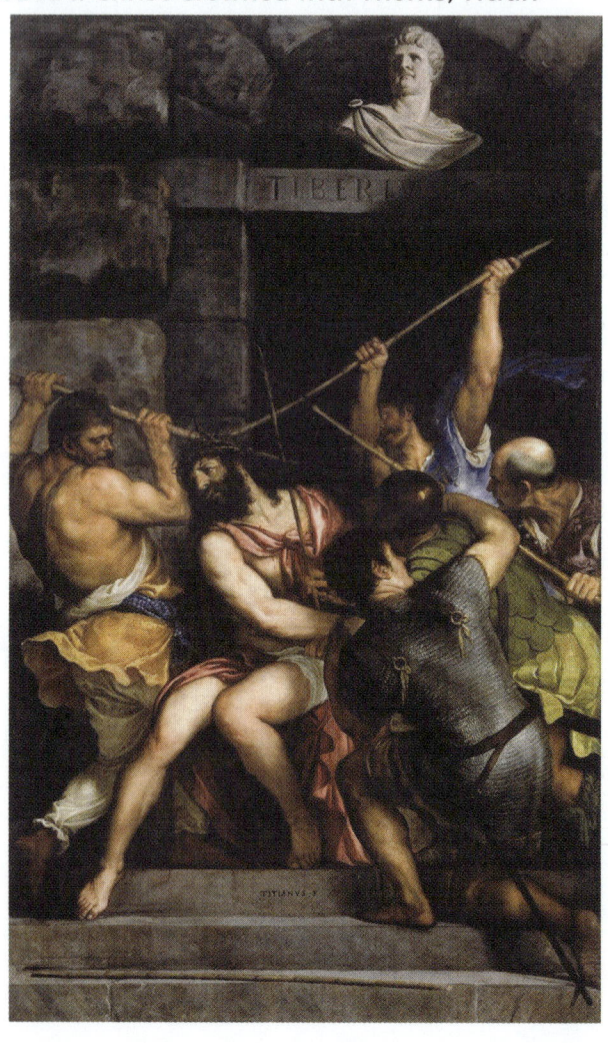

Reflect:
- The brilliant colors in the painting—blue, red, green, gold, and silver—add beauty to this painful scene. How can our suffering, when united to Christ, actually be beautiful? How can it add beauty to the world?
- The bust at the top of the painting is an image of Tiberius Cesar, the emperor of Rome at the time of Christ. Below, Jesus is being tortured. Yet, who is the real king in the painting? The image of Tiberius Cesar also might remind us of the moment in the Passion when the chief priests rejected Jesus with the words, "We have no king but Caesar" (John 19:15). Have there been times in our lives when we chose another king in our lives over Christ the King?
- Look at Jesus' face, especially his eyes. He is in utter anguish. What do you think he is thinking about?
- Notice how the men are violently putting the crown on Jesus' head. By doing this, they would have embedded the thorns in his head. He would have felt this pain all the way to his death. What wounds do you have that you might carry your whole life? How can you also bring these to the foot of the Cross?
- Notice the man in the chain mail placing his arm around the man beside him and whispering to him. What do you think he is saying to this man?
- How is Jesus, even though he is suffering at the hands of these men, in full control of the situation? Does it give you comfort and consolation knowing that Jesus is King and has full control over governments and his Church?

DAY 142

Today's Mystery: The Carrying of the Cross

Today's Prayer:
- Pray with today's sacred art in "*visio divina*," using as many or as few of the reflection questions as you find fruitful.
- Pray 1 decade of the Rosary (1 Our Father, 10 Hail Marys, and 1 Glory Be).

View Sacred Art: *The Procession to Calvary*, Pieter Bruegel

Reflect:
- There is so much happening in this painting that it is difficult to see where Jesus is, but he is right in the middle of the painting. Can the events of life sometimes feel overwhelming so that we have a hard time focusing on Jesus? What is happening to Jesus in the painting?
- The largest figures in the painting are the characters in the foreground on the right. They are Mary along with John and Mary Magdalene. Mary looks so pale and so sorrowful. Simeon said to her at the Presentation that a sword would pierce her heart. How would this event have pierced her heart?
- In the middle of the painting on the left, there is a character who is being pulled forward by soldiers while he leans backward and is pulled away from the soldiers by a woman, perhaps his wife. This could be Simon of Cyrene. He seems reluctant to help carry the Cross. When have we been reluctant to carry our crosses?
- Many people within the painting appear to be of the time and place when the artist painted this scene. Notice the windmill in the background! Why do you think the artist depicted this scene happening in his own time? In what way can we imagine this scene taking place in our own time?
- Notice the storm brewing in the distance, the ravens in the sky, and the animal bones in the lower right of the painting. What feelings do these images convey?
- Some characters within the painting do not seem to be aware or perhaps do not care about what is taking place. How are we sometimes unaware of the sacred around us? Have we ever been distracted with trivial things, missing out on pivotal moments where we could comfort or meet Jesus?

DAY 143

Today's Mystery: The Crucifixion

Today's Prayer:
- Pray with today's sacred art in "*visio divina,*" using as many or as few of the reflection questions as you find fruitful.
- Pray 1 decade of the Rosary (1 Our Father, 10 Hail Marys, and 1 Glory Be).

View Sacred Art: The Crucifixion

Reflect:

- Notice the rainbow and the sky opening as if to welcome Jesus. After the Flood, God sent a rainbow to represent the covenant he made (see Genesis 9:8–17). Why do you think the artist included a rainbow here?
- See Our Lady standing at the foot of the Cross on Jesus' right. Her garment matches the colors of the sky and the rainbow above. One of her titles is "Gate of heaven." How does she lead us to heaven?
- At the bottom of the painting, a man and a woman are depicted coming up from under the earth. Golgotha was called the "place of the skull" because it was believed that Adam's bones were buried there. These two figures are likely Adam and Eve. Jesus is the New Adam, and Mary is the New Eve. Does seeing Adam and Eve in this image help you to meditate on what Jesus has done for us?
- Notice that it looks like there is an earthquake happening. In the background, we also see people coming out of a tomb behind Jesus. Matthew's Gospel mysteriously writes that "the tombs also were opened, and many bodies of the saints who had fallen asleep were raised, and coming out of the tombs after his resurrection they went into the holy city and appeared to many" (Matthew 27:52–53). The bystanders in this painting look startled and frightened by the events taking place. How can we turn to Jesus and cling to his Cross when the events of life frighten us?
- See the bad thief on the right; a demon is taking his soul down to hell. Why is his soul taken to hell, but the other thief is saved?
- Notice the men casting lots for the tunic of Jesus. How was even this a fulfillment of what was prophesied regarding Jesus' death? (See Psalm 22.)

DAY 144

Today's Mystery: The Resurrection

Today's Prayer:
- Pray with today's sacred art in "*visio divina*," using as many or as few of the reflection questions as you find fruitful.
- Pray 1 decade of the Rosary (1 Our Father, 10 Hail Marys, and 1 Glory Be).

View Sacred Art: The Resurrection of Christ, Annibale Carracci

Reflect:
- Notice how Jesus looks victorious in this painting. How is death "swallowed up in victory" (1 Corinthians 15:54)?
- Notice in this painting how the tomb is sealed shut. The Gospel of Matthew recounts that the Pharisees asked for guards to be placed at the tomb to keep Jesus' body from being stolen by the Apostles and "made the tomb secure by sealing the stone" (see Matthew 27:62–66). Why does Matthew include these details in his Gospel? What does this depiction emphasize about Jesus' Resurrection?
- Notice the cross that Jesus is carrying, along with the white banner. This looks similar to the staff that John the Baptist is shown carrying in some paintings of the baptism of the Lord. How are these two mysteries connected?
- See how the angels are pushing the clouds aside. They are "parting the clouds" for Jesus. It might remind us of how God parted the waters of the Red Sea for the Israelites to walk through in the Exodus. How is the Resurrection a New Exodus?
- Several of the guards seem to be asleep. This depiction can remind us of how Jesus urged us to stay awake and be ready for his coming (see Mark 13:35–36). How are we to remain awake?
- One of the guards seems to be telling one of the chief priests what took place. Instead of believing that Jesus rose from the dead, the chief priests bribed the soldiers to lie and say, "His disciple came by night and stole him away while we were asleep" (Matthew 28:13). Why do you think they refused to believe? How can we guard ourselves from becoming hardhearted and refusing to believe what Christ has done for us?

DAY 145

Today's Mystery: The Ascension

Today's Prayer:
- Pray with today's sacred art in "*visio divina*," using as many or as few of the reflection questions as you find fruitful.
- Pray 1 decade of the Rosary (1 Our Father, 10 Hail Marys, and 1 Glory Be).

View Sacred Art: The Ascension, St. Mark's Basilica in Venice

Reflect:
- Notice how Jesus is holding the Cross. How has the Cross been glorified with Jesus? How is this a sign of his authority and his power?
- On the right is John the Baptist. Notice his red robe. It looks like a robe worn by a king. Why do you think he is dressed in this way instead of in the rough garments Scripture describes him as wearing during his ministry (see Matthew 3:4)?
- This mosaic is located above the main doors of St. Mark's Basilica in Venice, Italy, on the outside wall of the church. Pilgrims visiting the church see this mosaic as they enter the basilica's doors. Why do you think this is the scene that welcomes pilgrims into the basilica?
- Notice all the gold within the artwork. How does this represent heaven? What does it tell us about heaven?
- Notice how Mary and John the Baptist are adoring Jesus' face with looks of love. How can we adore Jesus and look at him with love today?
- Notice Jesus' side. It seems like it is dripping with blood. Why does Jesus still have his wounds in his glorified body in heaven?

DAY 146

Today's Mystery: The Descent of the Holy Spirit on Pentecost

Today's Prayer:
- Pray with today's sacred art in "*visio divina*," using as many or as few of the reflection questions as you find fruitful.
- Pray 1 decade of the Rosary (1 Our Father, 10 Hail Marys, and 1 Glory Be).

View Sacred Art: *Pentecost*, Jean Restout

Reflect:
- Who is at the center of the painting as the most prominent person? Why is this appropriate? What is Our Lady's relationship with the Holy Spirit? Has Mary already experienced an outpouring or overshadowing of the Holy Spirit?
- Mary is looking up into heaven, and she does not look at all surprised at what is happening. She almost looks as if she is in dialogue with someone above. Do you think she is interceding with her spouse, the Holy Spirit?
- The descent of the Holy Spirit is shown occurring in a very large room. Some scholars argue that this occurred at the Temple. Why might it be fitting for it to occur at the Temple?
- Notice how clouds completely cover the ceiling; it is as if heaven is coming to earth. How does heaven come to earth with the coming of the Holy Spirit? The clouds might remind one of the cloud in the Exodus, which rested on the Tabernacle, and the cloud which filled the Temple during Solomon's dedication. How are each of these people who have received the Holy Spirit now "temples"?
- Notice how the color red stands out in this painting. When does the priest wear red in the liturgy?
- Notice the faces of the disciples who are receiving the Holy Spirit. How would you describe their faces? What would you have felt if you were present there?

DAY 147

Today's Mystery: The Assumption of Mary

Today's Prayer:
- Pray with today's sacred art in "*visio divina*," using as many or as few of the reflection questions as you find fruitful.
- Pray 1 decade of the Rosary (1 Our Father, 10 Hail Marys, and 1 Glory Be).

View Sacred Art: The Assumption

Reflect:
- Mary has a crown of twelve stars around her head and the moon under her feet, referring to St. John's vision in Revelation 12:1. What might the twelve stars represent?
- See the serpent or dragon below Our Lady. How is Our Lady part of God's plan to defeat Satan (see Genesis 3:15 and Revelation 12)?
- Notice the little cherub thrusting a spear at the dragon with a smile on his face. This cherub looks more like a baby than a warrior, yet he is shown vanquishing the Enemy. How does God often use the lowly to overthrow Satan?
- Notice how some of the angels have musical instruments, as if there is music being played as Our Lady enters heaven, body and soul. Though we may not play instruments, how can we praise God more in our lives?
- We can see God the Father and the Holy Spirit as a dove. Why do you think Jesus is not pictured?
- Notice the different kinds of fruit in the gold framing the painting. What do you think these fruits represent? How was Our Lady's life fruitful? How can our lives bear more fruit when we imitate her?

DAY 148

Today's Mystery: The Coronation of Mary as Queen of Heaven and Earth

Today's Prayer:
- Pray with today's sacred art in "*visio divina*," using as many or as few of the reflection questions as you find fruitful.
- Pray 1 decade of the Rosary (1 Our Father, 10 Hail Marys, and 1 Glory Be).

View Sacred Art: *The Coronation of the Virgin*, Diego Velázquez

Reflect:

- Our Lady is being crowned by both God the Father and God the Son. The Holy Spirit is also shown above her head. What is Our Lady's relationship with each person of the Trinity? How can she guide us closer to the Holy Trinity?
- Notice the ray of light coming down from the Holy Spirit onto Our Lady through her crown. What other mysteries does this make you think of? When did the Holy Spirit come down on her?
- Jesus and God the Father are wearing purple robes, representing royalty. Also, God the Father holds an orb, and the Son holds a scepter. These are symbols of kingship. What details of the painting show that Our Lady has been given a share in this majesty? How does she reign with God in heaven?
- Notice how the figures of Jesus, Our Lady, and God the Father form a heart shape. Mary is pointing to her heart, as well. We have a well-known devotion and a feast day to honor Our Lady's heart. Why is her heart worthy of honor? What can we learn from her heart?
- Notice Our Lady's face. She is looking down in humility even though she is being crowned Queen of the Universe. How does she possess so much humility? What does this teach us?
- Perhaps Our Lady is looking down towards earth. What is she concerned about on earth? How is she the Queen of both heaven and earth?

DAY 149

Today's Mystery: The Annunciation

Today's Prayer:
- Pray with today's sacred art in "*visio divina*," using as many or as few of the reflection questions as you find fruitful.
- Pray 1 decade of the Rosary (1 Our Father, 10 Hail Marys, and 1 Glory Be).

View Sacred Art: *The Annunciation*, Henry Ossawa Tanner

Reflect:

- This painting is very different from Fra Angelico's. Our Lady looked like a queen in Fra Angelico's painting. Here she looks very ordinary. Why do you think the artist depicted her this way?
- Gabriel is shown simply as a ray of light, and the artist seems to emphasize the fact that angels are pure spirits. How do you think you would react when seeing an angel?
- Some have pointed out that the ray of light and the shelf behind it intersect to form the shape of a cross. The red tapestry in Mary's room might make one think of Christ's Passion also, since red is used in the liturgy on Good Friday. How is the Cross present in the Incarnation?
- Notice that the linens are not neat and tidy, nor is the rug. As we know from the Scriptures, the Holy Family's life was not without difficulty. Is God's will for our lives always neat and tidy?
- Look at Mary's face. What is her face saying? How does she conduct herself?
- If we look at the painting again as a whole, it is quite amazing to think the Incarnation happened at this poor, simple home. But is this often how God works?

DAY 150

Today's Mystery: The Visitation

Today's Prayer:
- Pray with today's sacred art in "*visio divina*," using as many or as few of the reflection questions as you find fruitful.
- Pray 1 decade of the Rosary (1 Our Father, 10 Hail Marys, and 1 Glory Be).

View Sacred Art: The Visitation

Reflect:
- Not all paintings of the Visitation show St. Joseph, but this painting shows that he accompanied Mary on her trip to see Elizabeth and Zechariah. It seems likely that St. Joseph would have accompanied Mary. Why would he have done this? He is shown bowing in reverence. Whom is he reverencing?
- Notice the two servants to the left of the painting. They do not seem particularly aware of what is happening before them but are busy doing other things. What are they doing instead? How can we prepare to welcome the Holy Family within our homes or show hospitality to those visiting us?
- See how Elizabeth is feeling for her unborn son; this would have been an automatic response when she felt the baby leap within her womb. Why did John the Baptist leap for joy when Mary spoke to Elizabeth? Notice how Elizabeth is pointing to Mary's womb. How is this a preview of the mission of John the Baptist?
- Mary has a sort of "glow" about her, and she is looking up to heaven as if to acknowledge that God is the one who has "done great things for her." Notice what her hands are doing. How do her hands express her Magnificat (see Luke 1:46–55)?
- Zechariah at this point cannot speak, because he did not believe the words of the angel who announced the coming of John the Baptist (see Luke 1:20). Do you think he believes now? Though he is silent, he can listen and ponder. What do you think he might be pondering in this painting?
- John the Baptist and Jesus are still in the womb—they are so little. However, how have their lives already impacted the people shown within the painting and all the people of the world?

DAY 151

Today's Mystery: The Nativity

Today's Prayer:
- Pray with today's sacred art in "*visio divina,*" using as many or as few of the reflection questions as you find fruitful.
- Pray 1 decade of the Rosary (1 Our Father, 10 Hail Marys, and 1 Glory Be).

View Sacred Art: *Adoration of the Shepherds*, Gerard van Honthorst

Reflect:

- See how the light in the scene is radiating from Jesus, lighting up the faces of those who are looking at him. How is this little baby the light of the world?
- Notice how Mary is presenting Jesus to the shepherds. How does Mary always present her son to us? How has she done this for you in your own life?
- Notice Jesus' arms and hands. What do they convey to the shepherds?
- See the joy on the shepherd's faces in seeing Jesus. How would you have felt if you were one of those shepherds who came to adore Jesus? See how Mary and Joseph look at Jesus. What do you think they were thinking? How do you think they would have felt upon seeing Jesus for the first time?
- The manger, in which Mary laid Jesus, was a feeding trough for animals. If we look closely at the bottom of the painting, on the left, we can see a ram eating the hay. What is the symbolism of Jesus' being placed in a manger?
- The shepherds look like they are dressed in more modern clothing that they would have worn in the first century. Why do you think the artist portrayed the shepherds in this way? Who would be the "shepherds" in our own day and age? Jesus is so humble; lowly surroundings and people do not seem to bother him. How is meditating on this image comforting?

DAY 152

Today's Mystery: The Presentation of Jesus in the Temple

Today's Prayer:
- Pray with today's sacred art in "*visio divina*," using as many or as few of the reflection questions as you find fruitful.
- Pray 1 decade of the Rosary (1 Our Father, 10 Hail Marys, and 1 Glory Be).

View Sacred Art: The Presentation

Reflect:
- At the top of the painting are two doves, held by a man whose cloak is blown by a gust of wind. The dove represents the Holy Spirit, and the huge gust of wind might make one think of Pentecost. How do you see the Holy Spirit present in this mystery of the Presentation?
- Jesus, shown in the center of the painting, does not look like a newborn baby; he looks older. He also looks like he is presenting himself. How does Jesus present himself, even though he is just a baby? What is his mission in coming as man?
- Mary is presenting her child to the high priest. Thirty-three years later, Jesus will be taken to Caiaphas, the high priest, the night before his death. Do you think the Presentation in the Temple could be a foreshadowing of what is to come?
- There are many people in this painting. Each of these people could have something that they are presenting along with Mary. Do you present your actions and sufferings to God and give them over to him with a daily morning offering?
- Notice the altar boys on the right. Why do you think the artist included them within the painting? How does the liturgy of the Church bring the mysteries of God to the present for us? How can we be present more fully to the mysteries within the liturgy?
- See the little girl looking at you on the left of the painting. The look she is giving is like an invitation to come into the painting and experience this mystery for yourself. How are we to approach these mysteries as little children? How can we be more childlike when praying the Rosary and meditating on these mysteries?

DAY 153

Today's Mystery: The Finding of Jesus in the Temple

Today's Prayer:
- Pray with today's sacred art in "*visio divina*," using as many or as few of the reflection questions as you find fruitful.
- Pray 1 decade of the Rosary (1 Our Father, 10 Hail Marys, and 1 Glory Be).

View Sacred Art: The Finding in the Temple

Reflect:
- Look at Mary in the painting and imagine losing your son or another loved one for three days. What do Mary's body language and her face convey? What do you think she is feeling right now as she sees Jesus?
- This event is told only in the Gospel of Luke. Most likely, Our Lady told Luke about this event and other events from Jesus' childhood. Why do you think this event was so special to Our Lady?
- Many of the figures in this painting seem to be dressed in the clothing of the artist's time and are holding books, not scrolls. Why do you think the artist depicted the teachers in the Temple in a contemporary way? How can we still ask questions of Jesus today in our studies and prayer, even though he has ascended into heaven?
- Notice the man on the right pointing to the Scriptures. His vestments look like a Catholic priest's vestments, not those of a first-century rabbi. Why do you think the artist depicted one of the teachers as a Catholic priest?
- Some of the teachers in the painting are not even looking at Jesus while he is teaching but just seem to be consumed with examining the texts. Are there ways we perhaps get overly consumed with questions or with texts and ignore Jesus' presence?
- Contrast Jesus' face with the faces of the teachers. Jesus looks serene, while the teachers have looks of consternation or perhaps a little confusion. Why do you think the teachers' faces look this way? Do you think they are aware that God incarnate is teaching them?

DAY 154

Today's Mystery: The Baptism of Jesus

Today's Prayer:
- Pray with today's sacred art in "*visio divina*," using as many or as few of the reflection questions as you find fruitful.
- Pray 1 decade of the Rosary (1 Our Father, 10 Hail Marys, and 1 Glory Be).

View Sacred Art: *The Baptism of Christ*, Andrea del Verrocchio and Leonardo da Vinci

Reflect:
- The Holy Trinity is depicted in this painting. At the very top of the painting, one can see the hands of the Father sending the dove, an image of the Holy Spirit, down upon the Son. How is the Holy Spirit active in Christ's ministry? How is he active in the ministry of the Church?
- Most likely, John immersed those being baptized in the Jordan River, but here he is depicted using a gold plate to pour water on Jesus' head to baptize him. Christ's baptism is often referred to as the "anointing" of Jesus and the beginning of his public ministry. How is it an anointing? How is our baptism a sort of "anointing" for us?
- As the dove descends, a voice is heard declaring the divine sonship of Jesus. For those of us who have also been baptized, do we remember that we are also beloved sons and daughters of God and that the Father is pleased with us?
- Notice the terrain around Jesus and John. It is very rocky and seems desert-like. After Jesus is baptized, he will first go into the desert. Why is this fitting?
- The Jordan River looks shallow and small here, and it really was not very big or impressive. Why does God use places or even people who are not grand or impressive to bring about his glory?
- Notice the angels ministering to Jesus and John by holding Jesus' clothes. We often forget how angels work with us closely to accomplish God's mission in our lives. How can we be more aware of their presence?

DAY 155

Today's Mystery: The Wedding at Cana

Today's Prayer:
- Pray with today's sacred art in "*visio divina,*" using as many or as few of the reflection questions as you find fruitful.
- Pray 1 decade of the Rosary (1 Our Father, 10 Hail Marys, and 1 Glory Be).

View Sacred Art: *The Wedding at Cana*, Gérard David

Reflect:
- Notice that it is not clear who the bridegroom is in the painting, but it is clear who Our Lord is. The bride's and bridegroom's names are not mentioned in the Gospel of John, either. Why do you think John omitted their names? Why did the artist depict the scene in this way?
- In Jewish tradition, the bridegroom was supposed to ensure there was wine for the celebration, yet it is Jesus who does this when the wine runs out. How does this show Jesus to be the Bridegroom?
- Our Lady looks at Jesus beseechingly to tell him, "They have no wine" (John 2:3). How does Mary intercede for all our needs and care for each of her children even in small matters?
- See Jesus' hand raised in a blessing. It looks like he is blessing the wine vessels. Where else do we see someone blessing wine in this way?
- See the large vessels. Each held twenty to thirty gallons (see John 2:6). Jesus turns water into an abundance of wine for the marriage feast. How has Jesus provided for your needs abundantly?
- Notice the people kneeling in prayer who do not seem to be part of the painting. Rather, they are meditating on this mystery. Notice that the figures in the painting are shown wearing medieval clothing that would have been worn at the time of the artist. Perhaps the artist depicted the painting this way to show us we should invite Christ into our marriages, in all times and all places. How can we invite Christ to be present in our marriages? How can Our Lady intercede for our marriages?

DAY 156

Today's Mystery: The Proclamation of the Kingdom and the Call to Conversion

Today's Prayer:
- Pray with today's sacred art in "*visio divina*," using as many or as few of the reflection questions as you find fruitful.
- Pray 1 decade of the Rosary (1 Our Father, 10 Hail Marys, and 1 Glory Be).

View Sacred Art: *The Adulterous Woman*, Lorenzo Lotto

Reflect:
- As you look at the painting, you might first notice how Jesus is putting his hand up to silence the men who are accusing the woman. "Satan" in Hebrew means "accuser." How has Jesus silenced the accuser in our lives?
- Contrast Jesus' face with those of the other men. What does Jesus' face express?
- Notice the different ways the men are accusing the woman. One man is pointing his finger in judgment. One is smiling. One is yelling. One is scowling. Have there been times when we, too, accused others or took pleasure in their wrongdoing?
- Notice the woman trying to cover herself; she feels ashamed. See the remorse and sorrow in her face. When have we also felt this shame and remorse and wanted to cover up what we have done? How can we give this sorrow for our sins to Jesus?
- In the Gospel account, Jesus reminds the men that they are sinners. How does remembering our own failings and our own sin help us to forgive others who have sinned, even those who have hurt us?
- Jesus says to the woman once all the men have left: "Neither do I condemn you; go, and do not sin again" (John 8:11). Jesus offers her forgiveness, not condemnation, yet he also wants to her to be transformed and not to sin again. Are there sins we are holding onto that we need to let go so we can walk in the new life Jesus is offering us in the Kingdom?

DAY 157

Today's Mystery: The Transfiguration

Today's Prayer:
- Pray with today's sacred art in "*visio divina*," using as many or as few of the reflection questions as you find fruitful.
- Pray 1 decade of the Rosary (1 Our Father, 10 Hail Marys, and 1 Glory Be).

View Sacred Art: *The Transfiguration*, Raphael

Reflect:
- Seeing Jesus depicted in this image might make us think of the Ascension. How did the Transfiguration point forward to the Ascension?
- Jesus took Peter, James, and John with him up the mountain. Look at these three Apostles at Jesus' feet. What are their reactions to seeing Christ glorified?
- The Transfiguration was meant to give consolation to Peter, James, and John and prepare them for Jesus' Crucifixion. How can we take moments of consolation and allow them to strengthen us for times of desolation?
- The bottom half of the painting depicts the healing of the boy who was possessed with a demon, which is described in Matthew 17. Why do you think Raphael combined the two scenes in this painting?
- The other nine Apostles are shown below in the painting, trying to exorcise the demon but to no avail. Notice the distress in their faces. Several are pointing to the mountain as if to say, "Jesus is on the mountain!" They probably felt alone in their struggle. Have you ever felt this way?
- After coming down from the mountain, Jesus frees the boy from the demon and says the Apostles' failure was due to their lack of faith. Do we have faith that Jesus is all-powerful even when things are going wrong in our lives?

DAY 158

Today's Mystery: The Institution of the Eucharist

Today's Prayer:
- Pray with today's sacred art in "*visio divina*," using as many or as few of the reflection questions as you find fruitful.
- Pray 1 decade of the Rosary (1 Our Father, 10 Hail Marys, and 1 Glory Be).

View Sacred Art: The Last Supper, Juan de Juanes

Reflect:

- This rendering of the Last Supper shows Jesus holding the Holy Eucharist. What Jesus is holding does not look like the bread on the table but rather like the Host at Mass. Why do you think the artist portrayed it in this way?
- Look at Jesus' face. He is shown looking at the viewer. Jesus said to his Apostles, "I have earnestly desired to eat this Passover with you before I suffer" (Luke 22:15). What is Jesus' face telling you?
- Notice where the Apostles are gazing. Except for Judas, they are all adoring Jesus in the Eucharist in their own ways. One of the Apostles, James the Lesser, is not looking at Jesus in the Eucharist, but he is pointing to him with both hands and looking at the Apostle next to him, Thomas. Why do you think he is doing this?
- Judas is shown on the right, with his back to the viewer. See the money bag that he is clasping. Have there been times when we have clung to our possessions, our pleasures, or our sins instead of accepting Jesus' gift of himself?
- Notice the basin and the water jar. What event happened on Holy Thursday night right before the institution of the Eucharist? How are these two events in a way connected?
- Notice how Jesus' halo is barely visible. His divinity is hidden in the Holy Eucharist. The hymn *Adoro Te*, by St. Thomas Aquinas, begins, "Devoutly I adore You, hidden Deity, under these appearances concealed." Why does God hide himself for us?
- As the Museo del Prado's website points out, "The chalice which appears in the centre of the table reproduces the one kept in Valencia Cathedral, considered to be the one used by Christ at the Last Supper." In fact, the artist who created this painting was from Valencia, in Spain. While we do not know for certain if this relic is the actual chalice used by Jesus, how do you think the artist was affected by it? How do these relics and holy objects of the Church enrich our faith?

DAY 159

Today's Mystery: The Agony in the Garden

Today's Prayer:
- Pray with today's sacred art in "*visio divina*," using as many or as few of the reflection questions as you find fruitful.
- Pray 1 decade of the Rosary (1 Our Father, 10 Hail Marys, and 1 Glory Be).

View Sacred Art: The Agony in the Garden

Reflect:
- Observe how fervently Jesus is praying. He had said to his Apostles, "My soul is very sorrowful, even to death" (Matthew 26:38). Have you ever prayed fervently for yourself or for a loved one amid great sorrow? Despite his sorrow, Jesus submits himself to the Father's will. How can we be more submissive to the Father's will?
- Here, we see an angel offering Jesus a chalice. In his prayer, Jesus refers to his suffering as a "chalice" (Matthew 26:39). What does the chalice make you think of?
- Notice the darkness in the painting, especially on the right side. If you look closely there, you can see Judas leading the soldiers in the darkness. What is the significance of this darkness?
- Notice the light shining on Jesus. The Gospel of John says, "The light shines in the darkness, and the darkness has not overcome it" (John 1:4). How is this portrayed within the painting?
- See how the Apostles are sleeping right in the front of the painting, even though Jesus has asked them to stay awake. How have we slept in prayer when we should have been awake? How can we comfort Jesus instead? How can we watch with him?
- Notice the grass and leaves in the painting. This betrayal happened in a garden. Think of the Garden of Eden. Are these two gardens—Gethsemane and Eden—connected? Were there betrayals in both?

DAY 160

Today's Mystery: The Scourging at the Pillar

Today's Prayer:
- Pray with today's sacred art in "*visio divina,*" using as many or as few of the reflection questions as you find fruitful.
- Pray 1 decade of the Rosary (1 Our Father, 10 Hail Marys, and 1 Glory Be).

View Sacred Art: *The Flagellation of Christ*, Caravaggio

Reflect:
- The Gospel of John tells us that Jesus said, "I am the light of the world; he who follows me will not walk in darkness, but will have the light of life" (John 8:12). Notice the light in the painting. Who is in the light and who are in the shadows? Why do you think the artist depicted the scene in this way? How might this painting illustrate Jesus' words?
- Jesus is shown here wearing the crown of thorns. The soldiers placed this crown on his head to mock him while they called him a king. Is Jesus a King? Is this crown of thorns the only crown he has? What does this say about who Jesus is?
- One of the men is grasping Jesus' hair, and another man is kicking Jesus' leg. We do not see Jesus being hit by the whips; we only see these acts of violence. Why do you think the artist depicted the scourging in this manner?
- Contrast Jesus' face with the face of the man holding his hair. What emotions do you see in Jesus' face, and what does his face say?
- Notice the pillar in the background. Although it is difficult to see, we can tell that it is strong. How is Jesus, in a way, like this pillar?
- The man at the bottom of the painting is preparing an instrument to scourge Jesus. We cannot see his face. How are we all, in a way, like this man when we sin?

DAY 161

Today's Mystery: The Crowning with Thorns

Today's Prayer:
- Pray with today's sacred art in "*visio divina*," using as many or as few of the reflection questions as you find fruitful.
- Pray 1 decade of the Rosary (1 Our Father, 10 Hail Marys, and 1 Glory Be).

View Sacred Art: *Ecce Homo*, Caravaggio

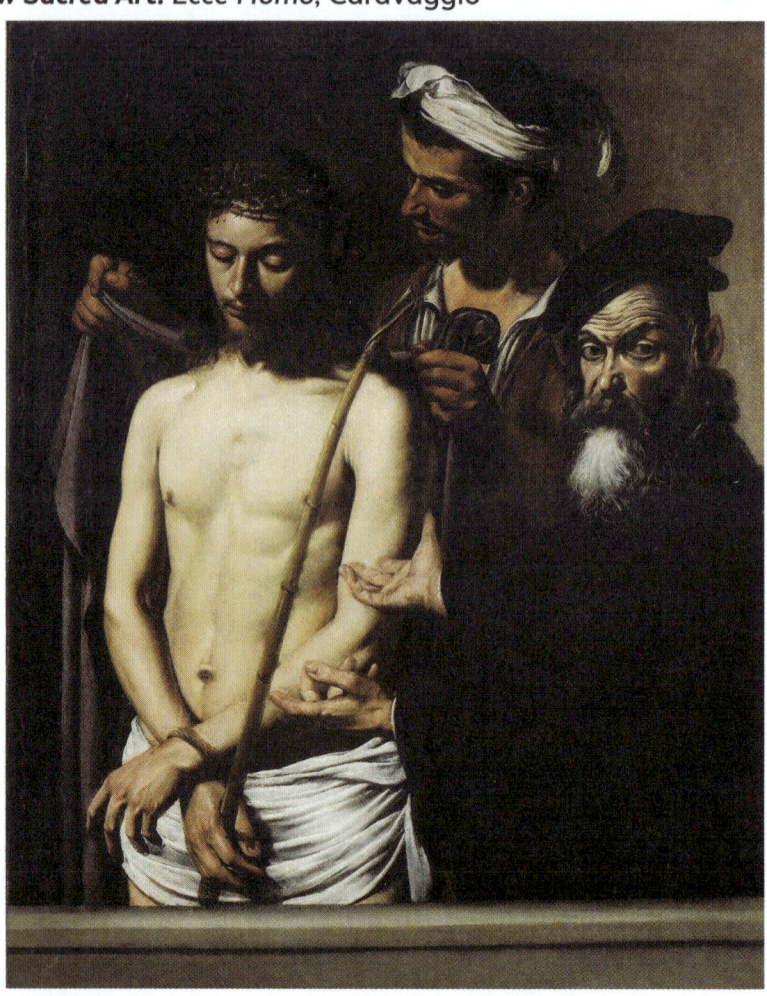

Reflect:
- This is a depiction of when Pilate presents Jesus to the people, saying "Behold the man!" (See John 19:5.) Notice that Jesus does not have a halo in this painting. Why do you think Caravaggio left this out of the painting?
- Notice how the man behind Jesus is covering him with a purple cloth, a sign of royalty. You can see in his face that he is mocking Jesus. How can we be better at defending Jesus' true kingship when we see him being mocked? Have you ever felt mocked because of your faith in Jesus? How can you comfort Jesus in his sorrow?
- It does not look like Pilate is wearing clothes of a first-century Roman. He looks like the artist is depicting him as a current-day politician. How can we be careful that politics do not become an idol? How can we be sure to trust more in Jesus' kingship than modern politics?
- Notice how Jesus' hands are tied by ropes like a criminal, even though he is the only one who is innocent. How can we be so blind as to bind God? When have we, in a sense, inhibited God from working in our lives or the lives of others?
- The only blood we see is that coming from the crown of thorns. Do you think this crowning could have caused Jesus more pain that his scourging, in a sense? Why or why not?
- Look at Pilate's face. What does his face express? Contrast his expression with the sorrow but also composure in Jesus' face. Does Jesus try to defend himself?

DAY 162

Today's Mystery: The Carrying of the Cross

Today's Prayer:
- Pray with today's sacred art in "*visio divina*," using as many or as few of the reflection questions as you find fruitful.
- Pray 1 decade of the Rosary (1 Our Father, 10 Hail Marys, and 1 Glory Be).

View Sacred Art: Christ Carrying the Cross, Orazio Gentileschi

Reflect:
- Notice Jesus' face. His eyes have a look of joy in them, and he is gently smiling at the woman who is showing compassion toward him. This may be a depiction of Our Lady, or it may be simply one of the women mentioned in the Gospel who wept for Jesus (see Luke 23:27–31). Would her presence have provided comfort to him?
- See how Jesus embraces his Cross. How can we find more peace in our suffering?
- The men next to Jesus want to move on and have an urgency about them. One of them is pointing away from Jesus. Jesus does not seem to be in a hurry. How can we be more like Jesus in this way?
- See how the woman's arms are open, as if she wants to embrace Jesus, who is holding his Cross. If this is a depiction of Our Lady, we can reflect on the fact that her cross was watching her Son suffer. How can we, like Mary, embrace our crosses?
- The woman is more visible because of the man behind her. His white shirt almost forms a halo around her head. How can other people, even people we least expect, make Jesus and Our Lady more visible to us?
- Notice the man next to Jesus. He looks angry, and his hand is clenched in a fist. Notice also the woman crying in the background, with her head bowed. How do their reactions to this scene differ? How is their reaction different from the reaction of the woman who is looking at Jesus? What do her hands and face convey? How can we keep our hands open and our eyes on Jesus?

DAY 163

Today's Mystery: The Crucifixion

Today's Prayer:
- Pray with today's sacred art in "*visio divina*," using as many or as few of the reflection questions as you find fruitful.
- Pray 1 decade of the Rosary (1 Our Father, 10 Hail Marys, and 1 Glory Be).

View Sacred Art: *What Our Lord Saw from the Cross*, James Tissot

Reflect:
- This rendering of the Crucifixion is unusual. We see in this painting what Christ saw from the cross. Why do you think the artist wished to depict the Crucifixion in this way? What is the first thing or person that strikes you?
- See all the people there to watch Jesus suffer and die. What are their different motivations for being there? How do they look differently at Jesus?
- Notice the tomb. What would you feel if you could see the place where you will be buried, as you were dying in agony? And yet, Jesus rose from the tomb on Easter Sunday. How does Jesus' death and Resurrection give us hope?
- Notice Jesus' feet at the very bottom of the painting. Have you ever thought about the scene you would want to see as you were dying? What would you want to see? What people would you want to surround you when you were dying?
- Notice Mary with her hands resting on her heart. Do you think she thought of the prophecy of Simeon that her heart would be pierced (see Luke 2:35)?
- Notice the two women near Mary, comforting her. Who are some of the people in your life who have comforted you during times of great sorrow? How can you be like these women for other people who are suffering?

DAY 164

Today's Mystery: The Resurrection

Today's Prayer:
- Pray with today's sacred art in "*visio divina*," using as many or as few of the reflection questions as you find fruitful.
- Pray 1 decade of the Rosary (1 Our Father, 10 Hail Marys, and 1 Glory Be).

View Sacred Art: *The Incredulity of St. Thomas*, Caravaggio

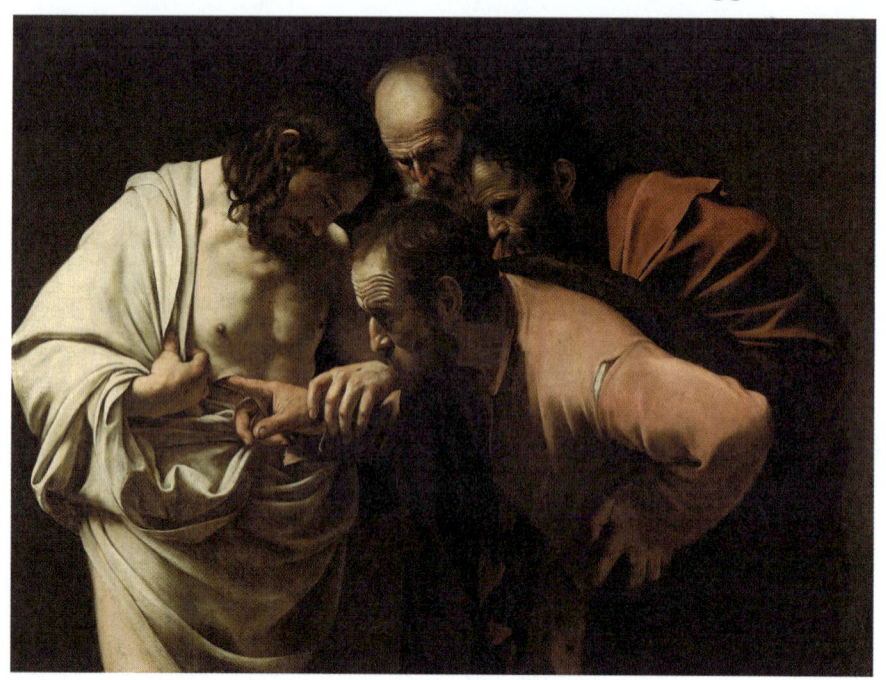

Reflect:
- See Thomas' finger in Jesus' side. Why do you think Caravaggio made the scene so graphic?
- Thomas tells the other Apostles, "Unless I … place my hand in his side, I will not believe" (John 20:25), but he does not say this to Jesus. Still, Jesus knows his need and his desire. How does Jesus also anticipate our needs even before we ask him?
- Notice how Jesus is guiding Thomas' hand to his side. How does Jesus gently lead us when we have weak faith? Look at Jesus' face. Does he look angry or frustrated with Thomas? How does Jesus often respond to our lack of faith?
- Look at Thomas' reaction in putting his finger in Jesus' side. What emotions does his face express? What do you think he is thinking?
- Elizabeth Lev, in her book, *How Catholic Art Saved the Faith: The Triumph of Beauty and Truth in Counter-Reformation Art*, makes the point, "The two apostles crowded over Thomas's shoulder suggest that he was not alone in his incredulity but was the only one who voiced it." How might it be good to voice our struggles to Jesus and ask him to strengthen our faith? Could it sometimes be beneficial to share our struggles with others we trust or with a spiritual director?
- Jesus said to Thomas, "Blessed are those who have not seen and yet believe" (John 20:29). How will we be blessed in believing Jesus, even though we have not yet seen him?

DAY 165

Today's Mystery: The Ascension

Today's Prayer:
- Pray with today's sacred art in "*visio divina,*" using as many or as few of the reflection questions as you find fruitful.
- Pray 1 decade of the Rosary (1 Our Father, 10 Hail Marys, and 1 Glory Be).

View Sacred Art: The Ascension

Reflect:
- Mary is shown here, along with the eleven Apostles, watching while Jesus ascends to heaven. Why do you think the artist included her in the painting? Do you think this moment would have been difficult for her?
- Notice the footprints in the earth where Jesus was standing. Why are these footprints significant?
- There are seven angels around Jesus. Is the number seven significant? How does Jesus still touch us today within his Church?
- Notice how Jesus is looking up and his hand is reaching up. It is as if he is calling us to heaven. How can this mystery strengthen our hope?
- See how Jesus is dressed in bright white with light radiating from him. Does this remind you of the Transfiguration? How was this moment foreshadowed within the Gospels?
- We are told in Acts of the Apostles that Jesus was taken up by a cloud (see Acts 1:9). What might be the significance of the cloud? Recall that God's presence among the Israelites was described as a cloud (see Exodus 40:34–38).

DAY 166

Today's Mystery: The Descent of the Holy Spirit on Pentecost

Today's Prayer:
- Pray with today's sacred art in "*visio divina*," using as many or as few of the reflection questions as you find fruitful.
- Pray 1 decade of the Rosary (1 Our Father, 10 Hail Marys, and 1 Glory Be).

View Sacred Art: *Pentecost*, Titian

Reflect:
- The man in the front right of the painting is holding what looks like a key. St. Peter is often shown holding a key. What does the key represent? How does Peter hold a special office among the Apostles?
- Notice that the ceiling is divided into seven sections, and each section has seven recessed sections. What is the significance of the number seven?
- See how there are three windows behind the dove. What does the number three represent? Even though it is the coming of the Holy Spirit, how are also the Father and Son involved?
- Notice the tongues of fire resting on each of the heads. We each receive the Holy Spirit at Confirmation. How is that sacrament a personal Pentecost for each of us?
- See how Mary is looking upward as if in ecstasy. One of the disciples is gazing at her face. How can we be more open to the Holy Spirit by meditating on Mary?
- Notice the man on the left with his arms extended towards the Holy Spirit, as if he is pleading. Do we plead for the Holy Spirit to be with us and inspire us in all that we do?

DAY 167

Today's Mystery: The Assumption of Mary

Today's Prayer:
- Pray with today's sacred art in "*visio divina,*" using as many or as few of the reflection questions as you find fruitful.
- Pray 1 decade of the Rosary (1 Our Father, 10 Hail Marys, and 1 Glory Be).

View Sacred Art: The Assumption

Reflect:
- See how Our Lady's large mantle is open to cover the people under her. How are we all under Our Lady's mantle and under her care?
- Notice how her hands are spread out as if to bring calm and peace to a situation. How has Our Lady brought peace and serenity to our lives?
- This is a depiction of a vision of St. Bonaventure, though St. Bonaventure is not shown here. Angels are writing down what he saw. How do you think our guardian angels help us in prayer?
- There seems to be a battle going on at the right of the painting. How can Our Lady help us in our battles with temptation? Recall the words of the *Memorare*, "Remember, O most gracious Virgin Mary, that never was it known that anyone who fled to thy protection, implored thy help, or sought thy intercession was left unaided." How have we seen this is true within history? How has Our Lady come through in your own life?
- The Holy Father with the papal tiara is standing below Our Lady. A king is kneeling beside him. Why is it important for leaders to look to Our Lady for guidance in their decisions?
- Our Lady is now in heaven body and soul, along with her son. How should this give us hope?

DAY 168

Today's Mystery: The Coronation of Mary as Queen of Heaven and Earth

Today's Prayer:
- Pray with today's sacred art in "*visio divina*," using as many or as few of the reflection questions as you find fruitful.
- Pray 1 decade of the Rosary (1 Our Father, 10 Hail Marys, and 1 Glory Be).

View Sacred Art: The Coronation of Mary

Reflect:

- Notice Mary's face. She is full of joy. How did her sorrow on earth turn into an abundance of glory and joy in heaven?
- There are many angels under and around Our Lady. Some look like they are lifting up the cloud on which she is kneeling. Even though she is by nature lower than the angels, she is higher than the angels by grace. How is this so? How is she Queen of the Angels? We each have a guardian angel here on earth to help us find our way and choose to follow God's will. Do you often think about how your guardian angel is adoring God? Do you ask for your angel's intercession and guidance?
- St. Joseph is kneeling below Mary and holding lilies. Notice how he is looking up and bowing to Mary. How did he serve Mary and Jesus during their earthly lives?
- Above St. Joseph is St. John the Baptist, holding a staff in the shape of a cross. Notice how St. John the Baptist is still pointing to the Lamb of God. How does this image encapsulate his whole mission?
- See the older woman on the right pointing to Mary. She looks like a person who perhaps was close to Mary during her earthly life and went before her into heaven. Perhaps this could be St. Anne, Mary's mother. How can parents imitate St. Anne in raising their children?
- Mary is kneeling down while she is being crowned, as if showing her submission to God's will. How did her yes to God in the Annunciation lead to her eventual coronation as Queen of Heaven and Earth?

DAY 169

Today's Mystery: The Annunciation

Today's Prayer:
- Pray with today's sacred art in "*visio divina,*" using as many or as few of the reflection questions as you find fruitful.
- Pray 1 decade of the Rosary (1 Our Father, 10 Hail Marys, and 1 Glory Be).

View Sacred Art: *The Annunciation,* Jan van Eyck

Reflect:
- The place where the artist depicts the Annunciation looks like a church. Why do you think the artist depicted the Annunciation in this way? As the National Gallery of Art's website points out, the event of the Annunciation "was reenacted by choirboys in church each December. Van Eyck's painting closely parallels a performance that" took place during the Medieval era. Although this Medieval custom of reenacting the Annunciation is no longer followed, how does the liturgy help us enter into the mysteries of Christ's life and Our Lady's life?
- As art critic Carol J. Purtle has pointed out, a viewer will notice that the church in this painting has a broken ceiling, then a high window typical of a more ancient building style, then features constructed in the more contemporary Gothic manner. Thus, we "see the building moving from a state of disrepair to its most recent historic style." This "indicate[s] a passage from the Old Law to the New." How does the Church continue to bring God's healing to us?
- Although they may be difficult to see in the painting, depictions of Old Testament stories and figures are included on the floor and on the walls. At the bottom edge of the painting is a depiction of David and Goliath, for instance. How does David foreshadow the coming of Christ?
- The dove descending onto Mary is a foreshadowing of Pentecost. As the National Gallery of Art's website points out, "The seven beams of light that carry the dove to Mary represent the seven gifts of the Holy Spirit: wisdom, understanding, right judgment, fortitude, knowledge, piety, fear of the Lord." How is Mary filled with the Holy Spirit even before Pentecost?
- Notice how Gabriel is dressed. He has a crown like a king and is wearing many beautiful jewels. The clothing he wears also looks like priestly vestments. Why is Gabriel dressed in this way? How does it declare who Christ will be?
- Gabriel is actually smiling as he greets Our Lady, and we do not often see the archangel depicted in this way. How is this a very joyful occasion?

DAY 170

Today's Mystery: The Visitation

Today's Prayer:
- Pray with today's sacred art in "*visio divina*," using as many or as few of the reflection questions as you find fruitful.
- Pray 1 decade of the Rosary (1 Our Father, 10 Hail Marys, and 1 Glory Be).

View Sacred Art: The Visitation, Church of the Visitation in Ain Karem

Reflect:

- This mosaic is located on the outside wall of the Church of the Visitation in Ain Karem in Israel, so it is one of the first things that pilgrims see on arriving at the church. Mary made the journey to this very spot, just as pilgrims continue to do today. The Latin words under the mosaic quote Luke 1:39: "In those days Mary arose and went with haste into the hill country, to a city of Judah." Why do you think Mary went "in haste" to visit Elizabeth?
- Joseph is not present in this depiction of the Visitation. But who accompanies Mary on her way to visit Elizabeth? There are six angels shown. The angels who are walking are wearing sandals, and one is leading the donkey. Why do you think they are depicted this way? What does this say about the mission of certain angels?
- Notice the path Mary is following. It is rocky, and we can see cacti growing. Even amid the joys of life, can we find that we are sometimes on a difficult journey?
- It does not say in Scripture that Mary traveled on a donkey to visit Elizabeth. Why do you think the artist included a donkey? What does this foreshadow?
- Notice the placement of Mary's hands. What do you think she is thinking about on her journey?
- Mary is wearing white with some purple underneath. These are different from the colors we often see Mary wearing. White is a color of purity; purple is a color of royalty. What does this say about Mary and the child she is carrying?

DAY 171

Today's Mystery: The Nativity

Today's Prayer:
- Pray with today's sacred art in "*visio divina*," using as many or as few of the reflection questions as you find fruitful.
- Pray 1 decade of the Rosary (1 Our Father, 10 Hail Marys, and 1 Glory Be).

View Sacred Art: *Nativity with St. Francis and St. Lawrence*, Caravaggio

Reflect:
- The artist included St. Lawrence, a third-century martyr, in this painting on the left and St. Francis of Assisi on the right. St. Francis and St. Lawrence were not actually present at the Nativity, yet they surely meditated on this mystery within their lives, perhaps even to the point of picturing themselves within the scene. How can you also picture yourself here? What do you see? What do you smell? What do you hear and touch? Is there anything you want to say to the people present here?
- Notice how Mary seems very relaxed, since she is not kneeling and her hands are not folded. She just seems to be enjoying gazing at Jesus. What does this depiction say to you?
- Observe the angel at the top of the painting, shown looking down at Jesus, pointing up to heaven, and carrying a banner that says in Latin "Glory to God in the highest." He seems to be communicating that God has become man. How can we give glory to God in thanksgiving for becoming man to save us?
- It is not made very clear in the painting which character is St. Joseph. Do you think he is the one sitting in front of Mary? Or is he the one standing with a hat and a staff? Why? While we do not know which character is St. Joseph, he is clearly in conversation with another man within the painting. What do you think they were talking about?
- Notice how Jesus is on the straw on the ground. He is God, and yet He is shown as the lowest and the most vulnerable. What can we learn from pondering Christ's meekness and humility?
- St. Francis had a special devotion to the Nativity, and he is credited with creating the first crèche. How can we show greater devotion to Christ in the Nativity?

DAY 172

Today's Mystery: The Presentation of Jesus in the Temple

Today's Prayer:
- Pray with today's sacred art in "*visio divina*," using as many or as few of the reflection questions as you find fruitful.
- Pray 1 decade of the Rosary (1 Our Father, 10 Hail Marys, and 1 Glory Be).

View Sacred Art: *Simeon's Song of Praise*, Arent de Gelder

Reflect:
- This painting is different from the other depictions of the Presentation we have seen. This painting just focuses on Our Lady, Simeon, and Jesus. Why do you think the artist wanted to depict this moment in this way?
- We see that Simeon is holding Jesus. Perhaps Mary knew of Simeon before she came to the Temple, but perhaps she did not. And yet, she let Simeon hold him. How has Mary, even though we are sinful and unworthy, loved us as her children and given us her son?
- This joyful mystery also contains sorrow, as Simeon prophesies that both Mary and Jesus will suffer. How are the joyful events in our life sometimes also mixed with sorrow? How can meditating on the Presentation help us in these moments?
- See how Jesus is looking at Mary. He loves her so much, and yet she will greatly suffer. Why, in his great love for her, does He not shield her from great suffering? Why does Jesus also not shield us from great suffering?
- If you look carefully, you can dimly see another figure in the dark background of the painting. He has a quill in his hand and looks like he is writing. Could this be St. Luke, who is the only one to record this event in his Gospel? It is widely believed that Luke interviewed Mary while writing his Gospel, and Mary told him the events from Jesus' childhood. How do you think Mary felt recounting this story to Luke?
- Simeon says that Jesus is "a light for revelation to the Gentiles" (Luke 2:32). How does the artist portray this prophecy in the painting?

DAY 173

Today's Mystery: The Finding of Jesus in the Temple

Today's Prayer:
- Pray with today's sacred art in "*visio divina*," using as many or as few of the reflection questions as you find fruitful.
- Pray 1 decade of the Rosary (1 Our Father, 10 Hail Marys, and 1 Glory Be).

View Sacred Art: *The Finding of the Saviour in the Temple*, William Holman Hunt

Reflect:
- Jesus is shown looking right at you, inviting you into the painting and into the mystery. What questions would you ask Jesus if you were there? What do you think he wants you to learn from this mystery?
- Most of the teachers are sitting on the ground listening to Jesus. How do we need to humble ourselves in order to listen to and learn from Jesus?
- Notice the beggar sitting outside of the Temple. Why do you think the artist included him in the painting?
- Notice how Mary is discreetly talking to Jesus. She asks him why he allowed her and St. Joseph to suffer by losing him for three days. How can meditating on this mystery help us when we are suffering?
- See how Our Lady's hand is near her heart and how Jesus is resting his hand on her arm. What insights do you think Our Lady had after meditating on this mystery within her heart?
- Notice St. Joseph's arm embracing Jesus and Mary. Knowing his mission was to protect Jesus and Mary, how do you think he would have felt losing Jesus for three days?

DAY 174

Today's Mystery: The Baptism of Jesus

Today's Prayer:
- Pray with today's sacred art in "*visio divina*," using as many or as few of the reflection questions as you find fruitful.
- Pray 1 decade of the Rosary (1 Our Father, 10 Hail Marys, and 1 Glory Be).

View Sacred Art: *The Appearance of Christ Before the People (The Apparition of the Messiah)*, Alexander Ivanov

Reflect:
- The Gospel of John recounts that John the Baptist sees Jesus from a distance and declared him to be "the Lamb of God" (John 1:29). This event is being portrayed here. What did John mean by saying that Jesus is the Lamb of God?
- Two of the future Apostles—John the Beloved and Andrew—hear these words of John the Baptist and become the first followers of Jesus. Andrew then brings his brother Simon, who will become Peter, to Jesus. Who are the people that we can bring to Jesus today, either in prayer or by sharing with them who Jesus is?
- This painting shows the clothes that John the Baptist wore, described in Matthew 3:4: "a garment of camel's hair, and a leather belt around his waist." The Old Testament prophet Elijah is described wearing similar clothing in 2 Kings 1:8. Why do you think John the Baptist wore those clothes?
- Some of the people shown here are naked because they have just been baptized. This might seem odd to us. However, what might this nakedness, or taking off one's clothes before being baptized, symbolize?
- Notice the different people within the painting—for instance, the young and the old, those on horseback and those walking. This painting shows John's mission "to bear witness to the light, that all might believe through him" (John 1:7). How did John fulfill his mission, which was prophesied centuries before he was born? How can you, like John the Baptist, bear witness to the light?
- The Gospel of Matthew recounts that many Pharisees and Sadducees go to John to be baptized, and John warns them to "bear fruit that befits repentance" (Matthew 3:8). How can we take these words to heart in our own lives?

DAY 175

Today's Mystery: The Wedding at Cana

Today's Prayer:
- Pray with today's sacred art in "*visio divina,*" using as many or as few of the reflection questions as you find fruitful.
- Pray 1 decade of the Rosary (1 Our Father, 10 Hail Marys, and 1 Glory Be).

View Sacred Art: *The Wedding at Cana,* Paolo Veronese

Reflect:
- This painting depicts a colorful scene. Not all the people shown seem to be aware of the miracle that has just taken place. Why does God work sometimes in a quiet, unassuming way? Are we sometimes unaware of the blessings being given around us?
- This marriage feast looks very loud and joyful with music playing and food being prepared and eaten. How do marriage feasts foreshadow the eternal wedding feast?
- See the servants pouring the wine into gold vessels to serve it. The jars that were filled with water were used for purification, not for holding wine. How is it fitting that Jesus used these jars of purification?
- Look at Our Lady's face. She seems serene and confident that Jesus can and will provide wine for the wedding feast. How can we be more confident in Jesus, as Mary was?
- Notice the face of the bride, in the left corner of the painting. The bride seems to be looking directly at you while you look at the painting. What do you think she is trying to tell you?
- On the left, we can see someone, next to the bride and groom, pointing to the wine, as if to make a remark about how good it is. When people ask you about your joy or hope, how can you be better at making "a defense to any one who calls you to account for the hope that is in you" (1 Peter 3:15)?

DAY 176

Today's Mystery: The Proclamation of the Kingdom and the Call to Conversion

Today's Prayer:
- Pray with today's sacred art in "*visio divina*," using as many or as few of the reflection questions as you find fruitful.
- Pray 1 decade of the Rosary (1 Our Father, 10 Hail Marys, and 1 Glory Be).

View Sacred Art: Christ in the Storm on the Sea of Galilee, Rembrandt

Reflect:
- This storm at sea is depicted as a terrible tempest. The waves are crashing against the boat. Have you ever had a "storm" in your life where you feared for your safety or the safety of a loved one?
- Look at the dark clouds overhead and the way the boat is tossed by the waves. The sea and the weather are out of our control. What is going on within your life that is truly out of your control that you can give to Jesus?
- Notice the different men in the boat. Some are trying to fix the sail. Some are just staring at the waves. Some are holding on for dear life. One man even seems to be hiding in the boat. However, some men go to Jesus to wake him up. What do you do when you are in the midst of a storm? Do you go to Jesus, do you try and fix it yourself, or do you even hide?
- The sun seems to be peeking out in the left corner of the painting, as if the storm is already calming down. Have you ever experienced a difficult situation that you did not think was going to end but that suddenly stopped? Can the storms in our life become calm again in an instant if Jesus wills it?
- Notice Jesus sleeping in the boat. Should the men have just let Jesus sleep and wait for the storm to end? Have there been times when it seems Jesus is asleep during your storm?
- The Gospel of Matthew tells us that the men in the boat were amazed that Jesus could control the storm (see Matthew 8:27). How does this event reveal who Jesus is to the disciples?

DAY 177

Today's Mystery: The Transfiguration

Today's Prayer:
- Pray with today's sacred art in "*visio divina*," using as many or as few of the reflection questions as you find fruitful.
- Pray 1 decade of the Rosary (1 Our Father, 10 Hail Marys, and 1 Glory Be).

View Sacred Art: *The Savior's Transfiguration*, Theophanes the Greek (attr.)

Reflect:
- Look at how the artist depicts Jesus' glory. Notice the perfect circle behind him and the rays that come from him. The rays of light almost look like a star behind Jesus. Do you think these shapes and rays are significant? What do they represent?
- Notice how Moses and Elijah are also standing on mountains. Both these men had encounters with God on mountains. What did God reveal about himself in his encounters with Moses at Mount Sinai? (See Exodus 19–20 and 24.) How might that be connected to the Transfiguration?
- What did God reveal about himself in his encounter with Elijah at Mount Carmel? (See 1 Kings 18:20–40). What did he reveal at Mount Horeb? (See 1 Kings 19:1–18.) How might those events be connected to the Transfiguration?
- Notice the little scenes depicted at each side of the icon. On the left, it looks like Jesus is leading the Apostles up the mountain. On the right, Jesus seems to be taking the Apostles down the mountain. How do you think this experience changed them?
- Notice how the Apostles are shown in the main part of the icon. The Gospel of Luke says that Peter, James, and John "were heavy with sleep but kept awake" (Luke 9:32). In the Garden of Gethsemane, these same three Apostles will be with Jesus and will not stay awake. Are these two events connected?
- Matthew's Gospel says that Jesus told Peter, James, and John to tell no one what they saw until he was raised from the dead. Why do you think Jesus wanted them to keep this mystery a secret?

DAY 178

Today's Mystery: The Institution of the Eucharist

Today's Prayer:
- Pray with today's sacred art in "*visio divina*," using as many or as few of the reflection questions as you find fruitful.
- Pray 1 decade of the Rosary (1 Our Father, 10 Hail Marys, and 1 Glory Be).

View Sacred Art: *Christ and the Disciples Before the Last Supper,* Henry Ossawa Tanner

Reflect:
- This painting simply shows Jesus with two of his disciples. In the Gospel of Luke we are told that Jesus sent Peter and John to get ready for the Passover and told them to follow a man with a jar of water into a house where they would eat the Last Supper (see Luke 22:7–13). Perhaps these instructions did not make sense to the disciples at the time. Have you ever been directed to do something you knew was right but that did not make sense to you? Did it become clearer later?
- One of the disciples has his hands folded and almost looks like he is beseeching Jesus about something. What do you think he is saying to Jesus? If you had been there, what would you have said to Jesus on the night of the Last Supper?
- Notice Jesus is holding a staff. What does this staff represent for you?
- Notice Jesus' white garment. At the Passover, the Jews were to sacrifice a lamb without blemish. How is Jesus' white garment significant?
- Look at the overall color of the painting. What mood does this color evoke for you? It seems to be the end of the day, right before night takes over. Knowing what is to come, how does this painting make you feel?
- The Last Supper took place in springtime, and the shadows of the trees show that the trees have no leaves. How do the bare trees remind us of the death that Jesus is about to undergo? How does his death lead to new life? Do the bare trees also suggest that new life?

DAY 179

Today's Mystery: The Agony in the Garden

Today's Prayer:
- Pray with today's sacred art in *"visio divina,"* using as many or as few of the reflection questions as you find fruitful.
- Pray 1 decade of the Rosary (1 Our Father, 10 Hail Marys, and 1 Glory Be).

View Sacred Art: *The Arrest of Christ (Kiss of Judas)*, Giotto

Reflect:
- In the center of this painting, Judas embraces Jesus. Though he is about to kiss Christ, this is the signal Judas has arranged to betray him. Why do you think Judas chose a kiss to point out the one to be arrested? Have you ever been betrayed by a friend? How can you comfort Jesus in his agony?
- See Jesus' eyes and how he is looking at Judas. What do his eyes and face express?
- This painting shows a violent scene with a crowd grasping clubs, spears, and torches. Does Jesus put up a fight when the soldiers come to take him? Yet, he says that an army of angels would come to his aid if he desired it (see Matthew 26:53). What does this tell us? How is Jesus completely in control of what is happening to him?
- See Peter cutting off the ear of the high priest's slave. One can see the ear falling to the ground. Why do you think Giotto depicted this scene in a gruesome way? It is odd to see someone with a halo cutting off someone's ear. What were Peter's intentions? What would you do if Jesus was being arrested in front of you?
- Notice the man pointing. On what charges is Jesus being arrested? How can this mystery strengthen you if you are ever attacked or accused unjustly?
- Look at the helmets of the crowd behind Jesus and Judas. They look like a dark cloud or even a swarm of flies. What thoughts do you have when you think of the soldiers swarming Jesus in this way? How can this scene move us to greater contrition for our sins?

DAY 180

Today's Mystery: **The Scourging at the Pillar**

Today's Prayer:
- Pray with today's sacred art in "*visio divina*," using as many or as few of the reflection questions as you find fruitful.
- Pray 1 decade of the Rosary (1 Our Father, 10 Hail Marys, and 1 Glory Be).

View Sacred Art: *The Flagellation of Our Lord Jesus Christ*, William-Adolphe Bouguereau

Reflect:
- Notice how Jesus is hanging, not standing up, in this painting. He looks like he has died, although we know that he will undergo much more suffering before dying on the Cross. This depiction can be a reminder that Jesus held nothing back in his Passion. All suffering offered up is a share in the sufferings of Christ on the Cross. How can we accept and offer up the suffering within our own lives in union with Christ's Passion?
- Jesus looks helpless here, but in his Passion, he was actually saving the whole world. How can reflecting on this mystery help us to trust Jesus more deeply, even when things seem out of control?
- Jesus' skin looks untouched. However, the red cloth on the ground might remind us of the blood that will be shed in the scourging. How can reflecting on this mystery and the blood that Jesus shed help us to have greater contrition for our sins, especially sins that violate the Sixth and Ninth Commandments?
- Both the men who are scourging Jesus have clenched fists. Why do you think this their hands are clenched this way? What emotions do you think they are experiencing?
- See the child looking away and his mother embracing him. What feelings are evoked for you when looking at this mother and child at Jesus' scourging? Could this mother represent Our Lady, who is our mother, coming to our aid when we have been guilty of sin and need to repent?
- Notice all the different people watching. Who do you think they are? Do you think they care for Jesus, or are just curious, or are taking pleasure in the scourging?

DAY 181

Today's Mystery: The Crowning with Thorns

Today's Prayer:
- Pray with today's sacred art in "*visio divina*," using as many or as few of the reflection questions as you find fruitful.
- Pray 1 decade of the Rosary (1 Our Father, 10 Hail Marys, and 1 Glory Be).

View Sacred Art: *The Crowning with Thorns*, Anthony van Dyck

Reflect:
- Look at Jesus' eyes. How does the artist depict him in this painting? How can meditating on the mystery strengthen us in patience?
- The man handing Jesus the reed is genuflecting, even though he does not acknowledge who Jesus actually is. Jesus' Kingdom, as he says to Pilate, "is not of this world" (John 18:36). Do we sometimes forget that Jesus' Kingdom is not of this world? Are we surprised sometimes by how the world treats Him and His Church? Should we expect suffering and persecution, knowing our true home is in heaven?
- Notice that several of these men look like old men. Old men are supposed to be wise. How are these old men foolish? How is Jesus the wise one in the painting?
- Jesus does not appear to be particularly bloody in this rendering of the crowning with thorns, yet one might notice the blood coming from his nose. How does this make you feel seeing that it looks like one of the men struck Jesus in the face?
- Look at the crown of thorns. The thorns are huge. Notice how the soldier has gloves on while he puts this crown on Jesus' head. Have we deliberately caused pain in others while being careful to avoid pain ourselves?
- Notice people trying to view Jesus from the outside. Who do you think these people are? Why would they want to watch Jesus being mocked in this way?

DAY 182

Today's Mystery: The Carrying of the Cross

Today's Prayer:
- Pray with today's sacred art in "*visio divina*," using as many or as few of the reflection questions as you find fruitful.
- Pray 1 decade of the Rosary (1 Our Father, 10 Hail Marys, and 1 Glory Be).

View Sacred Art: Christ Falls on the Way to Calvary, Raphael

Reflect:
- Though it may be difficult to see, both Jesus and Mary have tears streaming down their faces. Jesus' suffering was for our sake, to save us, and Mary suffered with him. Have we at times been indifferent to the sins we commit and the pain it causes Jesus and Mary?
- Notice how Mary gets down to be near Jesus with her arms outstretched. She is not standing but wants to get as close to Jesus as she can. How does our love for Jesus draw us to want to get as close to him as we possibly can in our suffering?
- Mary's and Jesus' eyes are locked into each other. They do not seem to notice what is happening around them. Have you ever shed tears of sorrow in seeing your loved ones suffer or struggle? How can we turn to Jesus and Mary in these moments?
- See the several women attending to Mary, helping her up and comforting her. How can we be present to Mary in her sorrow for her Son? How can we help other people in their sorrow?
- We can see Simon of Cyrene helping Jesus to carry his Cross. He looks disgusted by how the other soldiers are treating Jesus. One of the soldiers is brandishing a spear, and another is pulling Jesus by a rope. How can we be like Simon to those suffering in our lives?
- Jesus fell three times because of the weight of the Cross and because of his injuries. Here, it looks like he might have tripped on a large rock. When have you felt that your cross was too heavy to go forward? What have been the obstacles in your path? Who has helped you in moving forward and to continue to carry your cross?

DAY 183

Today's Mystery: **The Crucifixion**

Today's Prayer:
- Pray with today's sacred art in "*visio divina,*" using as many or as few of the reflection questions as you find fruitful.
- Pray 1 decade of the Rosary (1 Our Father, 10 Hail Marys, and 1 Glory Be).

View Sacred Art: *The Descent from the Cross*, Peter Paul Rubens

Reflect:

- Notice how Jesus' body looks grey and how the artist depicted death settling into his body. Why do you think the artist depicted Jesus in this way?
- See how Mary's face also looks grey and how it matches Jesus' skin. How did Mary, in a special way, share in Jesus' work of redemption?
- The Gospels do not mention Jesus being placed in his mother's arms after the Crucifixion, but it is one of the seven sorrows of Mary and one of the Stations of the Cross. How do you think Mary felt in holding her Son, who had just died? How do you think she was able to endure his Passion and death?
- See the items of the crucifixion at the bottom of the painting. Some of them are placed in a gold dish. How have these instruments, which were once objects to inflict torture, now become holy objects?
- See John holding Jesus as the men let him down from the cross. See how his head is placed right where Jesus was pierced. Where was John's head leaning during the Last Supper? How do we stay near Jesus' pierced heart?
- Notice the man richly dressed on the right who is helping to take Jesus down from the Cross. He is most likely Joseph of Arimathea, who was wealthy and who donated the tomb to be used for Jesus' burial (Matthew 27:57–60). Notice, as well, Mary Magdalene kneeling and simply caressing Jesus' arm. How might we show greater reverence to Our Lord in large ways like Joseph of Arimathea or in simple, small ways like Mary Magdalene?

DAY 184

Today's Mystery: The Resurrection

Today's Prayer:
- Pray with today's sacred art in "*visio divina*," using as many or as few of the reflection questions as you find fruitful.
- Pray 1 decade of the Rosary (1 Our Father, 10 Hail Marys, and 1 Glory Be).

View Sacred Art: *The Holy Women at Christ's Tomb*, Annibale Carracci

Reflect:
- Notice the sunrise in the background of the painting. These women wanted to get to Jesus' tomb as soon as it was permitted by Jewish law. What do they wish to do and why?
- See how one woman is holding a clay vase full of spices to anoint Jesus' body. Why is it important for us to show reverence and to adequately care for the dead?
- See the angel pointing to the empty tomb. The stone which covered the tomb has been moved away. We hear in the Gospels that Jesus entered rooms without opening the door, so he could have risen from the tomb and left the stone in place. Why do you think the angel moved away the stone?
- The angel has a bright glow and his clothes are white. Matthew recounts in his Gospel regarding the angel, "His appearance was like lightning, and his clothing white as snow" (Matt 28:3). Does his appearance remind you of someone else's appearance? Why does an angel appear in this way?
- Notice how the woman on the left looks startled and frightened. The angel tells the women, "Do not be afraid" (Matthew 28:5). Why do you think he says this?
- Notice the tree near the tomb. John's Gospel tells us that Jesus is buried in a garden (see John 19:41). Why is it fitting that Jesus was buried in a garden?

284   The Rosary in a Year Prayer Guide

DAY 185

Today's Mystery: The Ascension

Today's Prayer:
- Pray with today's sacred art in "*visio divina,*" using as many or as few of the reflection questions as you find fruitful.
- Pray 1 decade of the Rosary (1 Our Father, 10 Hail Marys, and 1 Glory Be).

View Sacred Art: *Appearance on the Mountain in Galilee,* Duccio

Reflect:
- Jesus had directed the Apostles to go to a mountain in Galilee, and they met Jesus there. Why do you think he chose a mountain? What other mysteries involve mountains?
- Notice how the Apostles are all grouped together in one group. Why do you think this is significant? How are they to be one?
- See how a couple of Apostles are holding books. Why do you think they are holding books? What does this represent?
- Notice Jesus' hands. He looks like he is teaching or instructing the Apostles. He says that they are to spread the Gospel (see Matthew 28:19–20). How do these men teach with Jesus' authority?
- Look at the Apostles' faces. They are all ordinary men, and some look worried or confused. Jesus tells them, "You shall receive power when the Holy Spirit has come upon you" (Acts 1:9). What is coming next for them? How is everything soon changed?
- Jesus tells these men they are his "witnesses" (Luke 24:48). The Greek word for "witness" is where we get the word "martyr." How are all these men going to be his martyrs and witnesses?

DAY 186

Today's Mystery: The Descent of the Holy Spirit on Pentecost

Today's Prayer:
- Pray with today's sacred art in "*visio divina*," using as many or as few of the reflection questions as you find fruitful.
- Pray 1 decade of the Rosary (1 Our Father, 10 Hail Marys, and 1 Glory Be).

View Sacred Art: *Pentecost*, Simone Peterzano (attr.)

Reflect:
- Notice that Our Lady is at the center of depictions of Pentecost. How is she an image of the Church? See Our Lady's face here. She looks deep in prayer. How is she interceding for the Church? How should we all pray to the Holy Spirit on behalf of our Church?
- The woman next to Our Lady is holding something. It looks like this figure is Mary Magdalene, who anointed Jesus' feet with oil before his Passion. How would receiving the Holy Spirit have given her great joy? Notice how Our Lady and Mary Magdalene both have their hands on their hearts. How did they both love Jesus so well? How can we imitate them?
- This image shows a crowd of different people. How does each person receive different gifts but still receives the one Holy Spirit (see 1 Corinthians 12:4)? What gifts of the Holy Spirit do you have?
- Notice the tongues of fire resting on the heads of those present. What does this fire represent? When has God manifested himself as fire?
- The disciples were fearful before the Holy Spirit fell on them. Afterwards, they spoke boldly about Jesus Christ. Are you sometimes filled with fear? How can you let the Holy Spirit come into these fearful moments? How can you speak more boldly about Jesus?
- Acts of the Apostles states that people from different regions heard the Apostles speaking in their own native languages. How does Pentecost unite the nations under one Spirit?

DAY 187

Today's Mystery: **The Assumption of Mary**

Today's Prayer:
- Pray with today's sacred art in "*visio divina*," using as many or as few of the reflection questions as you find fruitful.
- Pray 1 decade of the Rosary (1 Our Father, 10 Hail Marys, and 1 Glory Be).

View Sacred Art: The Assumption

Reflect:
- Notice Mary's empty tomb at the bottom of the image with Mary above it surrounded by angels. What mystery does this depiction remind you of? How are these mysteries connected?
- Flowers are in Mary's tomb instead of her body. Notice that the flowers are lilies and roses. These flowers represent love and purity. Why are these flowers appropriate for Our Lady?
- Notice how one of the Apostles has a book open in prayer. What do you think he was reading or praying?
- Our Lady is looking up, with her arms open. Do you think she was eager to see and embrace her Son?
- See all the men have different postures. Some are looking up, some have their arms open, some are looking into the empty tomb. How do you think they felt when they realized she had been taken up to heaven?
- Notice how the angels in the image are playing instruments. What do you think the joy and celebration in heaven was like when Our Lady came?

DAY 188

Today's Mystery: The Coronation of Mary as Queen of Heaven and Earth

Today's Prayer:
- Pray with today's sacred art in "*visio divina,*" using as many or as few of the reflection questions as you find fruitful.
- Pray 1 decade of the Rosary (1 Our Father, 10 Hail Marys, and 1 Glory Be).

View Sacred Art: Mary, Queen of Heaven and Earth

Reflect:
- Notice that Our Lady and Our Lord are wearing similar crowns. How does Mary reign with Jesus? One of Our Lady's titles is "Help of Christians." How is she truly our help?
- In the kingdom of David in ancient Israel, the queen was typically the mother of the king, not his wife. This artwork emphasizes Our Lady's motherhood, since she is holding the child Jesus. How is Mary the Queen in being the Mother of Christ?
- Here Mary is shown with the child Jesus on her lap. Is it comforting to see Jesus as a young boy? How are we considered children of Mary?
- Notice the beautiful angel under Mary holding a lily and pointing to her. How is Mary's purity fruitful? How can our purity lead to much fruit?
- There are many saints present here in this painting. Some of them are looking at Mary and honoring her. Others are ministering to different people. How are these saints honoring Mary as well? How can we do the same?
- The upper part of the image shows heaven where the saints are enjoying their heavenly reward. The bottom shows others working during their earthly lives. Notice how close heaven is to them. How is heaven present on earth? How do the saints help us in our earthly lives? Does this give you hope that you can become a saint?

PHASE 4
FINDING FOCUS

Days 189 – 208

INTRODUCTION

About This Phase

Now that you have practiced many ways of meditating on the mysteries of the rosary, it's time to enter into prayer without new materials. In this phase, we will independently meditate on each mystery for 10 minutes each day, drawing on our inner "library" or "archive" of knowledge, insight, and images that we have built up over the last phase. You may find a journal to be a helpful tool.

With the foundation we have laid and the prayer "muscles" we are exercising, we are building our capacity to pray more deeply and spontaneously so that the Rosary can connect us more and more with Our Lord and Our Lady, even as we are going about daily tasks.

By the end of this phase, you will have practiced independent meditation on each mystery of the Rosary. You will be prepared to meditate more naturally while praying a full Rosary in the days to come!

PRAY	• Every day of this phase, we will spend 10 minutes in silent personal reflection meditating on the day's mystery independently. • Every day of this phase, we will continue to pray 1 decade of the Rosary (1 Our Father, 10 Hail Marys, and 1 Glory Be).

Tips for this phase
- Remember that you can focus your meditation on persons, as you learned to do in phase 1; prayers, as you learned to do in phase 2; or mysteries, as you learned to do in phase 3.
- As St. Teresa of Avila wrote, "Contemplative prayer in my opinion is nothing else than a close sharing between friends;

it means taking time frequently to be alone with him who we know loves us" (quoted in *Catechism of the Catholic Church* 2709). When it is difficult to remain focused, take this saying to heart and ask the Lord to reveal himself to you in your meditation on the day's mystery.

- If you need a refresher on the meaning of the mystery or some insights associated with it, you can reference the meditation materials from the last phase (page numbers are provided).

DAYS 189–208

DAY 189

Today's Mystery: The Annunciation

Today's Prayer:
- Spend 10 minutes meditating on today's mystery.
- Pray 1 decade of the Rosary (1 Our Father, 10 Hail Marys, and 1 Glory Be).

Note:
The goal is to meditate independently (i.e., without Scriptures, reflections, or images in front of you or read to you), drawing on your inner "library" or "archive" that you have built up over the last phase. But if you have a hard time doing this with today's mystery and would like to look back to the Scripture, reflections, or images for this mystery, you can do so here:

This mystery's Scripture passage: page 67
This mystery's reflections: page 109, 139
This mystery's sacred art: page 173, 212, 252

DAY 190

Today's Mystery: The Visitation

Today's Prayer:
- Spend 10 minutes meditating on today's mystery.
- Pray 1 decade of the Rosary (1 Our Father, 10 Hail Marys, and 1 Glory Be).

Note:
If you would like to look back to the Scripture, reflections, or images for this mystery, you can do so here:

This mystery's Scripture passage: page 68

This mystery's reflections: page 110, 141

This mystery's sacred art: page 174, 214, 254

DAY 191

Today's Mystery: The Nativity

Today's Prayer:
- Spend 10 minutes meditating on today's mystery.
- Pray 1 decade of the Rosary (1 Our Father, 10 Hail Marys, and 1 Glory Be).

Note:
If you would like to look back to the Scripture, reflections, or images for this mystery, you can do so here:

This mystery's Scripture passage: page 69

This mystery's reflections: page 112, 142

This mystery's sacred art: page 176, 216, 256

DAY 192

Today's Mystery: The Presentation of Jesus in the Temple

Today's Prayer:
- Spend 10 minutes meditating on today's mystery.
- Pray 1 decade of the Rosary (1 Our Father, 10 Hail Marys, and 1 Glory Be).

Note:
If you would like to look back to the Scripture, reflections, or images for this mystery, you can do so here:
This mystery's Scripture passage: page 70
This mystery's reflections: page 114, 144
This mystery's sacred art: page 178, 218, 258

DAY 193

Today's Mystery: The Finding of Jesus in the Temple

Today's Prayer:
- Spend 10 minutes meditating on today's mystery.
- Pray 1 decade of the Rosary (1 Our Father, 10 Hail Marys, and 1 Glory Be).

Note:
If you would like to look back to the Scripture, reflections, or images for this mystery, you can do so here:
This mystery's Scripture passage: page 71
This mystery's reflections: page 115, 146
This mystery's sacred art: page 180, 220, 260

DAY 194

Today's Mystery: The Baptism of Jesus

Today's Prayer:
- Spend 10 minutes meditating on today's mystery.
- Pray 1 decade of the Rosary (1 Our Father, 10 Hail Marys, and 1 Glory Be).

Note:
If you would like to look back to the Scripture, reflections, or images for this mystery, you can do so here:
This mystery's Scripture passage: page 72
This mystery's reflections: page 118, 147
This mystery's sacred art: page 182, 222, 262

DAY 195

Today's Mystery: The Wedding at Cana

Today's Prayer:
- Spend 10 minutes meditating on today's mystery.
- Pray 1 decade of the Rosary (1 Our Father, 10 Hail Marys, and 1 Glory Be).

Note:
If you would like to look back to the Scripture, reflections, or images for this mystery, you can do so here:
This mystery's Scripture passage: page 73
This mystery's reflections: page 119, 149
This mystery's sacred art: page 184, 224, 264

DAY 196

Today's Mystery: The Proclamation of the Kingdom and the Call to Conversion

Today's Prayer:
- Spend 10 minutes meditating on today's mystery.
- Pray 1 decade of the Rosary (1 Our Father, 10 Hail Marys, and 1 Glory Be).

Note:
If you would like to look back to the Scripture, reflections, or images for this mystery, you can do so here:

This mystery's Scripture passage: page 73
This mystery's reflections: page 121, 150
This mystery's sacred art: page 186, 226, 266

DAY 197

Today's Mystery: The Transfiguration

Today's Prayer
- Spend 10 minutes meditating on today's mystery.
- Pray 1 decade of the Rosary (1 Our Father, 10 Hail Marys, and 1 Glory Be).

Note:
If you would like to look back to the Scripture, reflections, or images for this mystery, you can do so here:

This mystery's Scripture passage: page 74
This mystery's reflections: page 122, 153
This mystery's sacred art: page 188, 228, 268

DAY 198

Today's Mystery: The Institution of the Eucharist

Today's Prayer:
- Spend 10 minutes meditating on today's mystery.
- Pray 1 decade of the Rosary (1 Our Father, 10 Hail Marys, and 1 Glory Be).

Note:
If you would like to look back to the Scripture, reflections, or images for this mystery, you can do so here:

This mystery's Scripture passage: page 74

This mystery's reflections: page 125, 155

This mystery's sacred art: page 190, 230, 270

DAY 199

Today's Mystery: The Agony in the Garden

Today's Prayer
- Spend 10 minutes meditating on today's mystery.
- Pray 1 decade of the Rosary (1 Our Father, 10 Hail Marys, and 1 Glory Be).

Note:
If you would like to look back to the Scripture, reflections, or images for this mystery, you can do so here:

This mystery's Scripture passage: page 75

This mystery's reflections: page 126, 157

This mystery's sacred art: page 192, 232, 272

DAY 200

Today's Mystery: The Scourging at the Pillar

Today's Prayer:
- Spend 10 minutes meditating on today's mystery.
- Pray 1 decade of the Rosary (1 Our Father, 10 Hail Marys, and 1 Glory Be).

Note:
If you would like to look back to the Scripture, reflections, or images for this mystery, you can do so here:

This mystery's Scripture passage: page 76
This mystery's reflections: page 127, 158
This mystery's sacred art: page 194, 234, 274

DAY 201

Today's Mystery: The Crowning with Thorns

Today's Prayer:
- Spend 10 minutes meditating on today's mystery.
- Pray 1 decade of the Rosary (1 Our Father, 10 Hail Marys, and 1 Glory Be).

Note:
If you would like to look back to the Scripture, reflections, or images for this mystery, you can do so here:

This mystery's Scripture passage: page 76
This mystery's reflections: page 128, 160
This mystery's sacred art: page 196, 236, 276

DAY 202

Today's Mystery: The Carrying of the Cross

Today's Prayer:
- Spend 10 minutes meditating on today's mystery.
- Pray 1 decade of the Rosary (1 Our Father, 10 Hail Marys, and 1 Glory Be).

Note:
If you would like to look back to the Scripture, reflections, or images for this mystery, you can do so here:
This mystery's Scripture passage: page 76
This mystery's reflections: page 129, 161
This mystery's sacred art: page 198, 238, 278

DAY 203

Today's Mystery: The Crucifixion

Today's Prayer:
- Spend 10 minutes meditating on today's mystery.
- Pray 1 decade of the Rosary (1 Our Father, 10 Hail Marys, and 1 Glory Be).

Note:
If you would like to look back to the Scripture, reflections, or images for this mystery, you can do so here:
This mystery's Scripture passage: page 77
This mystery's reflections: page 130, 162
This mystery's sacred art: page 200, 240, 280

DAY 204

Today's Mystery: **The Resurrection**

Today's Prayer:
- Spend 10 minutes meditating on today's mystery.
- Pray 1 decade of the Rosary (1 Our Father, 10 Hail Marys, and 1 Glory Be).

Note:
If you would like to look back to the Scripture, reflections, or images for this mystery, you can do so here:

This mystery's Scripture passage: page 77

This mystery's reflections: page 132, 164

This mystery's sacred art: page 202, 242, 282

DAY 205

Today's Mystery: **The Ascension**

Today's Prayer:
Spend 10 minutes meditating on today's mystery.

Pray 1 decade of the Rosary (1 Our Father, 10 Hail Marys, and 1 Glory Be).

Note:
If you would like to look back to the Scripture, reflections, or images for this mystery, you can do so here:

This mystery's Scripture passage: page 78

This mystery's reflections: page 134, 165

This mystery's sacred art: page 204, 244, 284

DAY 206

Today's Mystery: The Descent of the Holy Spirit on Pentecost

Today's Prayer:
Spend 10 minutes meditating on today's mystery.
Pray 1 decade of the Rosary (1 Our Father, 10 Hail Marys, and 1 Glory Be).

Note:
If you would like to look back to the Scripture, reflections, or images for this mystery, you can do so here:
This mystery's Scripture passage: page 78
This mystery's reflections: page 135, 167
This mystery's sacred art: page 206, 246, 286

DAY 207

Today's Mystery: The Assumption of Mary

Today's Prayer:
Spend 10 minutes meditating on today's mystery.
Pray 1 decade of the Rosary (1 Our Father, 10 Hail Marys, and 1 Glory Be).

Note:
If you would like to look back to the Scripture, reflections, or images for this mystery, you can do so here:
This mystery's Scripture passage: page 79
This mystery's reflections: page 136, 169
This mystery's sacred art: page 208, 248, 288

DAY 208

Today's Mystery: The Coronation of Mary as Queen of Heaven and Earth

Today's Prayer:
- Spend 10 minutes meditating on today's mystery.
- Pray 1 decade of the Rosary (1 Our Father, 10 Hail Marys, and 1 Glory Be).

Note:
If you would like to look back to the Scripture, reflections, or images for this mystery, you can do so here:

This mystery's Scripture passage: page 80

This mystery's reflections: page 137, 171

This mystery's sacred art: page 210, 250, 290

PHASE 5
BUILDING UP THE DECADES

Days 209 – 335

INTRODUCTION

About This Phase

In the past two phases, we have learned different ways to meditate on the mysteries of the rosary and begun to practice independent meditation. Now, it is time to apply those skills and slowly increase the number of mysteries (and decades) we are praying each day!

First, we will begin meditating on the mysteries of the rosary *while praying the prayers.* This is an acquired skill. If you struggle with this, have no fear; there will be advice along the way!

Second, we will slowly add to the number of decades we are praying each day. We will pray two decades a day on Days 209–243, three decades a day on Days 244–273, four decades a day on Days 274–303, and five decades a day on Days 304–335.

By the end of this phase, you will have practiced personal meditation on each mystery of the Rosary. You will be prepared to meditate more easily while praying a full Rosary in the days to come!

PRAY	<ul><li>Every day of this phase, we will meditate on the day's mysteries while praying the prayers of the Rosary.</li><li>Every day of this phase, we will pray several decades of the Rosary, building up from 2 to 5 through the coming weeks.</li></ul>

Tips for this phase

- Combining meditation on the mysteries with the vocal prayers of the Rosary can be difficult. When struggling, ask the Holy Spirit and the Blessed Mother for help, and listen for advice from Fr. Mark-Mary!

- Don't be afraid to refer back to your notes or the materials for meditation if you seem to notice that you struggle with meditating on a particular mystery time and again.
- If you are keeping a journal, you will likely find new insights on the mysteries to add to your journal each time you pray the Rosary. This is part of the beauty of this prayer.
- Continue to keep up with the habit you built at the beginning of *The Rosary in a Year*, including praying at a consistent time of day that works for you. As the time commitment increases with more decades, this habit will ensure that you stick with your daily Rosary!

DAYS 209–335

DAY 209

Today's Mysteries:
- The Annunciation
- The Visitation

Today's Prayer: Pray 2 decades of the Rosary while meditating on today's mysteries.

DAY 210

Today's Mysteries:
- The Nativity
- The Presentation of Jesus in the Temple

Today's Prayer: Pray 2 decades of the Rosary while meditating on today's mysteries.

DAY 211

Today's Mysteries:
- The Finding of Jesus in the Temple
- The Baptism of Jesus

Today's Prayer: Pray 2 decades of the Rosary while meditating on today's mysteries.

DAY 212

Today's Mysteries:
- The Wedding at Cana
- The Proclamation of the Kingdom and the Call to Conversion

Today's Prayer: Pray 2 decades of the Rosary while meditating on today's mysteries.

DAY 213

Today's Mysteries:
- The Transfiguration
- The Institution of the Eucharist

Today's Prayer: Pray 2 decades of the Rosary while meditating on today's mysteries.

DAY 214

Today's Mysteries:
- The Agony in the Garden
- The Scourging at the Pillar

Today's Prayer: Pray 2 decades of the Rosary while meditating on today's mysteries.

DAY 215

Today's Mysteries:
- The Crowning with Thorns
- The Carrying of the Cross

Today's Prayer: Pray 2 decades of the Rosary while meditating on today's mysteries.

DAY 216

Today's Mysteries:
- The Crucifixion
- The Resurrection

Today's Prayer: Pray 2 decades of the Rosary while meditating on today's mysteries.

DAY 217

Today's Mysteries:
- The Ascension
- The Descent of the Holy Spirit on Pentecost

Today's Prayer: Pray 2 decades of the Rosary while meditating on today's mysteries.

DAY 218

Today's Mysteries:
- The Assumption of Mary
- The Coronation of Mary as Queen of Heaven and Earth

Today's Prayer: Pray 2 decades of the Rosary while meditating on today's mysteries.

DAY 219

Today's Mysteries
- The Annunciation
- The Visitation

Today's Prayer: Pray 2 decades of the Rosary while meditating on today's mysteries.

DAY 220

Today's Mysteries
- The Nativity
- The Presentation of Jesus in the Temple

Today's Prayer: Pray 2 decades of the Rosary while meditating on today's mysteries.

DAY 221

Today's Mysteries:
- The Finding of Jesus in the Temple
- The Baptism of the Lord

Today's Prayer: Pray 2 decades of the Rosary while meditating on today's mysteries.

DAY 222

Today's Mysteries:
- The Wedding at Cana
- The Proclamation of the Kingdom and the Call to Conversion

Today's Prayer: Pray 2 decades of the Rosary while meditating on today's mysteries.

DAY 223

Today's Mysteries:
- The Transfiguration
- The Institution of the Eucharist

Today's Prayer: Pray 2 decades of the Rosary while meditating on today's mysteries.

DAY 224

Today's Mysteries:
- The Agony in the Garden
- The Scourging at the Pillar

Today's Prayer: Pray 2 decades of the Rosary while meditating on today's mysteries.

DAY 225

Today's Mysteries:
- The Crowning with Thorns
- The Carrying of the Cross

Today's Prayer: Pray 2 decades of the Rosary while meditating on today's mysteries.

DAY 226

Today's Mysteries:
- The Crucifixion
- The Resurrection

Today's Prayer: Pray 2 decades of the Rosary while meditating on today's mysteries.

DAY 227

Today's Mysteries:
- The Ascension
- The Descent of the Holy Spirit on Pentecost

Today's Prayer: Pray 2 decades of the Rosary while meditating on today's mysteries.

DAY 228

Today's Mysteries:
- The Assumption of Mary
- The Coronation of Mary as Queen of Heaven and Earth

Today's Prayer: Pray 2 decades of the Rosary while meditating on today's mysteries.

DAY 229

Today's Mysteries:
- The Annunciation
- The Visitation

Today's Prayer: Pray 2 decades of the Rosary while meditating on today's mysteries.

DAY 230

Today's Mysteries:
- The Nativity
- The Presentation of Jesus in the Temple

Today's Prayer: Pray 2 decades of the Rosary while meditating on today's mysteries.

DAY 231

Today's Mysteries:
- The Finding of Jesus in the Temple
- The Baptism of the Lord

Today's Prayer: Pray 2 decades of the Rosary while meditating on today's mysteries.

DAY 232

Today's Mysteries:
- The Wedding at Cana
- The Proclamation of the Kingdom and the Call to Conversion

Today's Prayer: Pray 2 decades of the Rosary while meditating on today's mysteries.

DAY 233

Today's Mysteries:
- The Transfiguration
- The Institution of the Eucharist

Today's Prayer: Pray 2 decades of the Rosary while meditating on today's mysteries.

DAY 234

Today's Mysteries:
- The Agony in the Garden
- The Scourging at the Pillar

Today's Prayer: Pray 2 decades of the Rosary while meditating on today's mysteries.

DAY 235

Today's Mysteries:
- The Crowning with Thorns
- The Carrying of the Cross

Today's Prayer: Pray 2 decades of the Rosary while meditating on today's mysteries.

DAY 236

Today's Mysteries:
- The Crucifixion
- The Resurrection

Today's Prayer: Pray 2 decades of the Rosary while meditating on today's mysteries.

DAY 237

Today's Mysteries:
- The Ascension
- The Descent of the Holy Spirit on Pentecost

Today's Prayer: Pray 2 decades of the Rosary while meditating on today's mysteries.

DAY 238

Today's Mysteries:
- The Assumption of Mary
- The Coronation of Mary as Queen of Heaven and Earth

Today's Prayer: Pray 2 decades of the Rosary while meditating on today's mysteries.

DAY 239

Today's Mysteries:
- The Annunciation
- The Visitation

Today's Prayer: Pray 2 decades of the Rosary while meditating on today's mysteries.

DAY 240

Today's Mysteries:
- The Nativity
- The Presentation of Jesus in the Temple

Today's Prayer: Pray 2 decades of the Rosary while meditating on today's mysteries.

DAY 241

Today's Mysteries:
- The Finding of Jesus in the Temple
- The Baptism of the Lord

Today's Prayer: Pray 2 decades of the Rosary while meditating on today's mysteries.

DAY 242

Today's Mysteries:
- The Wedding at Cana
- The Proclamation of the Kingdom and the Call to Conversion

Today's Prayer: Pray 2 decades of the Rosary while meditating on today's mysteries.

DAY 243

Today's Mysteries:
- The Transfiguration
- The Institution of the Eucharist

Today's Prayer: Pray 2 decades of the Rosary while meditating on today's mysteries.

DAY 244

Today's Mysteries:
- The Agony in the Garden
- The Scourging at the Pillar
- The Crowning with Thorns

Today we begin praying 3 decades as we continue our "slow build."

Today's Prayer: Pray 3 decades of the Rosary while meditating on today's mysteries.

DAY 245

Today's Mysteries:
- The Carrying of the Cross
- The Crucifixion
- The Resurrection

Today's Prayer: Pray 3 decades of the Rosary while meditating on today's mysteries.

DAY 246

Today's Mysteries:
- The Ascension
- The Descent of the Holy Spirit on Pentecost
- The Assumption of Mary

Today's Prayer: Pray 3 decades of the Rosary while meditating on today's mysteries.

DAY 247

Today's Mysteries:
- The Coronation of Mary as Queen of Heaven and Earth
- The Annunciation
- The Visitation

Today's Prayer: Pray 3 decades of the Rosary while meditating on today's mysteries.

DAY 248

Today's Mysteries:
- The Nativity
- The Presentation of Jesus in the Temple
- The Finding of Jesus in the Temple

Today's Prayer: Pray 3 decades of the Rosary while meditating on today's mysteries.

DAY 249

Today's Mysteries:
- The Baptism of Jesus
- The Wedding at Cana
- The Proclamation of the Kingdom and the Call to Conversion

Today's Prayer: Pray 3 decades of the Rosary while meditating on today's mysteries.

DAY 250

Today's Mysteries:
- The Transfiguration
- The Institution of the Eucharist
- The Agony in the Garden

Today's Prayer: Pray 3 decades of the Rosary while meditating on today's mysteries.

DAY 251

Today's Mysteries:
- The Scourging at the Pillar
- The Crowning with Thorns
- The Carrying of the Cross

Today's Prayer: Pray 3 decades of the Rosary while meditating on today's mysteries.

DAY 252

Today's Mysteries:
- The Crucifixion
- The Resurrection
- The Ascension

Today's Prayer: Pray 3 decades of the Rosary while meditating on today's mysteries.

DAY 253

Today's Mysteries:
- The Descent of the Holy Spirit on Pentecost
- The Assumption of Mary
- The Coronation of Mary

Today's Prayer: Pray 3 decades of the Rosary while meditating on today's mysteries.

DAY 254

Today's Mysteries:
- The Annunciation
- The Visitation
- The Nativity

Today's Prayer: Pray 3 decades of the Rosary while meditating on today's mysteries.

DAY 255

Today's Mysteries:
- The Presentation of Jesus in the Temple
- The Finding of Jesus in the Temple
- The Baptism of the Lord

Today's Prayer: Pray 3 decades of the Rosary while meditating on today's mysteries.

DAY 256

Today's Mysteries:
- The Wedding at Cana
- The Proclamation of the Kingdom
- The Transfiguration

Today's Prayer: Pray 3 decades of the Rosary while meditating on today's mysteries.

DAY 257

Today's Mysteries:
- The Institution of the Eucharist
- The Agony in the Garden
- The Scourging at the Pillar

Today's Prayer: Pray 3 decades of the Rosary while meditating on today's mysteries.

DAY 258

Today's Mysteries:
- The Crowning with Thorns
- The Carrying of the Cross
- The Crucifixion

Today's Prayer: Pray 3 decades of the Rosary while meditating on today's mysteries.

DAY 259

Today's Mysteries:
- The Resurrection
- The Ascension
- The Descent of the Holy Spirit

Today's Prayer: Pray 3 decades of the Rosary while meditating on today's mysteries.

DAY 260

Today's Mysteries:
- The Assumption of Mary
- The Coronation of Mary as Queen of Heaven and Earth
- The Annunciation

Today's Prayer: Pray 3 decades of the Rosary while meditating on today's mysteries.

DAY 261

Today's Mysteries:
- The Visitation
- The Nativity
- The Presentation of Jesus in the Temple

Today's Prayer: Pray 3 decades of the Rosary while meditating on today's mysteries.

DAY 262

Today's Mysteries:
- The Finding of Jesus in the Temple
- The Baptism of the Lord
- The Wedding at Cana

Today's Prayer: Pray 3 decades of the Rosary while meditating on today's mysteries.

DAY 263

Today's Mysteries:
- The Proclamation of the Kingdom and the Call to Conversion
- The Transfiguration
- The Institution of the Eucharist

Today's Prayer: Pray 3 decades of the Rosary while meditating on today's mysteries.

DAY 264

Today's Mysteries:
- The Agony in the Garden
- The Scourging at the Pillar
- The Crowning with Thorns

Today's Prayer: Pray 3 decades of the Rosary while meditating on today's mysteries.

DAY 265

Today's Mysteries:
- The Carrying of the Cross
- The Crucifixion
- The Resurrection

Today's Prayer: Pray 3 decades of the Rosary while meditating on today's mysteries.

DAY 266

Today's Mysteries:
- The Ascension
- The Descent of the Holy Spirit on Pentecost
- The Assumption of Mary

Today's Prayer: Pray 3 decades of the Rosary while meditating on today's mysteries.

DAY 267

Today's Mysteries:
- The Coronation of Mary as Queen of Heaven and Earth
- The Annunciation
- The Visitation

Today's Prayer: Pray 3 decades of the Rosary while meditating on today's mysteries.

DAY 268

Today's Mysteries:
- The Nativity
- The Presentation of Jesus in the Temple
- The Finding of Jesus in the Temple

Today's Prayer: Pray 3 decades of the Rosary while meditating on today's mysteries.

DAY 269

Today's Mysteries:
- The Baptism of Jesus
- The Wedding at Cana
- The Proclamation of the Kingdom and the Call to Conversion

Today's Prayer: Pray 3 decades of the Rosary while meditating on today's mysteries.

DAY 270

Today's Mysteries:
- The Transfiguration
- The Institution of the Eucharist
- The Agony in the Garden

Today's Prayer: Pray 3 decades of the Rosary while meditating on today's mysteries.

DAY 271

Today's Mysteries:
- The Scourging at the Pillar
- The Crowning with Thorns
- The Carrying of the Cross

Today's Prayer: Pray 3 decades of the Rosary while meditating on today's mysteries.

DAY 272

Today's Mysteries:
- The Crucifixion
- The Resurrection
- The Ascension

Today's Prayer: Pray 3 decades of the Rosary while meditating on today's mysteries.

DAY 273

Today's Mysteries:
- The Descent of the Holy Spirit on Pentecost
- The Assumption of Mary
- The Coronation of Mary as Queen of Heaven and Earth

Today's Prayer: Pray 3 decades of the Rosary while meditating on today's mysteries.

DAY 274

Today's Mysteries:
- The Annunciation
- The Visitation
- The Nativity
- The Presentation of Jesus in the Temple

Today we begin praying 4 decades as we continue our "slow build."

Today's Prayer: Pray 4 decades of the Rosary while meditating on today's mysteries.

DAY 275

Today's Mysteries:
- The Finding of Jesus in the Temple
- The Baptism of Jesus
- The Wedding at Cana
- The Proclamation of the Kingdom and the Call to Conversion

Today's Prayer: Pray 4 decades of the Rosary while meditating on today's mysteries.

DAY 276

Today's Mysteries:
- The Transfiguration
- The Institution of the Eucharist
- The Agony in the Garden
- The Scourging at the Pillar

Today's Prayer: Pray 4 decades of the Rosary while meditating on today's mysteries.

DAY 277

Today's Mysteries:
- The Crowning with Thorns
- The Carrying of the Cross
- The Crucifixion
- The Resurrection

Today's Prayer: Pray 4 decades of the Rosary while meditating on today's mysteries.

DAY 278

Today's Mysteries:
- The Ascension
- The Descent of the Holy Spirit on Pentecost
- The Assumption of Mary
- The Coronation of Mary as Queen of Heaven and Earth

Today's Prayer: Pray 4 decades of the Rosary while meditating on today's mysteries.

DAY 279

Today's Mysteries:
- The Annunciation
- The Visitation
- The Nativity
- The Presentation of Jesus in the Temple

Today's Prayer: Pray 4 decades of the Rosary while meditating on today's mysteries.

DAY 280

Today's Mysteries:
- The Finding of Jesus in the Temple
- The Baptism of Jesus
- The Wedding at Cana
- The Proclamation of the Kingdom and the Call to Conversion

Today's Prayer: Pray 4 decades of the Rosary while meditating on today's mysteries.

DAY 281

Today's Mysteries:
- The Transfiguration
- The Institution of the Eucharist
- The Agony in the Garden
- The Scourging at the Pillar

Today's Prayer: Pray 4 decades of the Rosary while meditating on today's mysteries.

DAY 282

Today's Mysteries:
- The Crowning with Thorns
- The Carrying of the Cross
- The Crucifixion
- The Resurrection

Today's Prayer: Pray 4 decades of the Rosary while meditating on today's mysteries.

DAY 283

Today's Mysteries:
- The Ascension
- The Descent of the Holy Spirit on Pentecost
- The Assumption of Mary
- The Coronation of Mary as Queen of Heaven and Earth

Today's Prayer: Pray 4 decades of the Rosary while meditating on today's mysteries.

DAY 284

Today's Mysteries:
- The Annunciation
- The Visitation
- The Nativity
- The Presentation of Jesus in the Temple

Today's Prayer: Pray 4 decades of the Rosary while meditating on today's mysteries.

DAY 285

Today's Mysteries:
- The Finding of Jesus in the Temple
- The Baptism of Jesus
- The Wedding at Cana
- The Proclamation of the Kingdom and the Call to Conversion

Today's Prayer: Pray 4 decades of the Rosary while meditating on today's mysteries.

DAY 286

Today's Mysteries:
- The Transfiguration
- The Institution of the Eucharist
- The Agony in the Garden
- The Scourging at the Pillar

Today's Prayer: Pray 4 decades of the Rosary while meditating on today's mysteries.

DAY 287

Today's Mysteries:
- The Crowning with Thorns
- The Carrying of the Cross
- The Crucifixion
- The Resurrection

Today's Prayer: Pray 4 decades of the Rosary while meditating on today's mysteries.

DAY 288

Today's Mysteries:
- The Ascension
- The Descent of the Holy Spirit on Pentecost
- The Assumption of Mary
- The Coronation of Mary as Queen of Heaven and Earth

Today's Prayer: Pray 4 decades of the Rosary while meditating on today's mysteries.

DAY 289

Today's Mysteries:
- The Annunciation
- The Visitation
- The Nativity
- The Presentation of Jesus in the Temple

Today's Prayer: Pray 4 decades of the Rosary while meditating on today's mysteries.

DAY 290

Today's Mysteries:
- The Finding of Jesus in the Temple
- The Baptism of Jesus
- The Wedding at Cana
- The Proclamation of the Kingdom and the Call to Conversion

Today's Prayer: Pray 4 decades of the Rosary while meditating on today's mysteries.

DAY 291

Today's Mysteries:
- The Transfiguration
- The Institution of the Eucharist
- The Agony in the Garden
- The Scourging at the Pillar

Today's Prayer: Pray 4 decades of the Rosary while meditating on today's mysteries.

DAY 292

Today's Mysteries:
- The Crowning with Thorns
- The Carrying of the Cross
- The Crucifixion
- The Resurrection

Today's Prayer: Pray 4 decades of the Rosary while meditating on today's mysteries.

DAY 293

Today's Mysteries:
- The Ascension
- The Descent of the Holy Spirit on Pentecost
- The Assumption of Mary
- The Coronation of Mary as Queen of Heaven and Earth

Today's Prayer: Pray 4 decades of the Rosary while meditating on today's mysteries.

DAY 294

Today's Mysteries:
- The Annunciation
- The Visitation
- The Nativity
- The Presentation of Jesus in the Temple

Today's Prayer: Pray 4 decades of the Rosary while meditating on today's mysteries.

DAY 295

Today's Mysteries:
- The Finding of Jesus in the Temple
- The Baptism of Jesus
- The Wedding at Cana
- The Proclamation of the Kingdom and the Call to Conversion

Today's Prayer: Pray 4 decades of the Rosary while meditating on today's mysteries.

DAY 296

Today's Mysteries:
- The Transfiguration
- The Institution of the Eucharist
- The Agony in the Garden
- The Scourging at the Pillar

Today's Prayer: Pray 4 decades of the Rosary while meditating on today's mysteries.

DAY 297

Today's Mysteries:
- The Crowning with Thorns
- The Carrying of the Cross
- The Crucifixion
- The Resurrection

Today's Prayer: Pray 4 decades of the Rosary while meditating on today's mysteries.

DAY 298

Today's Mysteries:
- The Ascension
- The Descent of the Holy Spirit on Pentecost
- The Assumption of Mary
- The Coronation of Mary as Queen of Heaven and Earth

Today's Prayer: Pray 4 decades of the Rosary while meditating on today's mysteries.

DAY 299

Today's Mysteries:
- The Annunciation
- The Visitation
- The Nativity
- The Presentation of Jesus in the Temple

Today's Prayer: Pray 4 decades of the Rosary while meditating on today's mysteries.

DAY 300

Today's Mysteries:
- The Finding of Jesus in the Temple
- The Baptism of Jesus
- The Wedding at Cana
- The Proclamation of the Kingdom and the Call to Conversion

Today's Prayer: Pray 4 decades of the Rosary while meditating on today's mysteries.

DAY 301

Today's Mysteries:
- The Transfiguration
- The Institution of the Eucharist
- The Agony in the Garden
- The Scourging at the Pillar

Today's Prayer: Pray 4 decades of the Rosary while meditating on today's mysteries.

DAY 302

Today's Mysteries:
- The Crowning with Thorns
- The Carrying of the Cross
- The Crucifixion
- The Resurrection

Today's Prayer: Pray 4 decades of the Rosary while meditating on today's mysteries.

DAY 303

Today's Mysteries:
- The Ascension
- The Descent of the Holy Spirit on Pentecost
- The Assumption of Mary
- The Coronation of Mary as Queen of Heaven and Earth

Today's Prayer: Pray 4 decades of the Rosary while meditating on today's mysteries.

DAY 304

Today's Mysteries:
- The Annunciation
- The Visitation
- The Nativity
- The Presentation of Jesus in the Temple
- The Finding of Jesus in the Temple

Today we begin praying 5 decades. This is the last step in our "slow build"!

Today's Prayer: Pray 5 decades of the Rosary while meditating on today's mysteries.

DAY 305

Today's Mysteries:
- The Baptism of Jesus
- The Wedding at Cana
- The Proclamation of the Kingdom and the Call to Conversion
- The Transfiguration
- The Institution of the Eucharist

Today's Prayer: Pray 5 decades of the Rosary while meditating on today's mysteries.

DAY 306

Today's Mysteries:
- The Agony in the Garden
- The Scourging at the Pillar
- The Crowning with Thorns
- The Carrying of the Cross
- The Crucifixion

Today's Prayer: Pray 5 decades of the Rosary while meditating on today's mysteries.

DAY 307

Today's Mysteries:
- The Resurrection
- The Ascension
- The Descent of the Holy Spirit
- The Assumption of Mary
- The Coronation of Mary as Queen of Heaven and Earth

Today's Prayer: Pray 5 decades of the Rosary while meditating on today's mysteries.

DAY 308

Today's Mysteries:
- The Annunciation
- The Visitation
- The Nativity
- The Presentation of Jesus in the Temple
- The Finding of Jesus in the Temple

Today's Prayer: Pray 5 decades of the Rosary while meditating on today's mysteries.

DAY 309

Today's Mysteries:
- The Baptism of Jesus
- The Wedding at Cana
- The Proclamation of the Kingdom and the Call to Conversion
- The Transfiguration
- The Institution of the Eucharist

Today's Prayer: Pray 5 decades of the Rosary while meditating on today's mysteries.

DAY 310

Today's Mysteries:
- The Agony in the Garden
- The Scourging at the Pillar
- The Crowning with Thorns
- The Carrying of the Cross
- The Crucifixion

Today's Prayer: Pray 5 decades of the Rosary while meditating on today's mysteries.

DAY 311

Today's Mysteries:
- The Resurrection
- The Ascension
- The Descent of the Holy Spirit
- The Assumption of Mary
- The Coronation of Mary as Queen of Heaven and Earth

Today's Prayer: Pray 5 decades of the Rosary while meditating on today's mysteries.

DAY 312

Today's Mysteries:
- The Annunciation
- The Visitation
- The Nativity
- The Presentation of Jesus in the Temple
- The Finding of Jesus in the Temple

Today's Prayer: Pray 5 decades of the Rosary while meditating on today's mysteries.

DAY 313

Today's Mysteries:
- The Baptism of Jesus
- The Wedding at Cana
- The Proclamation of the Kingdom and the Call to Conversion
- The Transfiguration
- The Institution of the Eucharist

Today's Prayer: Pray 5 decades of the Rosary while meditating on today's mysteries.

DAY 314

Today's Mysteries:
- The Agony in the Garden
- The Scourging at the Pillar
- The Crowning with Thorns
- The Carrying of the Cross
- The Crucifixion

Today's Prayer: Pray 5 decades of the Rosary while meditating on today's mysteries.

DAY 315

Today's Mysteries:
- The Resurrection
- The Ascension
- The Descent of the Holy Spirit
- The Assumption of Mary
- The Coronation of Mary as Queen of Heaven and Earth

Today's Prayer: Pray 5 decades of the Rosary while meditating on today's mysteries.

DAY 316

Today's Mysteries:
- The Annunciation
- The Visitation
- The Nativity
- The Presentation of Jesus in the Temple
- The Finding of Jesus in the Temple

Today's Prayer: Pray 5 decades of the Rosary while meditating on today's mysteries.

DAY 317

Today's Mysteries:
- The Baptism of Jesus
- The Wedding at Cana
- The Proclamation of the Kingdom and the Call to Conversion
- The Transfiguration
- The Institution of the Eucharist

Today's Prayer: Pray 5 decades of the Rosary while meditating on today's mysteries.

DAY 318

Today's Mysteries:
- The Agony in the Garden
- The Scourging at the Pillar
- The Crowning with Thorns
- The Carrying of the Cross
- The Crucifixion

Today's Prayer: Pray 5 decades of the Rosary while meditating on today's mysteries.

DAY 319

Today's Mysteries:
- The Resurrection
- The Ascension
- The Descent of the Holy Spirit
- The Assumption of Mary
- The Coronation of Mary as Queen of Heaven and Earth

Today's Prayer: Pray 5 decades of the Rosary while meditating on today's mysteries.

DAY 320

Today's Mysteries:
- The Annunciation
- The Visitation
- The Nativity
- The Presentation of Jesus in the Temple
- The Finding of Jesus in the Temple

Today's Prayer: Pray 5 decades of the Rosary while meditating on today's mysteries.

DAY 321

Today's Mysteries:
- The Baptism of Jesus
- The Wedding at Cana
- The Proclamation of the Kingdom and the Call to Conversion
- The Transfiguration
- The Institution of the Eucharist

Today's Prayer: Pray 5 decades of the Rosary while meditating on today's mysteries.

DAY 322

Today's Mysteries:
- The Agony in the Garden
- The Scourging at the Pillar
- The Crowning with Thorns
- The Carrying of the Cross
- The Crucifixion

Today's Prayer: Pray 5 decades of the Rosary while meditating on today's mysteries.

DAY 323

Today's Mysteries:
- The Resurrection
- The Ascension
- The Descent of the Holy Spirit
- The Assumption of Mary
- The Coronation of Mary as Queen of Heaven and Earth

Today's Prayer: Pray 5 decades of the Rosary while meditating on today's mysteries.

DAY 324

Today's Mysteries:
- The Annunciation
- The Visitation
- The Nativity
- The Presentation of Jesus in the Temple
- The Finding of Jesus in the Temple

Today's Prayer: Pray 5 decades of the Rosary while meditating on today's mysteries.

DAY 325

Today's Mysteries:
- The Baptism of Jesus
- The Wedding at Cana
- The Proclamation of the Kingdom and the Call to Conversion
- The Transfiguration
- The Institution of the Eucharist

Today's Prayer: Pray 5 decades of the Rosary while meditating on today's mysteries.

DAY 326

Today's Mysteries:
- The Agony in the Garden
- The Scourging at the Pillar
- The Crowning with Thorns
- The Carrying of the Cross
- The Crucifixion

Today's Prayer: Pray 5 decades of the Rosary while meditating on today's mysteries.

DAY 327

Today's Mysteries:
- The Resurrection
- The Ascension
- The Descent of the Holy Spirit
- The Assumption of Mary
- The Coronation of Mary as Queen of Heaven and Earth

Today's Prayer: Pray 5 decades of the Rosary while meditating on today's mysteries.

DAY 328

Today's Mysteries:
- The Annunciation
- The Visitation
- The Nativity
- The Presentation of Jesus in the Temple
- The Finding of Jesus in the Temple

Today's Prayer: Pray 5 decades of the Rosary while meditating on today's mysteries.

DAY 329

Today's Mysteries:
- The Baptism of Jesus
- The Wedding at Cana
- The Proclamation of the Kingdom and the Call to Conversion
- The Transfiguration
- The Institution of the Eucharist

Today's Prayer: Pray 5 decades of the Rosary while meditating on today's mysteries.

DAY 330

Today's Mysteries:
- The Agony in the Garden
- The Scourging at the Pillar
- The Crowning with Thorns
- The Carrying of the Cross
- The Crucifixion

Today's Prayer: Pray 5 decades of the Rosary while meditating on today's mysteries.

DAY 331

Today's Mysteries:
- The Resurrection
- The Ascension
- The Descent of the Holy Spirit
- The Assumption of Mary
- The Coronation of Mary as Queen of Heaven and Earth

Today's Prayer: Pray 5 decades of the Rosary while meditating on today's mysteries.

DAY 332

Today's Mysteries:
- The Annunciation
- The Visitation
- The Nativity
- The Presentation of Jesus in the Temple
- The Finding of Jesus in the Temple

Today's Prayer: Pray 5 decades of the Rosary while meditating on today's mysteries.

DAY 333

Today's Mysteries:
- The Baptism of Jesus
- The Wedding at Cana
- The Proclamation of the Kingdom and the Call to Conversion
- The Transfiguration
- The Institution of the Eucharist

Today's Prayer: Pray 5 decades of the Rosary while meditating on today's mysteries.

DAY 334

Today's Mysteries:
- The Agony in the Garden
- The Scourging at the Pillar
- The Crowning with Thorns
- The Carrying of the Cross
- The Crucifixion

Today's Prayer: Pray 5 decades of the Rosary while meditating on today's mysteries.

DAY 335

Today's Mysteries:
- The Resurrection
- The Ascension
- The Descent of the Holy Spirit
- The Assumption of Mary
- The Coronation of Mary as Queen of Heaven and Earth

Today's Prayer: Pray 5 decades of the Rosary while meditating on today's mysteries.

PHASE 6
PRAYING TOGETHER

Days 336 – 365

INTRODUCTION

About This Phase

During the final thirty days of the year, we will pray a 5-decade daily Rosary, using the skills and tools we've developed throughout the year.

We will begin praying the 5-decade Rosary, including the introductory and concluding prayers. You have been preparing to pray a full Rosary as you slowly built up to saying 5 decades a day in the last phase. If you struggle with this, have no fear; there will be advice along the way!

In addition, we will start praying the mysteries associated with each day of the week, rather than assigned mysteries. This way, you will be praying the mysteries of the day with Catholics around the world.

By the end of this phase, you will have prayed a daily Rosary faithfully for a month, in addition to all the work you have done to build the habit and practice meditation. You will be praying the Rosary like never before!

| **PRAY** | Every day of this phase, we will pray a 5-decade Rosary, including the introductory and concluding prayers. We will meditate on the mysteries of the day as we pray the prayers of the Rosary. |

Tips for this phase

- If you have trouble remembering which mysteries to pray each day of the week, refer to the chart on the following page.
- The longer introductory and concluding prayers of the Rosary can be difficult to memorize. In the following pages, these prayers are printed out for you.
- At this point in *The Rosary in a Year*, you have faithfully been

praying for almost a year! If the time of day you selected is not working anymore due to the longer time commitment, don't be afraid to revisit and find a new time that works for you.
- We have included a chart for you in the following pages to fill in the mystery assignments for each day and track your progress as you finish the podcast.
- Keep up the habit. As we have discovered this year, there are so many rich graces available through the power of the Rosary. After the podcast ends, continue praying the Rosary for yourself, for your friends and relatives, and for the Church!

WHEN TO PRAY EACH SET OF MYSTERIES

- **Sundays**: glorious mysteries*
- **Mondays**: joyful mysteries
- **Tuesdays**: sorrowful mysteries
- **Wednesdays**: glorious mysteries
- **Thursdays**: luminous mysteries
- **Fridays**: sorrowful mysteries
- **Saturdays**: joyful mysteries

Optionally, the joyful mysteries may be prayed on Sundays in Advent, and the sorrowful mysteries may be prayed on Sundays in Lent.

DAYS 336–365

Every day, we will pray a 5-decade Rosary, including the introductory and concluding prayers. We will meditate on the mysteries of the day as we pray the prayers of the Rosary. You can fill out the chart on the following pages to remind yourself of the day's mysteries and keep track of your progress.

	Day of the Week	Mysteries to Pray Today
DAY 336		
DAY 337		
DAY 338		
DAY 339		
DAY 340		
DAY 341		
DAY 342		

Phase 6: Praying Together   363

	Day of the Week	Mysteries to Pray Today
DAY 343		
DAY 344		
DAY 345		
DAY 346		
DAY 347		
DAY 348		
DAY 349		
DAY 350		
DAY 351		
DAY 352		

	Day of the Week	Mysteries to Pray Today
DAY 353		
DAY 354		
DAY 355		
DAY 356		
DAY 357		
DAY 358		
DAY 359		
DAY 360		
DAY 361		
DAY 362		

Phase 6: Praying Together

	Day of the Week	Mysteries to Pray Today
DAY 363		
DAY 364		
DAY 365		

HOW TO PRAY THE ROSARY

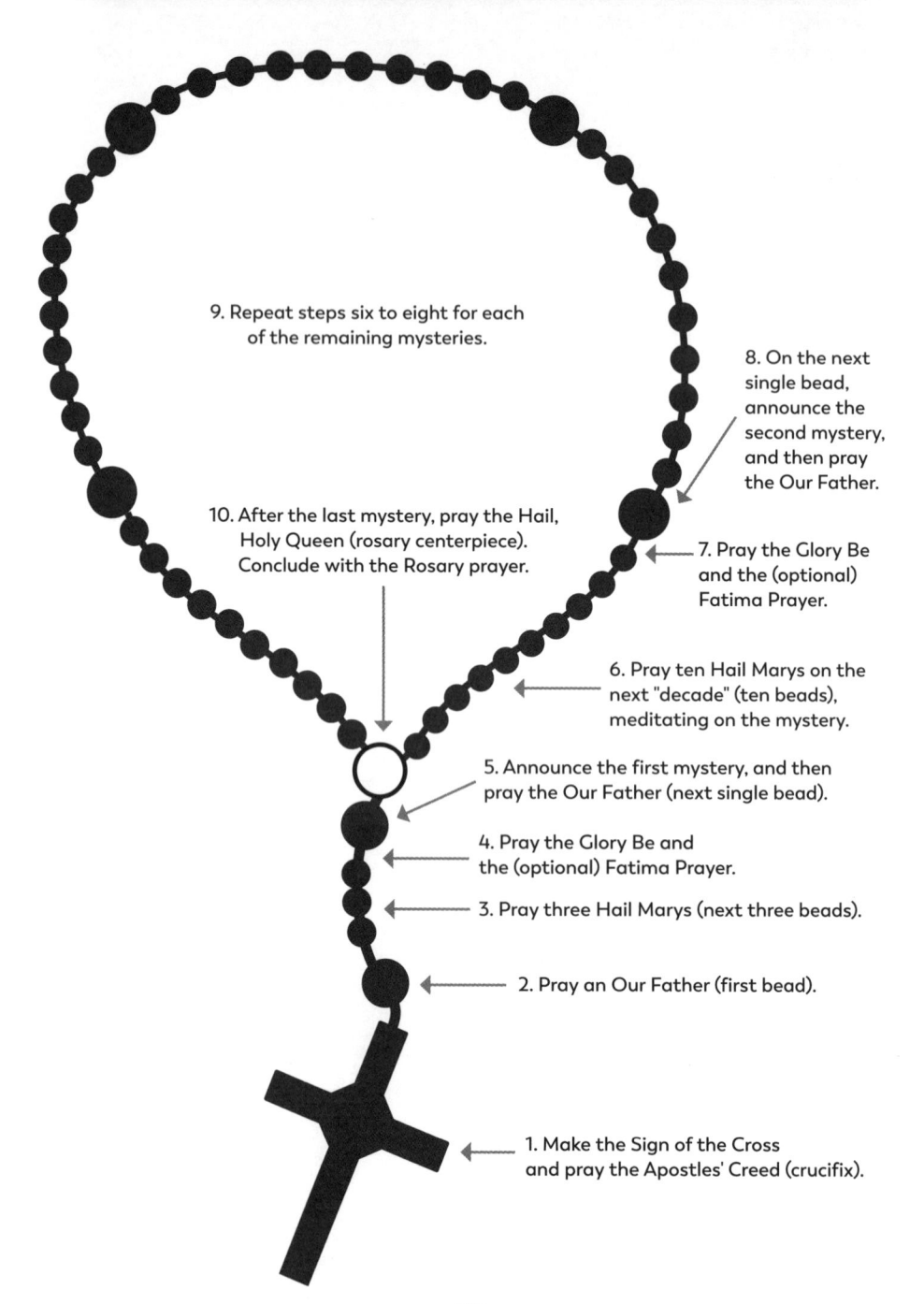

9. Repeat steps six to eight for each of the remaining mysteries.

8. On the next single bead, announce the second mystery, and then pray the Our Father.

10. After the last mystery, pray the Hail, Holy Queen (rosary centerpiece). Conclude with the Rosary prayer.

7. Pray the Glory Be and the (optional) Fatima Prayer.

6. Pray ten Hail Marys on the next "decade" (ten beads), meditating on the mystery.

5. Announce the first mystery, and then pray the Our Father (next single bead).

4. Pray the Glory Be and the (optional) Fatima Prayer.

3. Pray three Hail Marys (next three beads).

2. Pray an Our Father (first bead).

1. Make the Sign of the Cross and pray the Apostles' Creed (crucifix).

PRAYERS OF THE ROSARY

Apostles' Creed
I believe in God, the Father almighty, Creator of heaven and earth, and in Jesus Christ, his only Son, our Lord, who was conceived by the Holy Spirit, born of the Virgin Mary, suffered under Pontius Pilate, was crucified, died and was buried; he descended to hell; on the third day he rose again from the dead; he ascended into heaven, and is seated at the right hand of God the Father almighty; from there he will come to judge the living and the dead. I believe in the Holy Spirit, the holy catholic Church, the communion of saints, the forgiveness of sins, the resurrection of the body, and life everlasting. Amen.

Our Father
Our Father, who art in heaven, hallowed be thy name; thy kingdom come, thy will be done, on earth as it is in heaven. Give us this day our daily bread, and forgive us our trespasses as we forgive those who trespass against us; and lead us not into temptation, but deliver us from evil. Amen.

Hail Mary
Hail Mary, full of grace, the Lord is with thee. Blessed art thou among women, and blessed is the fruit of thy womb, Jesus. Holy Mary, Mother of God, pray for us sinners, now and at the hour of our death. Amen.

Glory Be
Glory be to the Father, and to the Son, and to the Holy Spirit, as it was in the beginning, is now, and ever shall be, world without end. Amen.

Fatima Prayer
O my Jesus, forgive us our sins, save us from the fires of hell, and lead all souls to heaven, especially those in most need of thy mercy.

Hail, Holy Queen

Hail, Holy Queen, Mother of mercy, our life, our sweetness, and our hope. To thee do we cry, poor banished children of Eve; to thee do we send up our sighs, mourning and weeping in this valley of tears. Turn, then, most gracious advocate, thine eyes of mercy toward us, and after this, our exile, show unto us the blessed fruit of thy womb, Jesus. O clement, O loving, O sweet Virgin Mary.

Rosary Prayer

God, whose only begotten Son, by his life, death, and resurrection, has purchased for us the rewards of eternal life, grant, we beseech thee, that meditating upon these mysteries of the Most Holy Rosary of the Blessed Virgin Mary, we may imitate what they contain and obtain what they promise, through the same Christ our Lord. Amen.

Prayer to St. Michael the Archangel

(Note: This beautiful prayer is not part of the Rosary, but it is sometimes prayed at the conclusion of the Rosary.)

St. Michael the Archangel, defend us in battle, be our protection against the wickedness and snares of the Devil. May God rebuke him, we humbly pray, and do thou, O Prince of the Heavenly Host, by the power of God, cast into hell Satan and all the evil spirits, who prowl throughout the world seeking the ruin of souls. Amen.

CONCLUSION

Congratulations!

You have completed *The Rosary in a Year (with Fr. Mark-Mary Ames)*! Praise God for the graces he has poured out upon you and everyone along this journey throughout the year. Don't stop now; continue to pray the Rosary each day and meditate on the lives of Jesus and Mary through this beautiful and centuries-old prayer!

SOURCES

Introduction: Address of Pope Benedict XVI for the Recitation of the Holy Rosary at the Basilica of St. Mary Major on May 3, 2008, vatican.va.

The Rosary in a Year Prayer Plan: Information about artwork marked with an asterisk (*) has not been fact-checked.

Litany of Loreto: "The Litany of Loreto," "The Holy Rosary," vatican.va, accessed August 26, 2024, https://www.vatican.va/special/rosary/documents/litanie-lauretane_en.html.

Note: "The Litany of Loreto takes its name from the Marian shrine of Loreto in Italy, where it is believed to have been used as far back as 1531. It was officially approved in 1587 by Pope Sixtus V, who suppressed all other Marian litanies used publicly. The Litany of Loreto is the only approved Marian litany. However, many more Marian litanies were and are in use, but are designated for private devotion, as is evident, for example, in the so-called *Officia Mariana*. Through the centuries at least 7 new invocations to Mary were added. Saint Pope John Paul II added 'Mother of the Church' in 1980, and 'Queen of families' in 1995. Pope Francis has now added three more." ("Pope adds three new invocations to the Litany of the Blessed Virgin Mary," Vatican News, June 20, 2020, vaticannews.va.)

Litany of the Sacred Heart and Litany of the Holy Name: From Charles J. Callan and John A. McHugh, *Blessed Be God: A Complete Catholic Prayer Book* (New York: P. J. Kenedy and Sons, 1925), archive.org/details/blessed-be-god-a-complete-catholic-prayer-book, capitalization and punctuation slightly revised and language slightly revised ("Holy Ghost" replaced with "Holy Spirit").

Mysteries of the Rosary: Gifts we pray for in the joyful, sorrowful, and glorious mysteries are adapted from *Le Secret Amirable du Très Saint Rosaire* by St. Louis-Marie Grignion de Montfort.

Day 1: St. Louis de Montfort, *The Secret of the Rosary*, trans. Mary Barbour (Bay Shore, NY: Montfort Publications; TAN Books and Publishers, 1987), 10.

Day 3: "Litany to the Sacred Heart of Jesus," accessed August 28, 2024, ewtn.com.

Day 5: "Pope adds three new invocations to the Litany of the Blessed Virgin Mary," Vatican News, June 20, 2020, vaticannews.va.

Day 6: Rev. Paolo Carta, "Padre Pio and the Immaculate Heart of Mary," accessed August 22, 2024, ewtn.com.

Day 7: Address of Pope Benedict XVI for the Recitation of the Holy Rosary at the Basilica of St. Mary Major on May 3, 2008, vatican.va.

Day 89: Bernard of Clairvaux, *Four Homilies in Praise of the Virgin Mother*, in Bernard of Clairvaux and Amadeus of Lausanne, *Magnificat: Homilies in Praise of the Blessed Virgin Mary*, trans. Marie-Bernard Saïd and Grace Perigo (Kalamazoo, MI: Cistercian Publications, 1979), 4.8–9 (page 53–54). © 1979 by Cistercian Publications, Inc. © 2008 by Order of Saint Benedict, Collegeville, Minnesota. Used with permission.

Day 90: Alphonsus Liguori, "On the Visitation of the Blessed Virgin" in *The Way of Salvation: Meditations for Every Day in the Year*, trans. Rev. James Jones (London: Keating and Brown, 1836), 1–2 (page 282–283), archive.org/details/TheWayOfSalvation1836, language slightly revised ("Holy Ghost" replaced with "Holy Spirit").

Day 91: Excerpts from St. Leo the Great, *Sermon 21 (On the Feast of the Nativity, I)*, trans. Charles Lett Feltoe, in *Nicene and Post-Nicene Fathers, Second Series*, ed. Philip Schaff and Henry Wace, vol. 12 (Buffalo, NY: Christian Literature Publishing Co., 1895), revised and edited for New Advent by Kevin Knight, www.newadvent.org, language slightly revised ("Holy Ghost" replaced with "Holy Spirit"). Courtesy of New Advent.

Day 92: Saint Cyril of Alexandria, *Homily 4*, in *Commentary on the Gospel of Saint Luke*, trans. R. Payne Smith ([Astoria, NY?]: Studion Publishers, 1983), 60–61. Used with permission.

Day 93: St. Augustine, *Sermons on Selected Lessons of the New Testament: Sermon 1* [LI. Benedictine Edition] sect. 17, 20, trans. R. G. MacMullen, in *Nicene and Post-Nicene Fathers, First Series*, ed. Philip Schaff, vol. 6 (Buffalo, NY: Christian Literature Publishing Co., 1888), revised and edited for New Advent by Kevin Knight, www.newadvent.org. Courtesy of New Advent.

Day 94: St. Ambrose, *On the Mysteries* 5.26, 27, trans. H. de Romestin, E. de Romestin and H. T. F. Duckworth, in *Nicene and Post-Nicene Fathers, Second Series*, ed. Philip Schaff and Henry Wace, vol. 10 (Buffalo, NY: Christian Literature Publishing Co., 1896), revised and edited for New Advent by Kevin Knight, www.newadvent.org. Courtesy of New Advent.

Day 95: St. Alphonsus Liguori, *The Glories of Mary*, 6.1 (p. 205–208), (New York: Edward Dunigan and Brother, 1852?), archive.org/details/TheGloriesOfMary1852.

Day 96: St. Augustine, *On the Sermon on the Mount* 1.1.2, trans. William Findlay, in *Nicene and Post-Nicene Fathers, First Series*, ed. Philip Schaff, vol. 6 (Buffalo, NY: Christian Literature Publishing Co., 1888), revised and edited for New Advent by Kevin Knight, www.newadvent.org. Courtesy of New Advent.

Day 97: Anastasius of Sinai, *Homily on the Transfiguration*, in *Light on the Mountain: Greek Patristic and Byzantine Homilies on the Transfiguration of the Lord*, trans. Brian E. Daley, Popular Patristics 48 (Yonkers, NY: St. Vladimir's Seminary Press, 2013), Kindle. Used with permission.

Day 98: *The Dialogue of the Seraphic Virgin Catherine of Siena*, trans. Algar Thorold, new and abridged edition (London: Kegan Paul, Trench, Trubner and Co., Ltd.: 1907), 238–239, archive.org/details/dialogueseraphi-00unkngoog.

Day 99: St. Alphonsus de Liguori, "Reflections and Affections on the Passion of Jesus Christ," in *The Passion and the Death of Jesus Christ*, ed. Eugene Grimm (New York: Benziger Brothers, 1887), 6.1 (p. 62–63), archive.org/details/ThePassionAndTheDeathOfJesusChrist.

Day 100: *Revelations of St. Bridget, on the Life and Passion of Our Lord and the Life of His Blessed Mother* (New York: D. & J. Sadlier & Co., 1862), chap. 16 (p. 56, 58–59), archive.org/details/RevelationsOfStBridget.

Day 101: St. Thomas Aquinas, *Commentary on the Gospel of Matthew: Chapters 13–28*, trans. Jeremy Holmes, ed. The Aquinas Institute, Latin-English Opera Omnia (Steubenville, OH: Emmaus Academic, 2018), 2350. Used with permission.

Day 102: Josemaria Escriva, "Second Station: Jesus Takes Up His Cross," in The Way of the Cross (Princeton, NY: Scepter, 2002). Used with permission.

Day 103: St. Alphonsus Maria de Liguori, "On the Fifth Dolour," in *The Glories of Mary*, 2nd ed., rev. Robert A. Coffin (New York: P. O'Shea, 1868?), 440–441, 444–445, archive.org/details/gloriesmary00ligugoog.

Day 104: "*Sancti Patris Nostri Joannis Chrysostomi Archiepisc. Constantinopolis exhortatio, sancta & magna dominica Paschae,*" in *Euchologion sive Rituale graecorum* (Venice, 1730), 565–566, babel.hathitrust.org. Courtesy of HathiTrust. Translated from Latin into English by Aaron Henderson. As noted at ewtn.com, this Easter homily is traditionally preached on Holy Saturday and is attributed to St. John Chrysostom.

Day 105: *The Summa Theologiae of St. Thomas Aquinas*, III.57.1, trans. Fathers of the English Dominican Province, 2nd and revised edition (1920), online edition 2017, newadvent.org, language slightly revised ("Holy Ghost" replaced with "Holy Spirit"). Courtesy of New Advent.

Day 106: St. Ambrose, *On the Holy Spirit* 14.168–170, trans. H. de Romestin, E. de Romestin and H. T. F. Duckworth, in *Nicene and Post-Nicene Fathers, Second Series*, ed. Philip Schaff and Henry Wace, vol. 10 (Buffalo, NY: Christian Literature Publishing Co., 1896), revised and edited for New Advent by Kevin Knight, www.newadvent.org. Courtesy of New Advent.

Day 107: Fulton J. Sheen, *Meditations on the Fifteen Mysteries of the Rosary* (St. Paul, MN: Catechetical Guild Educational Society, 1952; n.p.: Annunciation Books and Media, 2023).

Day 108: *Sermon 1: On the Assumption*, in *St. John Damascene on Holy Images: Followed by Three Sermons on the Assumption*, trans. Mary H. Allies (London: Thomas Baker, 1898), 169–170, archive.org/details/stjohndamasceneo00alliuoft.

Day 109: Excerpts from St. Gregory Thaumaturgus, *The First Homily: On the Annunciation to the Holy Virgin Mary*, in *Four Homilies*, trans. S. D. F. Salmond, in *Ante-Nicene Fathers*, ed. Alexander Roberts, James Donaldson, and A. Cleveland Coxe, vol. 6 (Buffalo, NY: Christian Literature Publishing Co., 1886), revised and edited for New Advent by Kevin Knight, www.newadvent.org, language slightly revised ("Holy Ghost" replaced with "Holy Spirit"). Courtesy of New Advent.

Day 110: Ambroise de Milan, *Traité sur L'Évangile de S. Luc: Livres I–VI; Texte Latin*, ed. Gabriel Tissot, Sources Chrétiennes (Paris: Les Éditions du Cerf, 1956), 2.19–20, 22–23, 26 (page 81–84), archive.org/details/traitsurlvangile0045ambr, translated from Latin into English by Aaron Henderson.

Day 111: *On the Miraculous Nature of the Nativity*, in *Sermons of St. Bernard on Advent and Christmas*, with an introduction by Rev. J.C. Hedley (London: R. & T. Washbourne, Ltd., and New York: Benziger Bros., 1909), 82–83.

Day 112: St. Alphonsus Liguori, *The Glories of Mary*, 2.6 (p. 458–461, 463–464), (New York: Edward Dunigan and Brother, 1852?), archive.org/details/TheGloriesOfMary1852.

Day 113: Saint Cyril of Alexandria, *Homily 5*, in *Commentary on the Gospel of Saint Luke*, trans. R. Payne Smith ([Astoria, NY?]: Studion Publishers, 1983), 64. Used with permission.

Day 114: St. Gregory of Nazianzus, *Oration 39* sect. 14–16, 20, trans. Charles Gordon Brown and James Edward Swallow, in *Nicene and Post-Nicene Fathers, Second Series*, ed. Philip Schaff and Henry Wace, vol. 7 (Buffalo, NY: Christian Literature Publishing Co., 1894), revised and edited for New Advent by Kevin Knight, www.newadvent.org. Courtesy of New Advent.

Day 115: John Henry Newman, *Sermons Bearing on Subjects of the Day* (London: Rivingtons, 1869), 31–33, https://archive.org/details/sermonsonsubject00newm.

Day 116: St. John Eudes, *The Life and the Kingdom of Jesus: A Treatise on Christian Perfection for Use by Clergy or Laity*, trans. a Trappist father in the Abbey of Our Lady of Gethsemani, with an introduction by Fulton J. Sheen (NY: P. J. Kenedy and Sons, 1947 [1946?]), 6.4 (page 251–253), archive.org/details/TheLifeAndKingdomOfJesusByEudes.

Day 117: St. Augustine, *Sermons on Selected Lessons of the New Testament: Sermon 28* [LXXVIII. Ben.] sect. 2-3, 6, trans. R. G. MacMullen, in *Nicene and Post-Nicene Fathers, First Series*, ed. Philip Schaff, vol. 6 (Buffalo, NY: Christian Literature Publishing Co., 1888), revised and edited for New Advent by Kevin Knight, www.newadvent.org. Courtesy of New Advent.

Day 118: St. Cyril of Jerusalem, *Catechetical Lecture 22 (On the Mysteries. IV.): On the Body and Blood of Christ* 1-6, 9, trans. Edwin Hamilton Gifford, in *Nicene and Post-Nicene Fathers, Second Series*, ed. Philip Schaff and Henry Wace, vol. 7 (Buffalo, NY: Christian Literature Publishing Co., 1894), revised and edited for New Advent by Kevin Knight, www.newadvent.org. Courtesy of New Advent.

Day 119: *The Fathers of the Church: A New Translation*, ed. Roy Deferrari, vol. 25, *Saint Hilary of Poitiers: The Trinity*, trans. Stephen McKenna (Washington DC: The Catholic University of America Press, 1954, 1968), 10.42 (page 429-431). Used with permission.

Day 120: *Diary of Saint Maria Faustina Kowalska: Divine Mercy in My Soul* (Stockbridge, MA: Marian Fathers of the Immaculate Conception of the Blessed Virgin Mary, 1987), 445.

Day 121: From chapter 47 in *Life of Christ* by Fulton J. Sheen.

Day 122: St. Thomas Aquinas, *Commentary on the Gospel of John: Chapters 9-21*, trans. Fabian Larcher, ed. The Aquinas Institute, Latin-English Opera Omnia (Steubenville, OH: Emmaus Academic, 2018), 2412-2414. Used with permission.

Day 123: *Revelations of St. Bridget, on the Life and Passion of Our Lord and the Life of His Blessed Mother* (New York: D. & J. Sadlier & Co., 1862), chap. 16 (p. 59-63), archive.org/details/RevelationsOfStBridget.

Day 124: St. Augustine, *Sermo VIII: In octava Paschatis ad infantes* 2, 4 (J. P. Migne, *Patrologia latina*, vol. 46 [Paris, 1842], 838–841), The University of Chicago Library *Patrologia Latina* Database Published by Chadwyck-Healey, Inc., lib.uchicago.edu, translated by Aaron Henderson.

Day 125: St. Augustine, *Sermons on Selected Lessons of the New Testament: Sermon 41* [XCI. Ben.] sect. 7–9, trans. R. G. MacMullen, in *Nicene and Post-Nicene Fathers, First Series*, ed. Philip Schaff, vol. 6 (Buffalo, NY: Christian Literature Publishing Co., 1888), revised and edited for New Advent by Kevin Knight, www.newadvent.org. Courtesy of New Advent.

Day 126: Alphonsus Liguori, "Novena of the Holy Ghost" in *The Way of Salvation: Meditations for Every Day in the Year*, trans. Rev. James Jones (London: Keating and Brown, 1836), page 247–249, language slightly revised ("Holy Ghost" replaced with "Holy Spirit").

Day 127: Bernard of Clairvaux, *On the Solemnity of the Assumption of the Blessed Virgin Mary: Sermon One*, in *Sermons for the Autumn Season*, trans. Irene Edmonds, rev. Mark Scott (Collegeville, MN: Cistercian Publications; Liturgical Press, 2016), 1–2 (page 14–15). Used with permission.

Day 128: John Henry Newman, "Mary Is the '*Regina Angelorum*,' the Queen of Angels," in *Meditations and Devotions of the Late Cardinal Newman* (New York: Longmans, Green, and Co., 1893), 29–30, digitalcollections.newmanstudies.org. Courtesy of National Institute for Newman Studies, Pittsburgh, PA, newmanstudies.org, newmanreader.org, and digitalcollections.newmanstudies.org.

Day 131: Caryll Houselander, *The Reed of God* (Notre Dame, IN: Christian Classics, 2020), 59–60.

Day 140: "Pilgrims Venerate Relic of Pillar Where Christ Was Scourged," April 3, 2015, National Catholic Register (website), ncregister.com.

Day 149: "'The Annunciation' by Henry Ossawa Tanner," Philadelphia Museum of Art, February 19, 2021, YouTube video, 1:16, youtube.com.

Day 155: Brant Pitre, *Jesus the Bridegroom: The Greatest Love Story Ever Told* (New York: Image, 2014), 43.

Day 157: "*Transfiguration* (Raphael)," Wikipedia, last edited June 25, 2024, 10:15, wikipedia.org.

Day 158: *The Aquinas Prayer Book: The Prayers and Hymns of St. Thomas Aquinas*, trans. and ed. Robert Anderson and Johann Moser (Manchester, NH: Sophia Institute Press, 2000), 69.

"*The Last Supper*," Museo del Prado (website), accessed August 29, 2024, museodelprado.es.

Day 160: "Violence and drama, Caravaggio's The Flagellation of Christ," Smarthistory: The Center for Public Art History, April 25, 2023, YouTube video, youtube.com.

Day 164: Elizabeth Lev, *How Catholic Art Saved the Faith: The Triumph of Beauty and Truth in Counter-Reformation Art* (Manchester, NH: Sophia Institute Press, 2018), 188.

Day 169: "The Annunciation: Jan van Eyck," National Gallery of Art (website), accessed August 21, 2024, nga.gov.

Carol J. Purtle, "Van Ecyk's Washington *Annuncation*: Narrative Time and Metaphoric Tradition," *The Art Bulletin* 81, no. 1 (1999): 117–119, https://doi.org/10.2307/3051290.]

"*Annunciation* (van Eyck, Washington)," Wikipedia, accessed August 2, 2024, wikipedia.org.

"Symbolism of van Eyck's 'Annuncation,'" "The Annunciation: Jan van Eyck," National Gallery of Art (website), accessed August 21, 2024, nga.gov.

ILLUSTRATION INFORMATION AND CREDITS

Day 129: Fra Angelico, *The Annunciation* (1426), in Museo Nacional del Prado, Madrid, Spain, GiorgioMorara/stock.adobe.com.

Day 130: Rembrandt, *The Visitation* (1640), in Detroit Institute of Arts, www.uni-leipzig.de./commons.wikimedia.org.

Day 131: "Vienna - Nativity paint in presbytery of Salesianerkirche," Renáta Sedmáková/stock.adobe.com.

Day 132: "The fresco of Presentation in the Temple in Chiesa di Santa Rita by Giulio Campi (1547)" (2016), Renáta Sedmáková/stock.adobe.com.

Day 133: "Mosaic of Jesus lost and found in the Temple," clamon/stock.adobe.com.

Day 134: "Padua - Baptism of Christ scene in church San Benedetto," Renáta Sedmáková/stock.adobe.com.

Day 135: Carl Bloch, *Wedding at Cana* (1870), in The Museum of National History at Frederiksborg Castle, Denmark, https://www.flickr.com/photos/the_bowyer_bible_genesis/39351375451/in/album-72157691583225345//commons.wikimedia.org

Day 136: James Tissot, *Healing of the Lepers at Capernaum* (1886–1894), Brooklyn Museum, Brooklyn Museum/commons.wikimedia.org.

Day 137: "Transfiguration on Mount Tabor, Votiv Kirche in Vienna," zatletic/stock.adobe.com.

Illustration Information and Credits   381

Day 138: "Vienna - Mosaic of Last supper - copy Leonardo da Vinci," [Giacomo Raffaelli, *The Last Supper* (1806–1814), in Minoritenkirche in Vienna, Austria (?)], Renáta Sedmáková/stock.adobe.com.

Day 139: "The painting of Prayer of Jesus in Gethsemane garden on the side altar in the Cathedral by Vicente Macip from end of 15. cent." (2022), Renáta Sedmáková/stock.adobe.com.

Day 140: "Rome - freco of Flagellation of Christ from Santa Prassede," Renáta Sedmáková/stock.adobe.com.

Day 141: Titian, *Christ Crowned with Thorns* (1542–1543), Web Gallery of Art/commons.wikimedia.org.

Day 142: Pieter Bruegel, *The Procession to Calvary* (1542), in Kunsthistorisches Museum Wien, Adam Ján Figel'/stock.adobe.com.

Day 143: "The fresco of Crucifixion in the church San Girolamo dei Croati by Pietro Gagliardi (1847-1852)," Renáta Sedmáková/stock.adobe.com.

Day 144: Annibale Carracci, *The Resurrection of Christ* (1593), Louvre, commons.wikimedia.org.

Day 145: "Ascension of Jesus Christ Mosaic," in St. Mark's Basilica, Venice, Italy, Jason Yoder/stock.adobe.com.

Day 146: Jean Restout, *Pentecost* (1732), in the Louvre, Art Renewal Center/commons.wikimedia.org.

Day 147: "Church of Santa Maria dell'Orto, in Rome, Italy," e55evu/stock.adobe.com.

Day 148: Diego Velázquez, *The Coronation of the Virgin* (c. 1645), in Museo Nacional del Prado, Madrid, Spain, Shalone/stock.adobe.com.

Day 149: Henry Ossawa Tanner, *The Annunciation* (1898), in Philadelphia Museum of Art, Philadelphia Museum of Art/commons.wikimedia.org.

Day 150: "The painting of Visitation in the church Chiesa dei Santi Severino e Sossio by Federico Maldarelli (1889)" (2023), Renáta Sedmáková/stock.adobe.com.

Day 151: Gerard van Honthorst, *Adoration of the Shepherds* (1622), in Pommersches Landesmuseum, Google Art Project/en.wikipedia.org.

Day 152: "The painting of Presentation of Jesus in the Temple in church kostel Svatého Havla by unknown baroque artist" (2018), Renáta Sedmáková/stock.adobe.com.

Day 153: "Paint of scene as Jesus Christ at age 12 teaching in the temple from St. Nicholas church on June 21, 2012 in Brussels," Renáta Sedmáková/stock.adobe.com.

Day 154: Andrea del Verrocchio and Leonardo da Vinci, *The Baptism of Christ* (c. 1470–1475), in Le Gallerie degli Uffizi, commons.wikimedia.org.

Day 155: Gérard David, *The Wedding at Cana* (1500–1510), in the Louvre, https://collections.louvre.fr/en/ark:/53355/cl010061836/commons.wikimedia.org.

Day 156: Lorenzo Lotto, *The Adulterous Woman* (1527–1529), in the Louvre, commons.wikimedia.org.

Day 157: Raphael, *The Transfiguration* (1516–1520), in Musei Vaticani, GiorgioMorara/stock.adobe.com.

Day 158: Juan de Juanes (Vicente Juan Masip), *The Last Supper* (1555–1562), in Museo Nacional del Prado, Madrid, Spain, corvalola/stock.adobe.com.

Day 159: "The painting of prayer of Jesus in Gethsemane garden in the Cathedral by Alessandro Maganza (1587-1589)" (2023), in Vicenza, Italy (?), Renáta Sedmáková/stock.adobe.com.

Day 160: Caravaggio, *The Flagellation of Christ* (1607), in National Museum of Capodimonte, commons.wikimedia.org.

Day 161: Caravaggio, *Ecce Homo* (c. 1605), in Palazzo Bianco, ugH0uYgOidL0bA at Google Cultural Institute/commons.wikimedia.org.

Day 162: Orazio Gentileschi, *Christ Carrying the Cross* (c. 1605), in Kunsthistorisches Museum Wien, restoredtraditions.com.

Day 163: James Tissot, *What Our Lord Saw from the Cross* (1886–1894), in Brooklyn Museum, Brooklyn Museum/commons.wikimedia.org.com

Day 164: Caravaggio, *The Incredulity of St. Thomas* (c. 1601), in Picture Gallery of Sanssouci, Germany, Google Arts and Culture/en.wikipedia.org.

Day 165: "The painting Ascension of the Lord in church Chiesa di Santa Maria del Carmine by Bernardino Gandino (1587 - 1651)" (2016), in Brescia, Italy (?), Renáta Sedmáková/stock.adobe.com.

Day 166: Titian, *Pentecost* (c. 1545), in Santa Maria della Salute, Venice, https://i.pinimg.com/originals/3c/cc/2a/3ccc2ae59bca826a0579c4b-011418ccf.jpg/commons.wikimedia.org.

Day 167: "The fresco of Assumption of Our Lady in the Vision of St Bonaventure in the church Chiesa di Santa Lucia del Gonfalone by Cesare Mariani (1863)," in Rome, Renáta Sedmáková/stock.adobe.com.

Day 168: "Gloire de Marie dans le Ciel. Giuseppe Mattia Borgnis. Eglise Sainte-Marie-Majeure. / Glory of Mary in Heaven. Santa Maria Maggiore. Italie" (c. 1725 ?), in Parish Church of Santa Maria Assunta, Santa Maria Maggiore, Italy (?), lemélangedesgenres/stock.adobe.com.

Day 169: Jan van Eyck, *The Annunciation* (c. 1434), National Gallery of Art, Washington, D.C., online collection/en.wikipedia.org.

Day 170: "Mosaic adorning the front of the Church of Visitation, depicting the scene of Mary's visit to Elisheb, Church of the Visitation in Ein Karem near Jerusalem, Israel," zatletic/stock.adobe.com.

Day 171: Caravaggio, *Nativity with St. Francis and St. Lawrence* (c. 1609), missing (stolen from Oratory of San Lorenzo in Palermo, Italy), Cuppoz/commons.wikimedia.org.

Day 172: Arent de Gelder, *Simeon's Song of Praise* (1700), in Mauritshuis, the Netherlands, commons.wikimedia.org.

Day 173: William Holman Hunt, *The Finding of the Saviour in the Temple* (c. 1855), in Birmingham Museum and Art Gallery, commons.wikimedia.org.

Day 174: Alexander Ivanov, *The Appearance of Christ Before the People (The Apparition of the Messiah)* (1837–1857), in Tretyakov Gallery, lgGqUffODe21kA/en.wikipedia.org.

Day 175: Paolo Veronese, *The Wedding at Cana* (1562–1563), in the Louvre, commons.wikimedia.org.

Day 176: Rembrandt, *Christ in the Storm on the Sea of Galilee* (1633), missing (stolen from Isabella Stewart Gardner Museum, Boston), www.gardnermuseum.org/en.wikipedia.org.

Day 177: Theophanes the Greek (attr.), *The Savior's Transfiguration* (c. 1403 ?), in Tretyakov Gallery (?), http://www.belygorod.ru/img2/Ikona/Used/218grek_preobrazhenie.jpg/commons.wikimedia.org.

Day 178: Henry Ossawa Tanner, *Christ and the Disciples Before the Last Supper* (1909?), Google Arts and Culture/commons.m.wikimedia.org.

Day 179: Giotto, *The Arrest of Christ (Kiss of Judas)* (c. 1305), in Scrovegni Chapel, Padua, Italy, wikiart.org.

Day 180: William-Adolphe Bouguereau, *The Flagellation of Our Lord Jesus Christ* (1880?), en.m.wikipedia.org.

Day 181: Anthony van Dyck, *The Crowning with Thorns* (1618–1620), in Museo Nacional del Prado, Madrid, Spain, https://www.museodelprado.es/en/the-collection/online-gallery/on-line-gallery/obra/the-crown-of-thorns//commons.wikimedia.org.

Day 182: Raphael, *Christ Falls on the Way to Calvary* (1515–1516), in Museo Nacional del Prado, Madrid, Spain, http://www.museodelprado.es/en/the-collection/online-gallery/on-line-gallery/zoom/1/obra/christ-falls-on-the-way-to-calvary/oimg/0//commons.wikimedia.org.

Day 183: Peter Paul Rubens, *The Descent from the Cross* (c. 1617), in Palais Beaux-Arts Lille, Sailko/commons.wikimedia.org.

Day 184: Annibale Carracci, *The Holy Women at Christ's Tomb* (c. 1600), in The State Hermitage Museum, St. Petersburg, Web Gallery of Art/commons.wikimedia.org.

Day 185: Duccio, *Appearance on the Mountain in Galilee*, (1308–1311), in Museo dell'Opera, Siena, Italy, Web Gallery of Art/commons.wikimedia.org.

Day 186: Simone Peterzano (attr.), *Pentecost*, (c. 1580?), in Basilica of Santa Eufemia, Milan, Italy (?), Renáta Sedmáková/stock.adobe.com.

Day 187: "Assumption of Mary - Stained Glass in Burgos Cathedral," jorisvo/stock.adobe.com.

Day 188: "The detail of fresco Mary Help of Christians in cupola of church Basilica Maria Ausiliatrice by Giuseppe Rollini (1889 - 1891)" (2017), in Turin, Italy (?), Renáta Sedmáková/stock.adobe.com.